MECHANICS·
MERCANTILE
LIBRARY.

Arthur F Mathews '06

The Island of Seven Cities

THE ISLAND OF

Paul Chiasson

SEVEN CITIES

Where the Chinese Settled

When They Discovered America

ST. MARTIN'S PRESS ❦ NEW YORK

Published by arrangement with Random House Canada, a division of Random House of Canada Limited

www.stmartins.com

ISBN-10 0-312–36186-6
ISBN-13 978-0-312-36186-0

First Edition: May 2006

10 9 8 7 6 5 4 3 2 1

TO MY FAMILY

CONTENTS

CHAPTER ONE

CUT STONES
IN THE WILDERNESS

FROM MY CHAIR in the front row, I looked around the Mumford Room of the Library of Congress in Washington at an assembly of people who were about to sit in judgment of me. It was May 16, 2005, and the library was hosting an international symposium on the early naval voyages of the Chinese, with a special emphasis on China's mapping of the globe before the European age of discovery had even begun. This notion had once seemed extremely controversial, but throughout the morning one speaker after another drew on genetic profiles, methods for determining latitude, original documents and centuries-old maps to present ideas that clearly had the power to reconfigure our history of the New World. The atmosphere was electric, as if all of us could see a window opening on the past and begin to make out something astonishing on the horizon.

Unlike the men and women around me, I was neither an archaeologist nor a historian. I was an architect from Toronto and had never imagined myself in this context—an accidental discoverer at best. But two years earlier I had stumbled on previously uninvestigated—and long-forgotten—ruins on a mountaintop on a small island in the North Atlantic, an island that happened to be the place where I was born and raised.

Waiting for my introduction, and a little anxious about speaking in front of such an audience, I cast my mind back to the stillness of the ruins, isolated on their abandoned mountaintop. I was only too aware that as soon as my presentation was over the arguments would begin about the various elements of this once vast settlement, the reasons for its construction and its demise, and the consequences of its forgotten history. For a last moment, I concentrated on the cut stones I'd discovered in the wilderness, the magnificence and the mystery of a site that until I stood to speak had been mine alone to experience.

At the end of my very first climb to the ruins, I'd sat gazing down over the open Atlantic, a vista that stretched farther and wider than my eye could take in. The ruined site below me, gently sloping towards the sea, held the marks of an ancient design. Its rectangular geometry had been cut sharply into the hillside, but was now softened on its edges by dense spruce forest. The ruined terraces and stone platforms stepping down the mountainside had been conceived and built with this panorama in mind. The stones had been untouched for centuries, and were covered in layers of lichen and mosses that still held the morning dew. Faint traces of mist lay in the hollows amid the ruins. It was a place of great beauty, approached by a long difficult road, and it struck me that it had been designed to ease the frightened spirits of people a long way from home.

Even in those first moments, I had known that these were not the remnants of a humble fishing outpost or farm or fortification, but of a lost settlement that had been inhabited by hundreds or thousands of people for decades—long before Columbus ever dreamed of sailing. After two years of historical investigation I had concluded that the settlement was Chinese. I was here to announce and describe this discovery for the first time in public. If the academics in this room believed me—if my years of intense work proved sound—then the vision we had been glimpsing on the horizon all day would suddenly come into view.

The session moderator called my name. The elderly couple who sat next to me leaned over and wished me good luck. I clutched my notes and walked to the podium.

The path that led me to that mountaintop began in 1993, when I discovered I was HIV-positive. At the time I believed I could lick the disease. I sat my family down and told them what it meant, but I told myself that I come from tenacious Acadian and Scots stock, pioneer blood that had helped build the communities of Cape Breton Island. I had moved from Washington two years earlier—giving up my teaching position at the Catholic University there—to Toronto. When I tested positive I met Dr. Anne Philips, an HIV specialist. She was the mother of three daughters and was married to another doctor, and her kindness and intelligence won my trust. In the mid-nineties, when drugs were just becoming an option and I was debating their pros and cons, she told me I would be dead in six months if I didn't start them immediately. I did and, as a result, was able to settle into a fulfilling career in Toronto as an architect and designer. I didn't look sick, after all. Someday, I believed, I would get better; someday this affliction would just go away.

By the end of the decade that sense of invincibility had dissipated. The virus had mutated to meet the onslaught of medications, and my strength was in decline. Yet perhaps as a consequence of HIV—and though I was not prone to romantic notions of death—I developed an increasing passion for the architecture of the past. Architecture was the discipline in which I had been trained, but now I found comfort in the evidence that ruins provided: nature will destroy even the most magnificent of human plans. I had limited time left to me, but there were still places that fascinated me and buildings I had never seen. I was hungry for ruins. I knew the architecture of the West: I'd taught it to university freshmen in one form or another for years, and I'd lived and studied in France and Italy. But the Middle East—Egypt's pyramids and the markets and mosques of Damascus—were still foreign to me. In the early spring of 2000 I'd persuaded my friend Beth to drive a rented car with me through the back roads of the region. With a suitcase full of guidebooks, we travelled from the Krak des Chavaliers in northern Syria to Petra in southern Jordan, then on to Egypt, the Sinai Desert, the Nile temples and the monuments of Karnak. We billed it as my last great adventure.

By the end of that year I found myself drawn to Cape Breton Island, the land of my birth. I had spent many childhood afternoons in the back seat of my grandparents' car as we toured rural roads and solitary graveyards in search of the island's history. My grandfather had retired, and the couple had the luxury of time and a grandson possessed of huge curiosity. We clambered together over the ruins of the French buildings of Île Royale—the Royal Island—which the English had destroyed in 1763. We read gravestones, hiked into high meadows, and ate ice cream as we drove home at night.

To play among the crumbled remains of ancient brick and stone walls built on a wild, rocky shoreline covered in thick fog was the definition of childhood wonder to me. Uniformed soldiers parading, cannons firing on pirate ships trapped in the fierce smoke of battle: it was all quite real, and I needed it again.

In the summer of 2001, while visiting my parents in Sydney, Cape Breton's largest town, I'd gone to inspect an old lighthouse on Boularderie Island, named after the Acadian family that once farmed the land. Here the eastern coast of Cape Breton juts out into the Atlantic Ocean at about the same angle your thumb makes when you stretch it out from your left hand. Where the first finger and the thumb might be imagined to meet, I stood looking across the Great Bras d'Or straits to the wild shore opposite, a vast hill of rock in dramatic

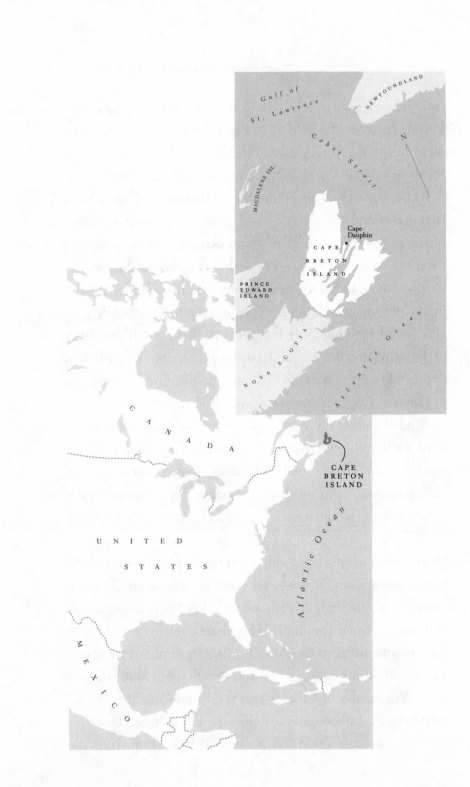

silhouette called Cape Dauphin. It was a part of the island I'd never encountered in any of my childhood explorations.

Back at my parents' house that day, I checked the bookshelves for whatever I could find on Cape Breton's history. I went to the Sydney library, where I had spent almost every Saturday morning as a child, to read histories of Cape Breton Island and check the indexes for anything that might have been written about that rock hill called Cape Dauphin. The story of the French—the Acadians as they came to be called—who pioneered the New World was the story of my own family. The tides and turns of the Americas during the seventeenth and eighteenth centuries were the same currents that had swept my family from their homes. For me, history had never been a story told by scholars: it was my story.

In 1524 the Italian explorer Giovanni Da Verrazano sailed up the Atlantic coast of North America in a French ship and, somewhere along that coast—possibly present-day North Carolina—named it Acadia, after the mythical Arcady. The Roman poet Virgil imagined Arcady to be a region of rustic beauty, cool springs and soft meadows, inhabited by a noble people living together in simple goodness. A sixteenth-century prose poem, "Arcadia," helped popularize the pastoral image, and to a Europe plagued by generations of war, it seemed that the romantic dream of peace might be found in this wilderness, a land where the old continent could begin anew.

In 1604 the young French explorer Samuel de Champlain attempted to establish a permanent colony in l'Acadie. He tried first on the coast of what is now Maine and then on the western shore of Nova Scotia. During these settlement attempts, the French came into contact with the Mi'kmaq, the local aboriginal nation, and began to trade for furs. L'Acadie became known as a place that might offer settlers a better life. Soon young men and women were arriving from France, mostly from the area around the port city of La Rochelle on the northwest coast. They made the journey in small ships in the early spring, and the crews and passengers hoped to see the New World by July. My family arrived in the 1650s in the person of Guyon Chiasson *dit* LaVallée, an unmarried farmer of twenty. In 1666 he married Jeanne Bernard, the second of his three wives, and one of the many children she bore was Sébastien Chiasson, my ancestor.

The Bay of Fundy has some of the highest tides in the world, which trap the ocean in the funnel-like bay and cover acres of land with the nutrients of the Gulf Stream. Using dykes and sluice gates to direct the flooding, the Acadians allowed these lands along the bay and the rivers to lie fallow for several years while rains and snow leached away the salt. The result was rich, flat soil perfect for agriculture, and the Acadian colonies grew and prospered.

As several generations passed, the Acadians' connection to France became tenuous. They were expert farmers now, and their wives gifted tenders of apple orchards. The Mi'kmaq people taught them hunting, fishing and the use of a local tree bark that could prevent and cure scurvy. Surviving the long, harsh winters became, with time, an Acadian skill, and the Acadians and the Mi'kmaq called each other brothers. Families intermarried and trust grew.

The emerging New England colonies of Britain had traded with the Acadians since the earliest years, and ships from Boston regularly sailed to Port Royal. As British relations with the native groups deteriorated, they resented the Acadians' friendship with the aboriginals and began to covet the rich Acadian farms. The Acadian homeland became a pawn in the imperial game being played out between France and England.

By the Treaty of Utrecht in 1713, France gave Acadia to the British. But the Acadians, who had lived in the area for more than three generations, considered themselves beyond the laws enacted in Europe. They were a peaceful people who called the British "nos amis les ennemis," our friends the enemies. Officially termed French Neutrals, they signed promises of neutrality with the new British commanders.

Such pledges were not enough to prevent the British from carrying out what is regarded as North America's first ethnic cleansing. By the middle of the eighteenth century they had deprived the French-speaking farmers of their rights and, in August 1755, they began to expel the Acadians from their land, using transports hired out of Boston. The new harvest and the fattened cattle were sold to pay for the deportations. The farms were then burnt. Over the next eight years, of eighteen thousand Acadians, some ten thousand lost their lives from shipwrecks, disease on board and smallpox epidemics after resettlement. When the French government complained of the high mortality rate, the British responded that it was not their fault but a consequence of the Acadians' "long voyage, their change of climate, their habits of body, their other disorders, and their irregularity and obstinacy."

In 1750, when the British plan of deportation started to become clear, my ancestor Jacques Chiasson was fifty-six years old. Jacques was the grandson of Guyon and the son of Sébastien, a member of the third generation of Chiassons to live in Acadia and the second generation to have known the shores of the New World as their only home. Together with his wife and eleven children, he escaped to Île St. Jean, which we now call Prince Edward Island. The family pioneered on the banks of a small coastal river, at a place called L'Étang des Berges. The soil was too sandy for farming, and Chiasson and his Acadian neighbours resorted to fishing. The 1755 purges passed them by.

Then, in the 1760s, the British took over their land there too. In 1763 Paul Chiasson, the thirty-six-year-old son of Jacques, with thirteen other Acadian families, made a bid to remove themselves from the English. They established Chéticamp on the western coast of what is now Cape Breton Island. On this barren shore, these pioneers—"Les Vieux Quatorze"—were left in peace. I was born on Cape Breton almost two centuries later.

My parents met at St. Francis Xavier University in Antigonish, Nova Scotia. My father, Alfred, was the star of the football and the hockey teams, and my mother, Joan, was the new beauty on campus. Their marriage in 1952 was a union in modern times of two cultures that had remained separate until the middle of the twentieth century.

My father is a twelfth-generation Acadian, born in Chéticamp. There were so many Chiassons in his village by then that individuals were known not only by their own first name but by their father's name and their father's father's name. My father was *Alfred à Thomas à Charles.* I would be called *Paul à Alfred à Thomas.*

My mother's family were Scottish pioneers on Cape Breton Island, and English is my mother tongue. It seemed normal to me that we had both a French-speaking and an English-speaking family. My mother learned to cook Acadian food, and we lived not far from Chéticamp, a place where old wharves were always alive with big wooden crates of lobsters. My sister, four brothers and I were raised with one foot in each of the two cultures that form the European roots of the island. The Scots came later than the Acadians but are so deeply grounded on the island that Cape Breton was known until a generation or two ago as one of the largest Gaelic-speaking communities in the world. At times the place seems saturated in tartans.

That summer day in 2001, after my visit to the lighthouse on Boularderie Island, my mother stopped to look through my pile of books and maps on the dining-room table. It was my habit to arrive at my parents' house for visits with a collection of books under my arm, mostly architecture and history.

"Why are you looking in these Cape Breton histories all of a sudden?" my mother asked.

"Just poking around. I think there's something over there, around St. Anns — a hill of rock called Cape Dauphin, right at the mouth of the bay on the southeast side."

"Of course. Cape Dauphin. The first Jesuit mission was at St. Anns, right there on that cape. The French were there really early, you know. They built a fort in—I think it was 1629, even before Louisbourg. It must have been small. They're always finding old things over there near Englishtown."

"Anybody write anything about that area around Englishtown?"

"Just a minute."

She went off, probably to the bookshelf in the study, and came back with a little clothbound book published in 1975 by James Lamb, and I settled down with Lamb's book in my favourite chair in the corner of the living room, next to a window.

Lamb's history concentrates on the south shore of the inner harbour and the area along the eastern shore of the bay, now a small town called Englishtown. But when discussing historical sites, he mentions the land at the opening of the bay: Cape Dauphin.

> Yet far and away the most intriguing and puzzling remains are those that abound in the wooded hills to the south . . . an ancient overgrown roadway, well ramped and graded, leading into the woods from the banks of the creek.

A built puzzle—just the sort of thing that attracts an architect with a weakness for the historical. Lamb mentions the ruins a second time.

> There are traces of wide and well-built roadways deep in these wooded hills, which may, of course, belong to

a much later era. But most baffling of all is the over-grown remains of a long, straight stone wall, which runs roughly east and west for a considerable distance. Was it intended as a defensive work, crowning the crest of the commanding ridge? It seems most unlikely, unless it was possibly associated with a blockhouse at each end, and yet it seems far too large and long and solid a work to be simply a farm enclosure.

He lists small relics found from the French period: cannon balls, bayonets, musket barrels, buckles and hobnails.

Yet all of these have been merely chance finds, of the most superficial nature. When you stroll today across the Englishtown pastureland, you walk among the tumbled remains of a puzzle of the most intriguing sort; a puzzle whose solution is half-guessed, but whose final clues are hidden by a paltry few inches of grass and topsoil. One can hardly wait to see this ancient conundrum made clear, as it must be, one day.

A conundrum. A conundrum on Cape Breton. I liked that.

I took the Lamb volume with me back to Toronto, finished reading it and called home. My mother answered the phone.

"Do you know anything more about Cape Dauphin? This book you gave me about St. Anns says something about unex-plained ruins in the hills. What's that about?"

"Yes. They're French."

"Really? Lamb didn't make that connection. To him the ruins were a mystery."

"No, no. They're French."

"He seems to know just about everything there is to know about the French occupation of the region."

"I thought it was quite a good little study."

"I wonder if the Acadians were involved? Lamb thought whatever was there was a conundrum, an architectural conundrum."

"Yes, the Acadians perhaps. But the French were in charge."

"Right. Well, anyway, I'm in the mood for a puzzle."

I searched out more histories of Cape Breton, and mentions of Cape Dauphin turned up again and again in my reading.

The geography of this isolated cape had clearly played a role in the island's early history. Both sides of the mountain at the seaward end are steeply sloped. Along the bay to the immediate southwest of Cape Dauphin, at the end of the road that runs along the shore of the narrow waterway called St. Anns Harbour, is the village of Englishtown. A long sandbar reaches from the opposite shore into the bay and almost touches the shore here. From early in the sixteenth century, just after John Cabot's discovery of the new coast, the sandbar had been used by European fishermen to dry their summer catch before returning to their home ports in the fall. By 1629 it was Port Dauphin, a solitary French military camp with forty soldiers and a single Jesuit missionary. Even today, there's no bridge across the gap of open water; a tiny ferry connects the highways

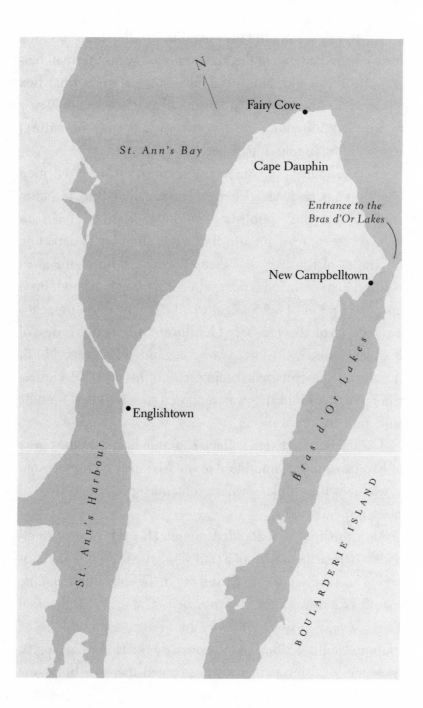

on either side during the summer. St. Anns Harbour has long been considered one of the best and most beautiful small harbours in the world, and, no doubt, this feature is what first attracted the attention of European sailors. It was not only easy to find but offered a safe port and a wealth of natural resources, including fresh water.

I came across a nineteenth-century history entitled "Beothuk and MicMac," from a series called "Indian Notes and Monographs" published in the *Journal of American Folklore*. Accompanying the article was an old map depicting the travels of Kluscap—Glooscap they called him—the great cultural hero of the Mi'kmaq, who, according to legend, lived on Cape Breton Island for centuries before the first Europeans arrived. Cape Breton schoolchildren still read stories of Kluscap, one of the best-known legends of eastern North America. I remembered reading tales of his great adventures when I was a child. He was supposed to have been friendly with animals.

The map interested me. Cape Dauphin had been the home of Kluscap and was important to the Mi'kmaq for that reason. It was shown as a place where someone special had lived, a place remembered.

After this find, I redoubled my search for historical references to the cape. I read of a trail along the shoreline that was said to end at a small cave carved out of the soft cliff face at the mouth of a tiny, almost dry river bed. The area is still called Fairy Cove, a curious reference in an area dominated since the nineteenth century by no-nonsense Scots. Archaeologists from the local museum had investigated the cave but came away with nothing. During the eighteenth century the Mi'kmaq were supposed to have organized nighttime raiding parties against English ships out of a cluster of small caves at Fairy Cove, now said to be haunted by the spirits of the Mi'kmaq and of the English they killed. The name alone suggests a lingering perception of the cape as a region of fairies, ghosts and visions from the underworld. When I asked my brother Gregory what he associated with Cape Dauphin, he could think only of the fairies who lived there. That sense of strangeness, combined with the area's importance to the native Mi'kmaq, seemed to have earned Cape Dauphin a peculiar respect among Cape Bretoners, though few have ever visited it.

What if there were the remains of an early French fort up on the mountain, earlier even than Louisbourg? Louisbourg, after all, was just an hour's drive down the coast. It had been the main French fortress in the North Atlantic during much of the early eighteenth century. In the spring of 2002 I ordered 1:50,000-scale topographic maps of the Cape Dauphin region through a Toronto supplier. When the maps arrived, I lined up St. Anns Harbour Map No. 11K/7 with the Bras d'Or Map No. 11K/8 to the east on the oversized stainless-steel table that dominates my small apartment. Standing back, I could envisage the topography of the region that stretched from Englishtown up to Cape Dauphin, a distance of less than ten kilometres. I was disappointed to find no indication of Lamb's walls or ruins along its slopes or summit. It didn't seem as if Englishtown—Port Dauphin, as it had been—was connected in any way with the summit of Cape Dauphin. Whatever it was that Lamb had seen or heard about on the summit must have been built sometime after Port Dauphin was vacated by the French in 1640. Yet, if it was a military installation, it must have been constructed before Louisbourg, which was started in the early 1720s and became the key French fort of Cape Breton Island.

I kept the maps on the table for a few days, and every now and then I'd stop and look at them. It occurred to me that, if there was something up there, it might be the remains of a chapel built by the Mi'kmaq. The Mi'kmaq had absorbed much of the Roman Catholic faith into their own religious system. Not far from Cape Dauphin, where the Bras d'Or Lake system stretches its fingers into the centre of the island, there is a tiny place called Chapel Island. The Catholic Mi'kmaq chapel there is still the site of important yearly pilgrimages. It is a simple wooden chapel, but an example of an actual Acadian-Mi'kmaq building project. A tiny chapel on the Cape Dauphin plateau top would have been enough to leave its mark on old maps, enough to be remembered in local legends, but not important enough to be included in general histories—and so may have been lost to modern memory and sight.

In August 2002 my parents had been married for fifty years and all the family—my sister and four brothers and their assorted spouses and children—had come from their various places in the country for the celebration. I flew down from Toronto to Halifax and rented a car, with the idea of spending a few days seeing more of the island before the party.

In the back of everyone's mind was my new prognosis. I had less than five years to live, and my family knew it. The blood factors that were supposed to be high were low, and the numbers that were supposed to be non-existent were climbing higher. I had lived with the often extreme side effects of HIV medication for almost ten years. My Toronto doctors now offered me a new combination of drugs, but after I'd listened to both sides of the debate, I decided enough was enough, I wouldn't even try. Death no longer frightened me, and I decided to enjoy the days that remained. I was back in Cape Breton Island, my own backyard, and the island could not have been more beautiful than it was that August—perhaps my last days of health in the land of my birth. I turned my attention to Cape Dauphin and began to plan a climb.

I knew from the maps that the only road leading to Englishtown ends in a farmer's field just beyond the town. The road couldn't go much farther along this coast or climb the north slope because the mountainside is too steep.

I had studied the opposite side of Cape Dauphin from the lighthouse on Boularderie Island. There had appeared to be a plausible route to the summit up that face. If there *was* some sort of road farther up the hill, it would have to be a road from the eastern side. Yet this location was on the opposite side of the cape from where the French had built Port Dauphin.

I assumed that where the cape was steepest, I would be able to snake back and forth up the cliffs. Whatever the case, it was important that I be able to walk up the mountainside. If it was impossible to climb, it would have been impossible to transport materials and labour to the summit. If there was no way up, Lamb's suggestion of ruins was nothing but rumour.

The morning of my parents' anniversary was warm and clear—such days are rare on an island noted for its long, wet winters and short, wet summers. I decided to take advantage of the weather.

   After breakfast I left my parents' house and drove the rental car out along the main highway that leads west from Sydney, along the coast to the Bras d'Or Lakes and Cape Dauphin. This highway is well travelled, well maintained and easy to drive. It quickly leaves behind the industrial centre, a once lovely region now blackened by a history of steel mills and coal mines, and winds through rolling hills. Water—lakes or rivers on one side and the ocean on the other—parcels the island into sections joined by bridges and ferry boats. Past these low-lying hills, the road crosses over the Seal Island Bridge, close to the narrow opening of the Bras d'Or Lakes. The bridge is long enough and high enough to have terrified me as a child, and I felt a small thrill of recollection as I crossed over. On the far side I wound along the base of Kelly's Mountain, which forms the higher extension of Cape Dauphin, with St. Anns Bay on one side and the Bras d'Or on the other. The main highway makes a sweeping curve as it begins to climb, and a small secondary road branches off to the right and follows the eastern shoreline of Cape Dauphin. I had been down this coastal road once, years before, but only part way. It had not seemed interesting, and now it appeared longer than I remembered. The car kicked up clouds of dust in my rear-view mirror as I followed the curves of the shoreline. Here and there were small houses, mostly summer places. At times I could see the far shore of Boularderie Island through breaks in the forest that lined the ocean side of the road. I drove past the remains of the small coal mine in New Campbellton, active in the nineteenth century and long since closed. I passed a row of pickup trucks parked neatly beside a wooden wharf in a small cove: lobster and crab fishermen were already out checking their traps.

Fifteen kilometres farther on, the road came to an end abruptly at a lone house at the tip of the cape. I had gone too far. From the topographic maps, I knew roughly where I needed to start my hike. I backed up along the road to where I thought there would be a more gradual climb.

Really, I was quite unprepared. In front of me was a relatively steep and heavily wooded mountain. I sat in the car a minute looking at it. But I'm a Cape Bretoner, I thought, imbibing a measure of fool's courage. I'm a local.

I could see an opening in the forest which had been cleared in the recent past. The good trees had been cut helter-skelter, the best ones trucked away and the smaller ones left to rot. It was an ugly scar, careless destruction by a weekend logging company. I looked back at the road. No one was in sight. I got out of the car and locked it, then walked through the clearing and started to climb.

I felt my way up from that small clearing. By the afternoon, I had only made it partway up and I was clinging to roots on the side of a steep and densely treed incline. It was hot, and I hadn't brought a compass, a map or water, but I was confident I wouldn't get really lost. I could go only up or down, and down would lead me back to the road and my car. Still, given the state of my health, I had been stupid. I was, after all, alone in the wilderness, and no one knew I was there.

I clambered over a fallen trunk, walked its length to a cluster of saplings that gave me easy handholds and hauled myself up. The undergrowth was somewhat less dense here. I stopped to catch my breath. A pair of chickadees hopped from branch to branch overhead. I looked up at them, and the sky beyond the canopy of dark conifers seemed unnaturally blue. I started climbing again, and my progress was easier. It was several minutes before I realized I was on a path.

I stopped and squinted at the underbrush to make sure it wasn't a trick of my imagination. No, I was on a path—overgrown, almost not there at all. But people had been here before me, and enough history had passed this way to leave a track. I felt immediately comforted. The sun was preparing to disappear over the summit above, and I would soon need to drive back to Sydney. My family was expecting me to appear in the dining room that evening, clean and dressed for the celebration. I looked up the path as it disappeared into the forest and felt a small sense of triumph. I had found something, hadn't I? The hike was a success. I'd come back some day, once I was better again and able to do this sort of thing.

Turning around, I started down the path. The faint track was walled with birch and maple trees that arched overhead, filtering the late afternoon sun. Beams shot through the branches, and a soft breeze from the ocean below made the path flicker in patterns. Bluebirds shrieked in the treetops and, suddenly, were quiet. I could hear nothing except for the rustle of the leaves.

I stopped. What was it? Something was catching my eye. As I looked around I could hear my own breathing. Ah, the rocks. The rocks that edged the path were not right—they weren't natural. I knelt to touch their edges. They were cut, hewn, straight. I carried on down the path. A hundred feet farther on the trees were thinner. Here I was able to see that the sides of the path were marked by the remains of low stone walls. The surface had been overgrown and the borders were almost lost, but this was—a road.

I sat down for a moment on a remnant of wall perhaps sixty centimetres in height and stared around me at what had been a well-constructed road about three metres wide. On either side were the remains of continuous stone walls. There was no doubt about it: this was the road that James Lamb had mentioned, the mysterious forgotten road up the mountain in Cape Breton. I stood and peered up and down its course as far as I could make it out. I was probably three-quarters of the way up the mountainside, and the road appeared to continue to the summit. So Lamb was right about the road. Could he have been right about the rest? I looked up the darkening slope and felt a shiver. The sun vanished behind the summit, and the woods were immediately darker. I started down again.

Five minutes later I stopped once more and touched the crumbling wall's cut edges to fix the stones in my memory, assure myself of their existence and reinforce my impression that this was no casual path snaking through a backwater wilderness. It was of consistent width, too wide for a country lane, and the walls marching along its sides were unlike anything in rural Cape Breton. They reminded me of walls in the English countryside or along narrow back lanes on Rhode Island. They were well made of angular stones, some no more finished than rough boulders, others cut in trapezoidal shapes to fit.

A road had been built—engineered—to go somewhere up on the mountaintop, to climb a steep and rocky slope. As an architect, I knew the road would have taken hundreds of men and many years to build. I looked up one more time, then down to where I could glimpse the waters of St. Anns Bay, far below me. I had found the first piece in a mystery it would take me two years of obsessive work to unravel.

CHAPTER TWO

FINDING THE
EDGES OF THE WORLD

AFTER I RETURNED to Toronto in August 2002, I could not
stop thinking about the sharp, cut edges of those stones in the
wilderness. For whatever reason, there was no historical
plaque at the base of the road and no photographs of it in
Canadian history books. In all likelihood the builders were the
French. It was a thrill to secretly contemplate the excitement
of helping restore an important French colonial site to public
recognition. But if I was going to establish who built the road,
I would have to be thorough—and thoroughness would mean
going back to the earliest European landings on these shores.

I was sure, if I looked hard enough, I'd find the records of that grand construction.

Despite a lifetime of voracious reading, however, my choice of profession was clear evidence that I am first and foremost a visual person. I'd already resorted to a set of topographical maps of Cape Dauphin, and the map of Kluscap's travels had been a delight. I now had the perfect excuse to indulge a private passion for history not just as it was written but as it was drawn, to see who had first inscribed Cape Breton on a map, and how they had pictured it.

Claudius Ptolemy, a second-century Greek citizen of the Roman Empire, is often referred to as the father of cartography. Writing from the library in Alexandria, Ptolemy, like many of his countrymen, thought of the world as a sphere. As a map-maker, he was the first European to impose a vertical and horizontal grid on his maps, a system that corresponds to our modern-day concept of latitude and longitude, the key to an accurate depiction of geography.

In 391, when the great library at Alexandria burned, Ptolemy's ideas were among the many that were lost. During the ensuing European Dark Ages, the science of cartography was kept alive by Muslim and Jewish scholars, primarily in the Middle East. The medieval Christian church decreed the world to be flat and rectangular, with Jerusalem at its centre and the whole surrounded by an abyss of water. The heavens were located above, and tropical lands were a boiling inferno in which no human could survive. Though Isidore of Seville, an early-sixth-century theologian and expert on the location of things holy, reported that heavenly Paradise lay in the farthest reaches of the Asian mainland, the regions yet unexplored by Europeans were generally believed to be inhabited by one-eyed monsters and big-footed demons. Gothic cathedrals were masterpieces of space, structure and light, but this was a dark time indeed for geography.

By the late thirteenth and early fourteenth century, however, map-makers began to draw maps that represented the observations of sailors who used the Mediterranean for trade, maps that showed more realistic outlines of European coast-lines. By the fourteenth century these early maps were including mysterious and miscellaneous islands out in the Atlantic. These islands at the very edge of Europeans' understanding of their world caught my imagination as I read. I made a note to keep watch for further reference to them.

In 1375 Abraham Cresques, a Jewish cartographer working in Spain, produced the Catalan Atlas, one of the best collections of late-medieval European cartography. Cresques had collected enough information to allow him to depict some of India and China, the Nile, parts of inland Europe, and the western coasts of France and Spain—and those miscellaneous Atlantic islands. European map-makers, it seemed, knew that something was out there, but they didn't yet know what it was or where. The islands were randomly placed, yet they served as a suggestion—or perhaps a reminder—to European powers that there might be a landfall beyond their western borders.

In 1380 the reports of Marco Polo were depicted on a map: the first time a European explorer's new discoveries were represented graphically.

———

The fifteenth century—the century before Europe's discovery of the New World—marked an evolutionary leap in European society's understanding of itself. Religion got out of the business of cartography, and maps became a critical record of what Western Europe actually knew, not just believed. For the first time, people attempted to place themselves in relation to their neighbours, their environment and other lands. The desire to understand became the driving force behind a new passion for exploration. For map-makers, the world was getting bigger, and the idea that it was flat and rectangular was replaced by the idea that it was flat and circular.

Meanwhile, a true precision had begun to appear on local sailing charts of European ports. The role of cartographers and navigators alike was to make the lucrative coastal trade safer and more predictable for mariners. Sailing charts were recorded by navigators in most of the important Atlantic and Mediterranean ports and were based on actual information gathered from returning sea voyagers. From this point forward, European sailing charts depicted with reasonable accuracy the entire Mediterranean, the west coast of Europe, England, Ireland and much of northern Africa. These first maps of the coastline not only gave form to the realities that European sea captains faced in their commercial trade routes but proved that the world could be drawn: they imposed the obligation of reality on those who set out to draw larger world maps.

A 1459 map commissioned by the King of Portugal was the first depiction of the world to incorporate newly reported lands with any realistic sense of proportion and correctness. That map, named the Fra Mauro Map after the Venetian monk who drew it, helped mark the beginning of modern European cartography. Fra Mauro's map, like other early world maps, attempted to show Europe, Africa and Asia as land masses—however vague—on a large scale. In the making of maps, this one was a huge advance.

Prince Henry the Navigator of Portugal, who died in 1460, just as the European age of discovery was beginning in earnest, fuelled a new passion for exploration that led directly to the voyages of Columbus and Cabot. His interest in navigation helped to reintroduce the works of Ptolemy to Europe, and his navigation school and library on the Atlantic coast of Portugal brought cartography alive again. His court was vibrant with new information, home to debates about the circumference of the globe and the size of the continents. Thanks in part to his initiatives, oceans became frontiers. By 1488 the Portuguese Bartholomew Dias, a sea captain and Henry's great-nephew, became the first European to round the Cape of Good Hope at the southern tip of Africa. In 1498 another Portuguese explorer, Vasco da Gama, rounded the Cape again and went on to reach the western coast of India, finally laying claim to a western sea route to Asia.

By the end of the fifteenth century, Africa was no longer a mysterious land mass with unknown limits: a sea route had been opened to Asia that skirted the continent. All of Europe had come to accept that the world was round.

The cartographer Martin Behaim had moved to Lisbon when he was twenty-five years old to immerse himself in the fascinating young science of cartography. Six years later, in

1492, back in his home city of Nuremberg and at the request of the city council, he produced a map to illustrate the great new things he had learned. This map was a globe, about 50 centimetres in diameter and meticulously crafted from flat sheets of paper cut to lie on the curved surface. A world once flat, the edges of which promised certain death to any ship so bold as to attempt to find its limits, was represented now by the safety of an endlessly navigable sphere.

The notion that there were islands off the European coast had been a Greek idea, popularized by Ptolemy. The Greeks believed that there was a place, located somewhere off the coast of Gibraltar, beyond which there could be no human habitation. The notion of a final marker at the edge of the world began to appear on newly drawn fourteenth-century maps. At first this mythical place was called the Island of Antilla and appeared on the 1367 navigational chart now in the Biblioteca Nazional at Parma. Antilla represented the limit of navigation—an unknown frontier, not yet an actual place. Eventually the name was attached to a location, an island in the Atlantic Ocean, believed by the map-makers to be real.[1]

1 Mythical islands continued to appear on European maps throughout the fifteenth century, but these islands became both fewer in number and more accurate in outline and position. Generations of cartographers shifted them around the Atlantic Ocean until, finally, an actual island would be reported and located, given a new name, and made part of the empire whose agents discovered and claimed it. The islands of Saint Brendan, for example, named after a sixth-century Irish monk who was said to have navigated the North Atlantic from Ireland, were positioned off the European coast by over a century of map-makers. Then, in the fifteenth century, the Azores were discovered off the coast of Portugal, whereupon the islands of Saint Brendan disappeared

This labelling was first done very tentatively on an anonymous chart from the early fifteenth century, and then more clearly on the 1424 Pizzigano chart and on a 1435 map called the Beccario Map. There it was shown as one of a group labelled as "Newly Reported Islands." For the first time the suggestion was made that this Antilla was populated, that it had settlements or centres of interest of some sort. The map indicated specific bays, depicted as small indentations along the otherwise straight coast. There were several of these bays and, within a generation of cartographers, the Benincasa Map of 1482 gave these bays place names: Aira, Ansalli, Ansodi, Con, Anhuib, Ansesseli and Ansolli. The Benincasa Map depicts a clear example of an island with seven named bays—seven distinct places.

About the same time as the Beccario Map—the early fifteenth century—a story began to circulate in Europe of an island on the other side of the Atlantic with actual cities. Martin Behaim included this legendary Antilla on the globe he constructed in 1492, which showed the world much as it was perceived by Columbus and his generation of European explorers. Below the drawing of the island, Behaim wrote: "In the year 734 of Christ, when the whole of Spain had been won by the heathen of Africa, the above island Antilla, called

from maps. The island of Brazil had been drawn on European maps as early as 1339. It was usually located somewhere in the oceans west of Ireland. In 1480 the English began sending out ships to look for it in the northern ocean, and the search for the mythical island stopped only when the name Brazil was chosen for the new land discovered in the South Atlantic by the Portuguese in 1500. Antilla was yet another of these legendary islands in the Atlantic: the name Antilla floated around on maps for a long while until it took on a real form and location in the Caribbean.

Seven Cities, was inhabited by an archbishop from the Porto in Portugal, with six other bishops, and other Christians, men and women, who had fled thither from Spain, by ship, together with their cattle, belongings and goods."

So the island of Antilla had become the Island of Seven Cities, the only island out in the northern Atlantic believed to hold non-native and apparently permanent settlements.

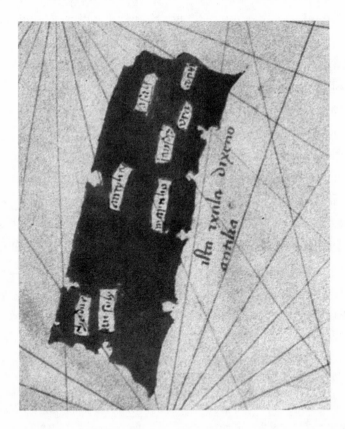

Detail of Pizzigano chart, 1424, showing the island of Antilla with seven large bays drawn along its coast.

Though these maps told a story unlike any other—of a lost but inhabited island far out in the Atlantic—they might have been no more helpful to me than the fables of the Holy Grail and the Lost Atlantis. After all, I was not looking for mythical islands. However, these maps, and others, soon led me back to Cape Breton Island. Giovanni Caboto, whom I'll write about in the next chapter, provided the links. Caboto, as it turned out, also mentioned the Island of Seven Cities. Indeed, he had reported finding it.

I discovered that this entire generation of explorers and geographers was exceptionally interested in the inhabited Island of Seven Cities. Cartographers were trying to place it, and adventurers made repeated voyages to locate it. European sailors, blown off course during storms in the North Atlantic, claimed to have visited it, but they were unable to find it again. One fact seemed indisputable in a period when few things were clear: Europeans believed that this mysterious island existed. They discussed it in official documents, and both Portugal and England launched expeditions to find it. The famous Spanish historian Bartolome de Las Casas reported that, in 1430, a Portuguese ship had been driven off course in the Atlantic and had landed on an inhabited island off the distant western coast of the ocean. The crew, worried that they would be held on the island, set sail as quickly as possible for Portugal, where they told their story to Prince Henry the Navigator, the man in Europe most interested in reports of new land across the Atlantic. Las Casas wrote that when Prince Henry asked these men to return to find the island, they refused.

Ferdinand Columbus claimed that his father, Christopher, knew the story of these shipwrecked sailors. "It is said that while the sailors were in church on that island," he wrote, "the ship's boys gathered sand for the firebox and found that it was one-third fine gold." The topic of gold was important to the older Columbus.

Then, in William Babcock's *Legendary Islands of the Atlantic* (1922), I found this quotation from the writings of a fifteenth-century historian named Galvano: "In this yeere also, 1447, it happened that there came a Portugall ship throught the streight of Gilbraltar; and being taken with a great tempest, was forced to runne westwards more then willingly the men would, and at last they fell upon an Island which had seven cities . . . The boatswaine of the ship brought home a little of the sand, and sold it unto a goldsmith of Lisbon, out of which he had a good quantitie of gold." It seems that these accounts by the younger Columbus and by Babcock represent two separate incidents, two different Portuguese ships, and two distinct reports of gold.

In 1475 the Portuguese initiated a new project to find the island. The king issued a royal charter granting Portuguese explorers any new islands they found. At the same time the charter removed an earlier distinction between inhabited and non-inhabited islands and referred, most specifically, to the Island of Seven Cities. The royal charter read in part:

> And it might happen that, in thus sending out to seek
> them (the new islands), his ships or people might find
> the Seven Cities or some other inhabited islands

which at the present time have not been navigated to
or discovered or traded with by my subjects, and it
might be said that the grant I have thus made must not
extend to them on account of their being thus inhabited. I declare by this charter that my intention and
purpose then at the time I thus gave them was that the
said charter comprises islands both inhabited and
uninhabited.

Both inhabited and uninhabited: the Island of Seven Cities
was theirs if they could find it. In 1486 another grant was
awarded to Fernão Dulmo, a Portuguese explorer and "gentleman of our lord the King's household and Captain of the
island of Terceira" who, according to the royal charter, "came
to us and told us how he wished to discover a large island or
islands or mainland by the coast, which is supposed to be the
Island of Seven Cities."

At first I could find nothing of what had actually happened
to these early attempts to discover the Island of Seven Cities.
Then I came across shipping documents from the harbour at
Bristol on the west coast of England that recorded unsuccessful attempts as early as 1480 to find Atlantic islands. The
English too, as it turned out, had the same stories of the same
mysterious islands and of the Island of Seven Cities. As I'll
describe in the next chapter, they continued to look for these
islands until the end of the century.

Christopher Columbus was known to have been interested in
the Island of Seven Cities as early as 1474, almost twenty years

before his voyage. He had consulted a Florentine cosmographer named Toscanelli on the possibility of a voyage to the west. Toscanelli sent him back a copy of a letter he had received earlier which recommended "the island of Antilla, which you call seven cities," as a possible resting point on the western route to Asia. According to Ferdinand Columbus, one of his father's motives for seeking the Indies "was his hope of finding before he arrived there some island or land of great importance." One of the islands of most interest was "this island some Portuguese showed on their charts under the name of Antilla," an island the Portuguese believed was "the Island of Seven Cities, settled by the Portuguese at the time of the Moors."

The older Columbus worked as a cartographer in Lisbon with his brother in 1485 and knew the science of maps. Most historians believe that he drew all or some of his own map of the world, as he understood it, sometime before the year 1492, probably about 1490. We still have that map: a single sheet of vellum measuring 70 by 110 centimetres, now in the Bibliothèque nationale de France in Paris. Much of the information it contains seems to have been compiled earlier, in the city of Louvain, in what is now Belgium. Columbus depicted much of western Europe, parts of the west coast of Africa following the new Portuguese discoveries, and many of the mythical Atlantic islands, including the islands of Saint Brendan and the Island of Brazil. I read that he had made particular note of the Island of Seven Cities. He apparently drew it with great detail and labelled it with an inscription: "Here is the island of the Seven Cities, now a colony of the Portuguese, according to the Spanish mariners."

——

I was in the Map and Atlas Section of the Toronto Reference Library. It had already been a long morning of dead ends, references and leads that had gone nowhere. It was well after the lunch hour, and I was hungry. The Columbus Map of 1490 does not play an important role in the history of early European cartography and is seldom referenced by historians, so I was having a difficult time finding a reproduction of it. I asked the librarian to recheck the catalogue to see if there was a source I had missed. Could it be somewhere else in their collection? He walked me down the aisle of atlases and map files to the last few shelves, a small section of historical atlases, and, without even checking a call number, pulled out a thin, illustrated book, *The Atlas of Columbus and the Great Discoveries.* "It might be in here," he said. I'd been looking for a single map, not an entire atlas, but there, as I opened the book, was a reproduction of the 1490 map—a good reproduction, in colour, clear and easy to read.

I laid the book open on one of the multi-drawered map cases. I stood and stared at the map for a very long time. Thoughts of food, or of anything else, vanished. In many ways it echoed the moment when I noticed I was standing on a stone road on Cape Dauphin.

The Columbus Map located the Island of Seven Cities farther north than the earlier positions for Antilla. Unlike other maps, however, here the island was drawn in careful detail as a distinct grouping of three islands, a large one and two smaller islands arranged below and beside it. I was astonished to see that this depiction matched both the shape and the orientation

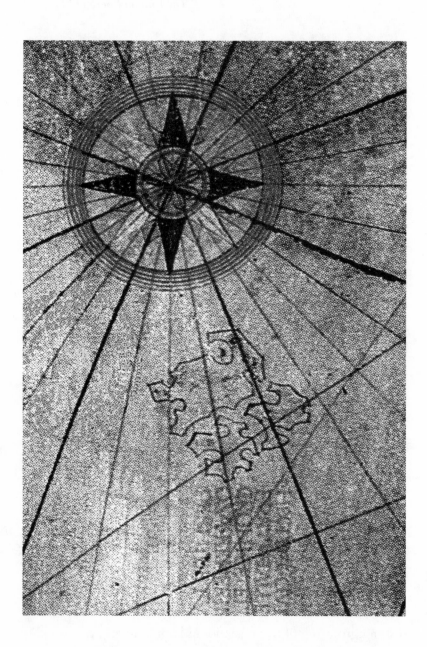

The Island of Seven Cities, as depicted on the Columbus Map of 1490,
matches the shape and orientation of Cape Breton Island.

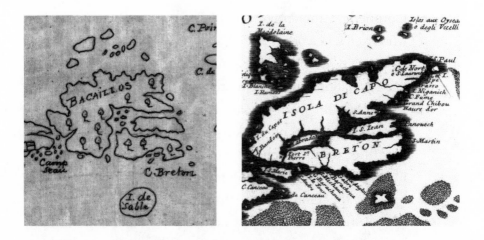

Lescarbot's rendering of Cape Breton Island, drawn in 1604 (above left); and Coronelli's Cape Breton from 1692.

of Cape Breton Island. Cape Breton is a single island, but it is split up by a lake system that snakes deeply into its core, dividing it into three distinct land masses that can easily be mistaken for individual islands. The axis of the long, thin land mass is at approximately a 45-degree angle, northeast to southwest, and the two smaller land masses lie beside and slightly below the long land mass. There is always water to be crossed. Here, on Christopher Columbus's map, I seemed to be looking at that very place.

I compared the Columbus Map to later maps of Cape Breton drawn in different periods and by other cartographers. Two maps stuck out. One had been drawn by Marc Lescarbot, a Parisian lawyer and adventurer who lived in Acadia during the winter of 1604, at the colony's very beginnings. The other was drawn almost a hundred years later in 1694 by Vincenzo

Coronelli, a monk and one of the great early cartographers who lived and worked among the splendour of the Papal court in Rome. One French map-maker, one Italian—from different generations, almost from different periods—but both men had drawn the island in an almost identical way. On both men's maps the central lake system divided the larger island into three distinct sections, with a pattern and an orientation like that shown on the Columbus Map. All three men were drawing the same island. But Columbus was drawing the Island of Seven Cities. His drawing was dated around 1490, before his first voyage. Lescarbot and Coronelli were drawing Cape Breton Island.

Now I began to search in earnest for other stories of overseas colonies—even before Columbus.

While the Island of Seven Cities legend was circulating through Europe, another less well-known story of a similar North Atlantic island was also current. In 1558 an Italian account of newly discovered northern lands was printed in Venice. The book was a compilation of fragments of information gathered from letters written over several generations by the Zeno family, an old and well-respected Venetian family of politicians and adventurers who did not appear to concoct silly fables. The author of the book was Nicolo Zeno. He recounts how, late in the fifteenth century, a fisherman had told his grandfather Antonio of a new land on the other side of the ocean, beyond Iceland and Greenland, which included two islands, Estotiland and Drogio. After several generations of recounting, however, the story as Nicolo Zeno finally recorded it contained much confusion and geographic vagueness. A reference to Zeno's book I found in an eighteenth-century history called it "the most puzzling in the whole circle of literature."

It may have been a case of not being able to see the forest for the trees. Even with the story's imprecise geography, experts agree that it refers to the northeastern coast of North America. Because there are indeed two large islands — Newfoundland and Cape Breton Island — on the northeastern coast, I read the Zeno stories. The narrative made no reference to the Seven Cities legend, but I found it described a settlement that was very similar to the cities of the legend. Zeno recounted a fisherman's elaborate description of an island where he been shipwrecked with five others after their boat had been blown off course during a violent storm at sea. It was the same sort of story the Portuguese had reported to Prince Henry: fishing ships driven by bad weather in the North Atlantic to a sophisticated island, a place where the Portuguese crews went to church with the inhabitants, discussed the political intrigues of Europe and, as two different versions of the stories relate, collected gold dust in the sand. Nicolo Zeno called the island Estotiland. The fisherman reported that they had been taken to "a fair and populous city, where the king of the place sent for many interpreters, but there were none could be found that understood the language of the fishermen, except one that spoke Latin." Then, after a brief description of the island's geography, the fisherman continued: "The inhabitants are very intelligent people and possess all the arts like ourselves; and it is believed that in time past they have had commerce with our people, for he said that he saw Latin books in the king's library, which they at this present time do not understand. They have their own language and letters."

After that, reports of the fair and populous city of Estotiland disappear from the records, never to appear again. The Island of Seven Cities would soon do the same, but not before it entered European history for one final and mysterious time.

CHAPTER THREE

JOHN CABOT: A FATHER EFFACED

I HADN'T EXPECTED my search to take me back to times before the European discovery of the Americas and for it to produce so much material from the Late Middle Ages. I had, however, expected to read about Giovanni Caboto, or John Cabot as we know him, who used to appear in the opening pages of every Canadian schoolchild's history textbook.

In 1497 King Henry VII of England sent Cabot, an Italian sea captain, navigator and adventurer, in search of "various islands" in the North Atlantic. Although Cabot had been born in Genoa, he moved to Venice and became a naturalized citizen there in 1476. In the late fifteenth century Venice was the commercial trading centre of Europe. Genoa, on the opposite Italian coast, was also one of the most important maritime powers in the Mediterranean. Both cities were perfectly suited for the concentrated study of the modern art of ocean navigation. The Genoese developed early maps and were foremost in the knowledge of legendary islands and overseas voyages—and that was their legacy to the young Cabot. In Venice, Cabot encountered Arab traders, then considered some of the best navigators in the world. Unlike most fifteenth-century European men who went adventuring, Cabot had travelled widely throughout the Mediterranean and even into the Middle East. By the time of his English-sponsored voyage in 1497, he could not have been better trained for his task.

Cabot left the west-coast English port of Bristol around May 20, 1497, with enough provisions to last eight months. He sailed west to Ireland and then out across the open Atlantic, landing on the shores of North America after thirty-five days, at the end of June. The shape and nature of the coastline was unknown to him. Its southerly regions had been visited by Columbus but not mapped. One land form looked much like another. It was a confusing place, and early explorers left confusing descriptions of it. The possible course Cabot followed, what currents and winds he used, the place of his first landfall, and where he planted the English King's standard—all these items he reported without specific locations. With one exception: Cabot made the specific claim that he had found the Island of Seven Cities.

Immediately on Cabot's return to Bristol in August 1497, foreign ambassadors sent out letters to their European courts advising their rulers of the new discovery. No report from Cabot himself has survived. However, from those ambassadors' reports we know that he spent a month along the coast and made at least one foray into the interior to survey the countryside and to plant the English flag.

In 1956 the American scholar L.A. Vigeras turned up a single English letter in the Spanish archives, making it one of the most recent additions to the long Cabotian bibliography. An English merchant in Bristol, John Day, had written the letter in the months following Cabot's return, addressed to the Lord Grand Admiral of Castile. The Spanish Lord Grand Admiral was none other than Christopher Columbus.

> Your Lordship's servant brought me your letter. I have seen its contents and I would be most desirous and most happy to serve you . . . I am sending the other book of Marco Polo and a copy of [the description of] the land which has been found. I do not send the map because I am not satisfied with it, for my many occupations forced me to make it in a hurry at the time of my departure; but from the said copy your Lordship will learn what you wish to know, for in it are named the capes of the mainland and the islands, and thus you will see where land was first sighted, since most of the land was discovered after turning back. Thus your Lordship will know that the cape nearest to Ireland is 1800 miles west of Dursey Head

which is in Ireland, and the southernmost part of the
Island of the Seven Cities is west of Bordeaux River,
and your Lordship will know that he landed at only
one spot of the mainland, near the place where land
was first sighted, and they disembarked there with a
crucifix and raised banners with the arms of the Holy
Father and those of the King of England, my master;
and they found tall trees of the kind masts are made,
and other smaller trees, and the country is very rich in
grass. In the particular spot, as I told your Lordship,
they found a trail that went inland, they saw a site
where a fire had been made, they saw manure of animals which they thought to be farm animals, and they
saw a stick half a yard long pierced at both ends,
carved and painted with brazil, and by such signs
they believe the land to be inhabited . . . They left
England toward the end of May, and must have been
on the way 35 days before sighting land . . . They
spent about one month discovering the coast and from
the above mentioned cape of the mainland which is
nearest to Ireland, they returned to the coast of
Europe in fifteen days . . . I kiss your Lordship's
hands, Johan Day.

Given Columbus's earlier interest in the Seven Cities, it is
hardly surprising that John Day should have written to him.

Day reported to Columbus that Cabot believed "the southernmost part of the Island of the Seven Cities is west of
Bordeaux River." That reference was more specific than any-

thing I had found. Cabot was using a method common among fifteenth-century navigators in reporting new locations. By linking a freshly discovered place in the New World to that of a known location on the European coast, mariners were able to specify its latitude and thus to find it again

Latitude is the distance north or south of the equator measured in regular parallel increments. To remain on the same degree of latitude while sailing, a navigator must maintain a consistent angle between the horizon and the North Star. If the angle he measures remains the same night after night, the ship is travelling in a straight line parallel to the equator. When that angle changes, his ship has veered north or south. To measure the angle between the ship and the sky, navigators of Cabot's era needed only a large protractor with an eyepiece for sighting the North Star (the point of reference changed in the Southern Hemisphere). Unlike the determination of longitude, a complicated skill that came much later to European navigators, no elaborate time-keeping or calculations were required.

John Cabot claimed that the Island of Seven Cities matched the latitude of the Bordeaux River in France. Bordeaux is located just inland from the French coast on the tip of the estuary of what is now called the Gironde River but was then known as the Bordeaux River. Its latitude was familiar to Cabot's generation of navigators and was already marked on early sailing charts as 45° 35' north. On the other side of the Atlantic Ocean, the most southerly tip of Cape Breton Island is a tiny peninsula called Isle Madame. Its latitude is 45° 33' north—less than four kilometres difference from that of the Bordeaux River. Cabot had discovered the Island of Seven

Cities for the English and, within a few years, it was to be called Cape Breton, the cape of the English.

Before Cabot's voyage, Europeans had suspected that land existed far out in the North Atlantic, but, other than the Viking site at l'Anse aux Meadows in Newfoundland, there are no records, ruins or even stories of any earlier settlements along this northern coast of the New World. Cabot found what had, until then, existed only in myth or as seemingly speculative outlines on maps. For the first time a European mariner had discovered the island of the legend and had given an exact location on a map.

At first, I wondered if Cabot's reference to the Seven Cities wasn't a mistake, a fluky misunderstanding of some sort. But in *The Cabot Voyages and Bristol Discovery under Henry VII*, James Williamson cited a letter to the Duke of Milan, one of two written in 1497 by Raimondo di Soncino, an Italian living in London. The writer confirmed that Cabot had "discovered the Seven Cities." In July 1498 Pedro de Ayala, the Spanish ambassador to Great Britain, sent a report to Ferdinand and Isabella of Spain. His letter advised that the English King had decided to give further support to Cabot because of the ongoing search for the Seven Cities. The document alleged that Cabot had brought back proof to the King that he had found land.

I had found three independent sources for Cabot's discovery: an English merchant to Christopher Columbus, an Italian diplomat to the Duke of Milan, and a Spanish nobleman to the King and Queen of Spain. This was an impressive list of influential people to whom the man's discovery was communicated. Cabot had credentials, and it seems that people listened to him. At the very end of the fifteenth century, at least for a few years, he was known throughout Europe as the mariner who had finally found the inhabited Island of Seven Cities on the other side of the Atlantic.

The reports of Cabot's discovery made reference to a legend that attributed specific characteristics to that place. The island was inhabited, and it supported a culture that had established an infrastructure of streets and roadways. As claimed in the few stories from shipwrecked fishermen, its people built large buildings, had libraries and could discuss the intricacies of European politics.

I was now devoting the better part of every day to my historical detective work. Whenever I came up for air, I felt in desperate need of a sounding board to test my reasoning and to prod me onward. My father and mother, my siblings and their spouses, and my good friends Beth and Rob were at this point the only people I felt comfortable sharing my research with. As often as I could, I laid out my work for them, seeking reassurance that I wasn't merely chasing phantoms.

Shortly after I came across the Cabot letters, my brother Gregory was in from Halifax on business. I met him and Gerard, who lives in Toronto with his wife, Debra, and their two children, for supper at Rodney's Oyster Bar.

I pulled out my file of Cabot letters as we sat down. There were five of them in total. While we were waiting to be served, I passed them out, and my brothers studied them. I said they all pointed in a similar, if somewhat confusing, direction, and I wanted the opinions of two people who would not be shy about letting me know if I wasn't making sense.

"All right," Gregory said. "So let's add up what Cabot found."

"He claims he found the Island of Seven Cities," I said. "He set out to find it and, when he got back, he said he found it."

Gregory nodded. "Okay. How about he was trying to look good?"

"You mean exaggerated his findings? This was one of the foremost navigators of his day. No one expected one hundred percent success, everyone knew these voyages were shots in the dark, but would he put his reputation at stake by lying? And he had a crew of eighteen. All of them would have been witnesses."

"Maybe he thought nobody'd find out," Gerard suggested.

"Yet he gave the island coordinates as accurately as it was possible to do at that time—accurate enough that you could still get there today by following his instructions. The one thing these explorers really knew how to do was determine latitude. They didn't lack the time to shoot the North Star and probably did so every clear night."

The oysters arrived, small, tender and salty from the Bras d'Or Lakes.

"You have to remember what it would mean to say you'd found the Island of Seven Cities. It was a legend everyone knew. It wasn't like saying, 'I found a lot of wooded hills, and the fishing was good.' It was saying you found that well-known but mysterious place on the other side of the Atlantic, the place with the cities."

"But your problem is that none of your various letters that mentioned Cabot's discovery of the Island of Seven Cities explain why everyone accepted that he'd discovered what he said he had," Gregory said.

"Correct. Other than reporting the claim, the documents are mute as to what he actually saw."

"Do you think he *did* find something other than trees and fish, Paul?"

"Well, we know he found evidence of logwood dye and domestic animals. Those are both out of place for a wilderness shore. And, of course, he saw evidence of human occupation."

"That's not surprising, is it?" Gerard pointed out. "There were native people everywhere."

"No, not surprising at all. But they were nomadic people, not farmers."

Gerard read out a passage I'd underlined in one of the letters. "Certain snares which were spread to take game and a needle for making nets, and he found certain notched [or felled] trees so that by this he judges that there are inhabitants."

"You would have been able to find signs of human occupation anywhere along the coast of either Newfoundland or Cape Breton," I said. "The Beothuk in Newfoundland or the Mi'kmaq in Cape Breton—anywhere on the coastline Cabot sailed—would have had summer camps. But something led Cabot and his crew to believe that seven cities, or at least *some* cities, had been built there. Otherwise he never would have made such a widely reported claim."

"What do you think, Paul?" Gregory asked. "Ruins?"

"Perhaps. The remains of an advanced civilization would have given Cabot a clue that this was the legendary island."

"But there *is* no public record of his seeing any ruins."

"No, there isn't. In fact, there are no direct writings of Cabot whatsoever. But he was sure enough of what he found to stake his reputation on it, to tell the King of England and to allow the news to be reported to Italy and Spain. At such-and-such a precise latitude, along the coast of what was later to be called North America, he had found the Island of Seven Cities."

The next morning I went back to the library and looked over my sources. There *were* a few unusual things about the Cabot claims, puzzles more than clues. From John Day's report to Columbus, I knew that Cabot had claimed to have seen the droppings of farm animals, but neither the Mi'kmaq nor the Beothuk had domestic animals before the coming of Europeans. Nor did they have the dye colour Cabot referred to as "brazil" in the letter sent to the Duke of Milan by Raimondo di Soncino. In the fifteenth century, brazil (derived from the Italian word for "glowing coals") was the name given to a hard red wood imported from Ceylon through Alexandria. A dye extracted from the wood produced various shades of red. During the Middle Ages this dye, though expensive, was widely used for both painting and the dyeing of cloth. Cabot, from his years in Venice, would have been familiar with it as a valuable trade good.[1]

---

1 The Portuguese found a species of tree in South America that produced a similar dye, and the name attached itself to the newly discovered country.

I looked back at the Italian ambassador's letter to the Duke of Milan. He wrote that Cabot and his crew "think that brazil wood and silks are native there." Cape Breton is a relatively cold, rocky region and home to mostly spruce and pine. Brazil wood is similar to teak or mahogany, the dark red hardwoods usually found in warmer climates with lush growing conditions. There are some birch, oak and maple trees among the short evergreen forests on Cape Breton, but no teak or mahogany. Cabot may conceivably have mistaken the colour of brazil wood for that of a local wood dye. But silk? I had somehow missed the reference to it. Silk was something Cabot could hardly mistake. It was a rare and exotic fabric produced almost exclusively in Asia. Woven from the long, thin filaments spun by cocooning moths, the strong fibres reflect light, so that cloth woven from them shines in a way that sets it apart from the other, more commonly used fibres of the period. John Cabot, as a trader working out of Venice, would have known silk.

It was curious that there were no descriptions of grand buildings or anything whatsoever to support Cabot's assertion. Yet the man had nevertheless given his discovery a specific location and taken responsibility for his claims. He reported them to his sponsor and benefactor, and those reports appear in a number of significant government documents written just after his return. We know that in the months after that return, he was widely recognized in England as an important explorer and adventurer. Yet, given all that, the story of John Cabot's first ocean voyage had almost disappeared from history within a generation. According to a second Letters Patent, a royal decree allowing an explorer to explore, which was awarded to Cabot by the English King and dated February 3, 1498, he may have made a second voyage of discovery that year. If he did, it is generally supposed that he never returned. Very little documentary evidence remains of that second voyage and, by 1500, John Cabot appears to have been dead or missing. How, I wondered, could his achievements have been obscured so quickly?

Certainly John Cabot's explorations were somewhat overshadowed by Columbus's discoveries five years earlier. Being second, Cabot's claims of discovery must have seemed less important and more malleable in the recounting. But, most surprisingly, the chief recounter appears to have been his own son, Sebastian.

After Cabot disappeared, Sebastian's career blossomed during the following decades and in several European countries. By 1509 he had made at least one voyage to find an Arctic passage to Asia, though this endeavour was unsuccessful. When Sebastian returned from the voyage, he found that his patron, King Henry VII, had died. The new king, Henry VIII, did not share his predecessor's interest in maritime discoveries. A lull in English overseas exploration followed and, during that time, Sebastian Cabot's failed Arctic voyage became linked with his father's 1497 voyage. Sebastian's stories of Arctic visits to cold northern lands of polar bears and ice floes became confused with his father's claims.

After the unsuccessful Arctic voyage, Sebastian Cabot was employed as a map-maker for the English government and, by 1512, he had been appointed as a captain in the Spanish navy. By 1518 he was a *pilot major* for Spain. His job was to examine future Spanish mariners in their knowledge of navigation and cartography, a role that would have given him a great deal of influence over an entire generation of young mariners. During this period he was approached by both England and Venice to lead naval expeditions to the New World, but nothing came of these plans.

By 1526 we find Sebastian at the head of a well-equipped Spanish fleet that hoped to open a new route to the East by following the Portuguese navigator Ferdinand Magellan's explorations. But four years later Sebastian Cabot returned with his broken-down expedition, having accomplished nothing. His leadership came under question, and his handling of the fleet resulted in heavy fines being levied against him. For several years he was banished to a Spanish colony in Morocco. Then he returned to England at the King's request and appears to have remained an active figure in the exploration business, at least as a landlubber. He kept alive his contacts and intrigues with both Spain and Venice and maintained a presence on the London waterfront. One 1556 report, written by ship's master Steven Borough, has Sebastian at the harbour to wish that captain success in a new adventure. It provides insight into the figure Sebastian Cabot had become.

> The 27 being Monday, the right Worshipfull Sebastian Cabota came aboard our Pinnasse at Gravesende, accompanied with diverse Gentlemen, and Gentlewomen, who after that they had viewed our Pinesse, and tasted of such cheer as we could make them aboard, they went on shore, giving to our mariners

right liberal rewards: and the good old Gentleman
Master Cabota gave to the poor most liberal almes,
wishing them to pray for the good fortune, and pros-
perous success of the *Serchthrift*, our Pinnesse . . .
He and his friends banqueted, and made me, and
them that were in the company great cheer; and for
the very joy that he had to see the towardness of our
intended discovery, he entered into the dance himself, among the rest of the young and lusty company:
which being ended, he and his friends departed
most gently, commending us to the governance of
almightly God.

Sebastian Cabot died the following year.

I found extensive documentation compiled during the
younger Cabot's rise to prominence. And more than one
writer claimed that Sebastian Cabot had "repeatedly and
deliberately misrepresented his role" on his father's expedition
of 1497. His 1508 voyage to northern Labrador gave him some
of the credentials he must have craved, and the voyage allowed
him to share in his father's image as an important explorer,
navigator and mariner. However, the desire to bask in that
shared fame led to the clouding of his father's legacy. He
appears to have confused his father's first landfall with a
description of his own failed Arctic trip. He credited the 1497
landing to "John Cabot, the Venetian, and Sebastian Cabot
his son." But at the time of John Cabot's discoveries, Sebastian
was fourteen years old, no more than a cabin boy if he was
even on the voyage. The documents and reports of the period

made it clear that the son exaggerated his participation to the point of falsehood. The only early voyage Sebastian Cabot actually may have led was his failed Arctic mission. I came across an early printed map, the so-called Paris Map of 1544, produced when printed sheets were just beginning to be available for widespread distribution. The map was drawn originally, at least in part, under Sebastian Cabot's control and supervision. He wrote the legend that described the first landfall of 1497 as being made at a place "very sterile" with "many white bears." This map opened the door to hundreds of years of mistaken speculation on Sebastian Cabot's role as a grand explorer, years that subtly relegated his father's position, and his father's discoveries, to a footnote.

After Sebastian Cabot's claims were included on the Paris Map, his stories were buttressed by later accounts of his father's voyage that omitted John Cabot's role altogether. Who would not believe a son? The fact was that Sebastian's adult life had positioned him to advance his version of events. His account, viewed as fact until relatively recently, muddied the already unclear waters surrounding his father's discoveries. Sebastian Cabot's claims found their way into history books and were not dispelled until more documents began to surface during the nineteenth century.

This confusion of fact and fiction became combined with the mistaken but stubborn notion that John Cabot's voyage had been an unsuccessful English attempt to find a western route to Asia. This idea served to position the elder Cabot in a minor, dead-end role in North American exploration. In history after written history, John Cabot's voyage is depicted as a failure—a failure to find something he wasn't even looking for. As documents from the period make clear, his voyage was not to seek out a route to the East but to search for the legendary islands believed to be located in the North Atlantic. Sailors from Bristol had tried to make this find in the past, but now John Cabot, "who is a very good mariner and has good skill in discovering new islands," was going to make an attempt. Given that his plan and his purpose was to find these islands, he was successful indeed. He did find the Island of Seven Cities.

Five hundred years after his discovery, John Cabot is recognized as the first European explorer to set out with a specific aim and to reach that goal, as clearly defined in an official Letters Patent issued by a royal court. Unlike the explorations of Columbus, Cabot's voyage was a complete success. He found what he was looking for. We know that he returned with news of that success to the courts of Europe. When he brought back those stories of legendary islands where silk and dye wood were found, Henry VII granted him a second Letters Patent, with the provision that he might "take at his pleasure six English ships."

After the brilliant success of Cabot's voyage of discovery, his claim received attention for about a generation. Then it was forgotten. In 1499 no word arrived from his new mission, and in that same year the last instalment of Cabot's royal pension was paid. He vanished from official records. Any reports he made to the King of England about his findings on the Island of Seven Cities also vanished. After he was gone, his son Sebastian talked on for years about a frigid and barren coastline, squelching any further English passion for the legendary island.

A map, believed to have been drawn in 1508, shows the Seven Cities displaced from their island home to an area along the coast of North America and south of present-day New England. The seven cities are indicated by tiny bishop's mitres, shown as various settlements along the coast. The legend of the Seven Cities lost its cohesiveness, and the image of this unusual island, alone in the vast ocean, faded away.

By 1530, just thirty-three years after Cabot's discovery, a region simply called the Seven Cities was thought by the Spanish to be located in an area of what is now the southwestern United States, then Spanish territory. At a time in the New World when Spain was beginning to expand her conquests northward, rumours circulated of large permanent settlements and a sophisticated indigenous population living in the region on which the Spanish had set their sights. Inexplicably, those rumours became connected with the legendary Seven Cities. The story was similar to the original legend of a land settled by seven fugitive bishops, and, during the 1530s, it was widely circulated in New Spain. In the spring of 1539, with the existence of these cities substantiated by vague local reports, a Franciscan friar, Marcus de Niza, was sent by the Spanish authorities to search for the Seven Cities. The friar returned in the late summer with a report of immense walled cities and multi-storey houses studded with precious stones. He was describing the pueblos of the Zuni Nation, in an area of New Mexico set in a spectacular vast landscape of coloured cliffs and high, flat-topped hills. Unfortunately, Friar Marcus claimed he had been told of a valley near these cities where the inhabitants used golden vessels every day. He had seen nothing himself, but this was the sixteenth century, and Europeans were impassioned by thoughts of gold in the New World.

For his work, Friar Marcus was awarded the office of "Provincial of the Franciscan Order of New Spain." Almost instantly "all the pulpits of the order resounded with the stories of such wonderful marvels discovered by the new father provincial."

The legend of the Seven Cities, with constant retelling, had become more and more fantastic. As it was recounted from one church congregation to the next, the Spanish became more sure of its truth, and their gold lust grew stronger. In the spring of 1540 an expeditionary force was organized in New Spain to find the Seven Cities under the command of Francisco Vasquez Coronado, the explorer credited with discovering the Grand Canyon. With a Spanish army of three hundred well-equipped soldiers and hundreds of auxiliaries drawn from local native allies, Coronado went in search of the mysterious cities of Friar Marcus. Two years later the company returned empty-handed, having marched through much of the southwest United States. The expedition had been a fiasco. That marked the end of the Seven Cities legend in New Spain.

I continued my search nonetheless and found the island on a few later maps—the Desceliers Map of 1546, the Ortelius Map of 1570, the Mercator Map of 1587—all important names in the history of sixteenth-century European map-making.

Mercator's map, drawn by a man whose ideas would change the science of cartography in Europe, showed the Island of Seven Cities as a small, randomly placed island off the southern coast of America. Within a generation, though, the legendary island had disappeared from geography entirely.

It was clear from the documents I was finding—all originals or first-generation translations—that the unravelling of the legend had started just after John Cabot's voyage of discovery in 1497. When Cabot returned to Bristol, it was reported throughout Europe that the Island of Seven Cities had finally been found. The matter was so important at the time that it was the subject of official government dispatches. Yet, in little more than a decade, the island was to acquire a reputation as an icy wasteland. Then it was forgotten.

CHAPTER FOUR

LOST BROTHERS

THE TORONTO REFERENCE LIBRARY has copies of most published early Canadian documents, and they are easily accessible. I was able to order everything online, make the thirty-minute walk from my apartment, and find the books and documents waiting for me there when I arrived. Having exhausted the cartographic evidence, I moved on to survey the history of the east coast in detail, record by record and report by report, searching for the builders of my road.

New information has always been a key to power, and the rulers of countries interested in maritime expansion regarded news from the distant reaches of the unexplored Atlantic as crucial information. Word of Cabot's claims was eagerly received in Portugal, where Lisbon had a well-established maritime trade link with Bristol.

Henry the Navigator was the Portuguese prince who, in pursuing his dream of new discoveries, had surrounded himself with navigators, astronomers and map-makers. He made the first Western attempt at a concentrated and logical program for the planned exploration of new sea routes into the unknown. His collection of experts studied maps and sea charts and organized new reports from returning mariners. His court became the catalyst behind much of the Portuguese exploration that followed his reign, as the country's sailors, like their English counterparts, continued their exploration of the northern Atlantic. Cabot's stories of new lands fuelled a passion there that already existed.

By the Treaty of Tordesillas in 1494, Pope Alexander VI had divided any newly found overseas lands into two zones of Roman Catholic influence: the Spanish zone west of an imaginary north-south line, approximately 60° west longitude, and the Portuguese zone east of that line. By a curious coincidence, the line passed through Cape Breton Island, effectively marking the island as a transitional zone, a beginning and an ending, a no-man's land.

Three years after Cabot's return, the King of Portugal issued a Letters Patent to the nobleman Gaspar Corte-Real, granting him feudal rights over any lands he might discover within the limits of Portuguese ownership in the Atlantic. In the early summer of 1500, Corte-Real made his first exploratory voyage into territories granted to Portugal: the northeast coast of the Americas. He reached the east coast of Greenland in early June. His ship—there may have been two—went on to explore sections of both the east and the west coasts, far enough north for him to describe Greenland as the "region of the white bears" even in mid-summer. He also came into contact with the native people, describing them in this way:

> [They are] very wild and barbarous, almost to the extent of the natives of Brazil except that these are white. By exposure to the cold, however, they lose this whiteness with age and become more or less brown. They are of medium height, very active and great archers. For javelins they make use of bits of wood burned at the ends which they throw as well as if they were tipped with steel. These natives clothe them-selves in skins of animals, which are plentiful in that region. They live in rocky caves and in thatched cot-tages, have no laws and are great believers in augury. They maintain the order of marriage and are extremely jealous of their wives.

Like the natives of the rest of the northern coast, these people were not builders, nor did they have metal tools.

Corte-Real returned to Lisbon in the autumn of 1500, before the North Atlantic winter set in. The following May, with the continued support of the Portuguese King, he set out again, this time with three vessels. He sailed past the ice-packed waters of Greenland to the coast of Labrador, and then south along the coast of what is now Newfoundland. In the first week of September he ordered two of his three ships to return to Lisbon. He decided to remain along the coast with hopes of continuing his exploration southward. The two ships left Corte-Real and his crew on the coast of Newfoundland, and he was never seen again.

The Corte-Reals, however, were a family of brothers — young men, all maritime adventurers. Not surprisingly, in the spring of the following year, 1502, Miguel Corte-Real set out from Lisbon in search of Gaspar.

Miguel Corte-Real's three ships arrived on the coast of Newfoundland by the end of June. Here they split up, each set to explore a separate section of the coast in search of the older brother. After scouring the Newfoundland coast, two of the three ships returned to the location where they had agreed to meet, but the third ship, carrying Miguel, was never seen again.

Coming as I did from a close family of brothers raised to understand the dangers of the ocean, the pain of the Corte-Reals was tangible to me, and the little-known saga became a true romance. After the ships returned without Gaspar or Miguel, an older Corte-Real brother, Vasqueanes, petitioned the Portuguese King to renew the search, but the possibility of losing more ships and loyal subjects to an enterprise fraught with unfathomable dangers was deemed unwise. No more ships were sent in search of the missing brothers.

Beyond its melancholy outcome, the Corte-Real stories contained an interesting detail. Unlike Cabot's ships, the ships that returned from the original Corte-Real voyage brought back cargo. The Venetian ambassador to Portugal,

Pietro Pasqualigo, claimed that the adventurers had captured fifty natives on this newly discovered coast. After the
first vessels arrived back in Lisbon, he sent a letter to his
brothers in Italy in which, besides describing the natives'
animal-skin clothing and their stone knives, he noted that,
being "tall and well-built," they were "admirably calculated
for labour." The unsuspecting natives were sold in the lucrative Lisbon slave markets, adding their lives to the rich trade
the Portuguese already carried on with Africa. Beyond
slaves, the newly explored coast was a source of valuable
timber—raw material for the expanding Portuguese shipbuilding industry.

According to the Pasqualigo letter, the ships' commander
had described one of the natives as wearing a pair of silver earrings "certainly made in Venice," while another carried part of
a gilt sword which the commander declared "unquestionably
came originally from Italy."

Now, here was something to consider. To claim that these
objects were of Italian origin, and specifically Venetian, implied
that they were foreign, ornate and mysterious. Venice was the
greatest trading power in the Mediterranean, with warehouses in Alexandria and links to the remote East. Venetian
associations were exotic associations. The earrings and sword
were not native goods. They were Venetian—not typically
European. They were found and brought back to Lisbon
well before there was any known European trade in the
North Atlantic. Fishermen don't carry gold swords.

Not surprisingly, the promise of new commodities such as
slaves and timber overshadowed these small but curious

details. The Portuguese may have believed that the two little treasures were remnants of John Cabot's voyage, only four years earlier: Cabot and his crew of eighteen men could have left behind a pair of ornate silver earrings and a gilded sword. Yet that would seem unlikely. Cabot's was not a grand voyage and, save for a large cross and the English flags he may have raised on the shore, the documents that record it never mention trade goods or any objects being left behind.

Reading these reports five centuries later, I could conclude only that the sword and the silver earrings were of neither Portuguese nor English design but were strange looking and were found during the summer of 1501 along the North Atlantic coast at a time before European trade had begun. These objects found by the Corte-Real brothers, together with the mysterious island so carefully depicted on the Columbus Map of 1492 and John Cabot's claim to have discovered the Island of Seven Cities, led me to wonder if there hadn't been a history to this narrow piece of coastline even before the first European voyages. The Europeans certainly seemed to have suspected it.

As the early legends of cities, of libraries and gold dust in the sand passed from memory, the records of new explorations continued to make unusual claims. For most of Europe, every third day was a time of fasting. As a result of these religious decrees, no meat, and sometimes not even meat products such as milk, eggs, butter or cheese, could be eaten by the faithful. Fish was not considered meat and was free of restriction. To supply this need, fishermen of the sixteenth century, from France, Portugal and England, developed a thriving summer fishing industry on the Grand Banks, off what is now New-foundland and Cape Breton. After the Corte-Real brothers, the Portuguese maintained their nominal entitlement to the coastline of Cape Breton, and their claims continued to appear in official documents, at least until the French began exploration along this coast in 1534. In 1506, for instance, the Portuguese government levied a royal tax of ten percent on the fish caught off this coast.

In 1520 there was a renewed Portuguese interest in explo-ration of these waters and possibly an early attempt at a perma-nent year-round colony. In the summer of that year, Joao Alvares Fagundes, a fisherman from the town of Vianna along the northern coast of Portugal, made an official voyage of dis-covery to the Americas under the auspices of the Portuguese King Manuel. The only actual reference I could find to the fate of this voyage—an English commentary on the early Portuguese voyages written by the Reverend George Patterson and published in 1890 in the *Proceedings and Transactions of the Royal Society of Canada*—suggested that Fagundes visited the coast somewhere between Newfoundland and Nova Scotia. After his return to report his success to the King, he was given a Letters Patent granting him ownership of the lands he had visited, bordered to the south by the land then owned by the Spanish—which at that time was most of the rest of North America—and to the north by what was seen as the Corte-Real family claim—present-day Newfoundland. The King awarded Fagundes what must be one of the oddest pieces of real estate given to an early explorer by royal decree. "And furthermore it is our pleasure to give and grant him, in the above-mentioned manner with legal right and inheritance, the white and black soap-houses of the said lands and islands." "Saboarias, brancas e pretas" is how the original document reads. What were these black and white *saboarias*, or soap factories? I had no idea.

At this point, history is unclear. Fagundes may have made this second voyage with the expectation of beginning a year-round settlement. A Portuguese report written fifty years later claimed that two vessels under his command and with the support of certain noblemen from Vianna had sailed in hopes of establishing a colony in the northeastern lands of the New World. The report claims that, on this second voyage, after losing their vessels along the coast of North America, Fagundes and his shipwrecked colonists were said to have settled "at Cape Breton, at the beginning of the coast that runs north, in a beautiful bay where there are many people and goods of much value." No more was heard from them, and their attempt disappeared from future records. The news of the colony was believed to have been relayed back to Portugal by "the Basques who continued to visit that coast in search of the many articles to be obtained there, who bring word of them and state that they [the settlers] asked them to let us know how they were, and to take out priests; for the natives are submissive and the soil very fertile and good." This information was all that made its way into the report written fifty years later.

I couldn't ignore the reference to the location of the Fagundes settlement, which matched Cape Dauphin. The location was at the "beginning of the coastline that runs north," the open hinge at which the east coast of Cape Breton changes direction.

If Fagundes ever actually made this second journey and if

his group of settlers ever actually existed, it was clear to me that the small size and ragtag condition of their expedition—two small vessels shipwrecked on a wilderness coast, leaving no records behind except a lone mention in a single report delivered second-hand from the Basques—rendered any connection with the road I had found up the side of Cape Dauphin all but impossible. The scale of construction of the road was too massive to be accomplished by two tiny boats of shipwrecked pioneers. During the sixteenth century—and this could be said even up to the late nineteenth century—the magnitude of such a project was beyond the ability of any European private enterprise. It was a project that would have taken royal decrees, involved a good part of the country's workforce and left in its wake much more than a single mention in a foreign report.

The reference in the King's charter to "Saboarias, brancas e pretas" led later historians to believe that Fagundes had planned to manufacture soap in the New World. That was hard to believe. I reread the charter, and the reference was clear. It was not a new production that Fagundes was to engage in, neither a new factory nor a new undertaking. These were existing buildings—black and white buildings of some sort. They were already there. The charter was not about the manufacturing of soap but the ownership of pre-existing buildings. Fagundes was simply being given them, with "legal rights and inheritance." Although I could find no

OPPOSITE: *Cape Breton Island showing the settlements at the seven primary bays. Cape Dauphin is located at the point where the coast "runs north."*

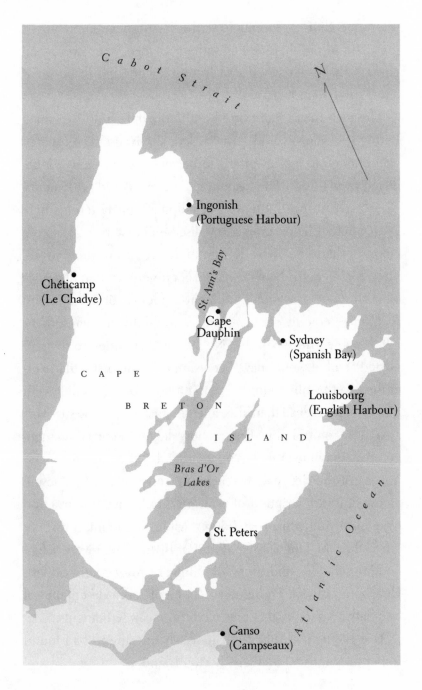

Cabot Strait

N

Ingonish
(Portuguese Harbour)

St. Ann's Bay

Chéticamp
(Le Chadye)

Cape
Dauphin

Sydney
(Spanish Bay)

C A P E

B R E T O N

Louisbourg
(English Harbour)

I S L A N D

Bras d'Or
Lakes

Atlantic Ocean

St. Peters

Canso
(Campseaux)

reference that explained how the Portuguese knew about these buildings before Fagundes's voyage, they were real enough to be described and important enough to be referenced in the contract.

The idea that a scant one hundred people from two small Portuguese ships would have settled, survived and prospered well enough to ask for priests to be sent over to them contradicted everything I knew about early New World settlements. The first European attempts at colonization lasted a single winter before being ravaged by disease and starvation. Those colonies that did survive left multiple records of their adventures, even lengthy books. A single document, written fifty years after the fact, was not significant evidence of a successful Portuguese colony, one large and lasting long enough to have left notable ruins behind. No, if the Fagundes settlement existed at all, it would have been similar to the first settlements of the seventeenth century: at most a tiny coastal hamlet, with more residents dead than alive after the first winter, the survivors anxious to return home. But the story did for the first time mention real, tangible buildings on the island. Other than the grand images of the Seven Cities legends, this was the first actual architectural description of a clearly non-native construction type: black and white soap-houses. More important, it was not phrased in the language of legend or myth. These were actual buildings that Fagundes was inheriting, by royal decree no less. Here in an official Portuguese document was a description of non-native buildings that preceded European settlements.

The Portuguese, like the English before them, had found something unusual on Cape Breton Island.

CHAPTER FIVE

AFTER THE PORTUGUESE

FOR THE NEW GENERATION of European navigators in the early years of the sixteenth century, the world was knowable — and the most fascinating place still to be known in that world was the other side of the Atlantic Ocean. Immediately after the great voyages of Columbus and Cabot, the Spanish King commissioned Juan de La Cosa, the official cartographer of Spain, to depict the new lands that the two explorers had reported finding. The result was the La Cosa Map of 1500, the first attempt by a European at an accurate and logical depiction of the American coastline based on the reports of actual explorers. If La Cosa had to work from verbal, often vague, visual description, he was at least fortunate in this respect: his information came directly from the two original sources.

After Cabot returned from his voyage, he drew a map and built a small globe based on his discoveries. In the letter that Raimondo de Soncino sent to the Milanese Duke in December 1497, just four months after Cabot's return, de Soncino wrote of "Messer Zoane Caboto" that "this Messer Zoane has the description of the world in a map, and also in a solid sphere, which he has made, and shows where he has been."

In what appears to be an attempt to address the duke's fears and doubts, de Soncino makes it clear that Cabot "tells all this in such a way, and makes everything so plain, that I also feel compelled to believe him. What is much more, his Majesty, who is wise and not prodigal, also gives him some credance, because he is giving him a fairly good provision, since his return, so Messer Zoane himself tells me."

A copy of those discoveries was sent by the Spanish ambassador in London to the Spanish King in July and then on to La Cosa's studio. It was probably in La Cosa's hands by the autumn of 1498. Cabot's original map and globe have disappeared, as have the copies that were sent to Spain, but the La Cosa Map still exists, uncovered in a Paris antique store in 1833. It is the first map we have to show what Cabot actually reported and, not surprisingly, has become one of the most studied European maps of these early discoveries. La Cosa's map showed the Seven Cities—*Citra Setemb*—as no longer an island but vaguely located much farther inland. For the area around Cape Breton and Newfoundland, La Cosa drew a simple jagged line for the coast and added five English flags, suggesting that Cabot had landed five times. One section of this coast, the small piece of land that was to become known as Cape Breton, La Cosa labelled as *Cauo Descubierto* — "the cape that was discovered." I checked every source I could find and every reference was clear: "Cauo Descubierto" referred to Cape Breton, or at least a part of what is now Cape Breton Island. But I was genuinely puzzled. Was Juan de La Cosa ignoring Cabot's claim to have found the Seven Cities? His map appeared to move the Island of Seven Cities from where Cabot reported finding it and, instead, marked that place as "the cape that was discovered."

The La Cosa Map effectively dissociates the popular medieval legend of Portuguese cities from what Cabot actually found. It must have been clear to Cabot that he had not found a community of Portuguese bishops and their flock. He made no mention of long-lost families and reported no return to Europe or news of what they must have endured. The settlement on Cape Breton appeared to have been something else entirely.

But I wondered if La Cosa's use of the term *descubierto* might not be significant. I would have missed it had it not been highlighted by Samuel Eliot Morison, a recognized historian of the period, in his book *Portuguese Voyages to America in the Fifteenth Century*. As Morison points out, *descubierto* refers to something that has been found, but there are two slightly different meanings. In one sense, the word refers to something that someone went looking for and found. La Cosa

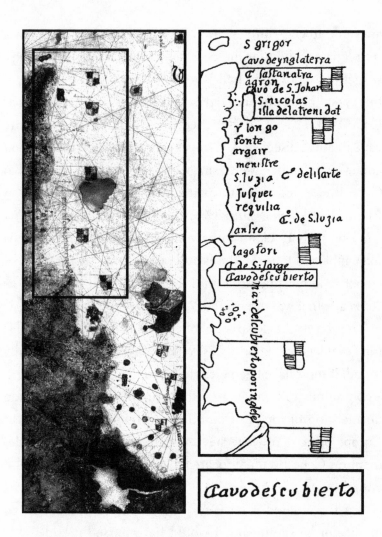

The La Cosa Map of 1500 (above left) incorporated the discoveries of both Christopher Columbus and John Cabot in its depiction of the New World. Above right is a sketch of the indicated area of the map, showing Cabot's five landings, each marked with an English flag. Cape Breton Island is labelled as "Cauo descubierto"—the "cape that was discovered."

uses it in this way when he labels the entire newly discovered coastline "mar descubierto por inglese"—the sea discovered by the English. This was what they had set out to find and they had found it. However, *descubierto* can also refer to a land already discovered—one discovered in the past by someone else. Used in this sense, it would imply that Cabot simply happened upon a site that was already discovered. The Portuguese have used this interpretation to help support their own notion that a Portuguese settlement existed in the Americas that predated Cabot. As Morison says, "the leading historians of Portugal and of Brazil assert it; leading schools and universities of both countries teach it; and educated people generally believe in it."

I realized this interpretation might have significance. There's little reason to believe in a previous Portuguese settlement: neither the Corte-Real brothers nor Fagundes were yet to make their voyages, and there is scant evidence of other Portuguese overseas activity. But this favoured meaning of the term *descubierto* raises the possibility that Cabot found a place *already* discovered.

A close examination of the La Cosa Map offers further support for this interpretation. Cabot spent more than a month sailing along the coast. He discovered a great deal, and the map makes this clear by representing the bays, rivers and even small islands that he reported. The map shows five distinct English flags at places where Cabot was believed to have landed, planted the flag and claimed for the King. Along with the five flags, there are over a dozen place names along the coast: specific locations given the same importance, the same

notation, and the same size as "cauo descubierto." In cartographic terms, then, this "cape that was discovered" appears to
have been simply another of the many places that Cabot
found along the new English coast.[1]

The La Cosa Map suggests that Cabot found "a cape that
was discovered," but perhaps not by Cabot and not by the
Portuguese. I had to allow the possibility that the great Cabot
had discovered something, but not all the pieces. He told
what he knew to La Cosa, and the map-maker called attention to it; that was all he could do. The way in which La Cosa
labelled this section of the map suggests it was a special place,
a cape different from the others, a place that was discovered.
Was it in this context—as a place that had already been
found—that Cape Breton Island was first mapped as a real
place? What is known for sure is that this tiny island was one
of the earliest located, identified and mapped regions in the
New World.

Soon after John Cabot's discovery in the name of the
English King, cartographers began to refer to the island as
Cape Breton, the "Cape of the English." It appeared on a 1516
map labelled as *C. dos Bretoes*, and, during the early decades
of the sixteenth century, it showed up on various other maps as
C. de bertom, *C. de bretton*, *C. del breton*, and *C. breton*.

But whatever its name, from the very beginnings of the
European history of North America, Cape Breton has been a

1 Scholars have since tried to make a connection between Cabot's notation and
what Sebastian Cabot referred to on a 1544 map as *prima vista* (and *prima tierra
vista*)—"the first land seen." However, Sebastian's knowledge of his father's
voyage and his understanding of the New World are questionable at best.

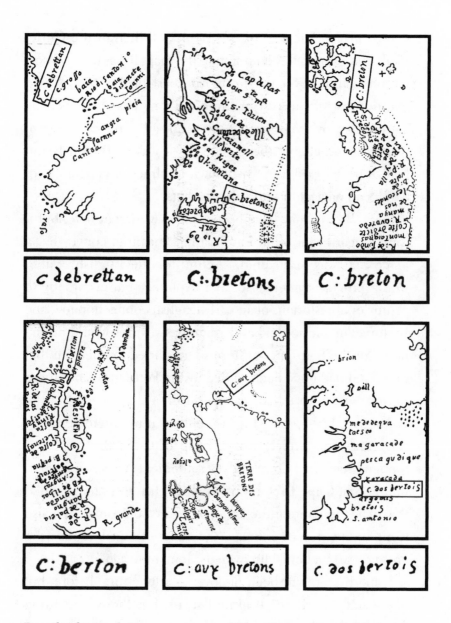

Details of six early European maps of Cape Breton Island. Clockwise from top left: Verrazano, 1529; Rotz, 1535; Deslien, 1541; Lopo Homem, 1554; Desceliers, 1546; Harlien, 1542.

known place. The reports of Cabot, and then of the Corte-Reals and Fagundes, had put it on the map. It was to become a familiar landfall on the northern coast of the New World before most of the rest of the continent was even seen by Europeans. By 1524, when Verrazano sailed up the coast of what was to become the United States, Cape Breton Island had been mapped and was known to almost a generation of European navigators and cartographers.

Cape Breton may have been a place worthy of note, but it wasn't clear to me what La Cosa had meant to convey by "a place that was discovered." Acting for the English, Cabot would provide evidence to later explorers and eventually to centuries of historians of an early English connection to Cape Breton. The Corte-Real and Fagundes voyages would do the same for the Portuguese. Stories had started to circulate that the island had once been settled by the Portuguese, but those stories must have relied heavily on the earlier legend of the Portuguese bishops. By the sixteenth century there certainly was confusion over the ownership of Cape Breton. Even though there were no records of settlement, Verrazano, when sailing past Cape Breton on his return trip to France, called the area "the Land of the Britons." More confusingly, he also went on to describe it as "the land of Lusitanians [the Portuguese]," a land "discovered a long time ago."

Cape Breton had been discovered a long time before, but discovered by whom? It almost seemed as though anything found on the island was blamed on the last explorer to step on its shores. Cabot was given the credit for having left behind the silver earrings; the Portuguese were assigned responsibility for having left their mark; the Corte-Real family was thought not only to have discovered Newfoundland but to have left two brothers behind on its shores; and a single report spoke of Fagundes's settlers, whom the Basques were said to have visited. But there were no actual records of any clearly identified party who stayed for any length of time.

By 1533 France had successfully petitioned against the Treaty of Tordesillas, the papal bull that had divided the New World between Portugal and Spain to the exclusion of all other countries. France argued that this law should refer only to the then-known lands and that the ownership and riches of any new lands were to be determined by exploration, discovery and permanent occupation by any European power. One year after Pope Clement VII opened the oceans to new discoveries, France took advantage of the change. In 1534 the French explorer Jacques Cartier, another brilliant navigator, sailed up the St. Lawrence River to the region that is now Quebec. He took possession of the northern part of the continent in the name of the French King by erecting Christian crosses in the several places he landed. These crosses were powerful symbols of European—and Christian—power. The cross that the French raised along the shores of the St. Lawrence, deep in the heart of the Iroquois Nation, was a towering ten metres high.

The following year Cartier returned to what was now called New France with three ships and a crew of 110 in hopes of beginning a permanent, year-round French colony in the wilderness, in the region of Quebec. During their first Canadian winter, twenty-five of Cartier's men died of scurvy.

This death rate and lack of preparedness were typical of the earliest European attempts at settlement, and one of the reasons I came to discount the early Portuguese claims that the Corte-Real brothers or Fagundes had ever managed to make a settlement. Cartier returned to France in the spring with what remained of his crew, enough to man only two of the three original ships. He limped home as living proof that Europeans were not prepared for the harsh Canadian winters, when the lakes were frozen and the ground hidden under a thick layer of snow from November to March. It was during this second voyage in 1535 that Cartier made his only visit to Cape Breton Island. It appears to have been no more than a brief sail along the northern tip of the island. There is no record that he landed.

In May 1541 Cartier made his third and final voyage to the New World, this time with five ships. Again he sailed up the St. Lawrence River to an area not far from where he had camped on his second voyage. The Iroquois, now cautious of these new settlers, surrounded Cartier's camp and kept the French, many of whom had again been stricken by scurvy, in a constant state of siege for the winter. By the spring of 1542, with thirty-five of his men reported killed by the Iroquois, Cartier realized the futility of the project. Abandoning camp, he sailed back along the St. Lawrence, out past Newfoundland, and on to France, leaving the New World behind for the last time.

The first French settlements in Acadia, early in the seventeenth century, would suffer the same fate as Cartier's attempts. But the French were groping towards the heart of North America, and Cartier's discoveries had opened up exploration of the continent. Sailing by the coast of Cape Breton Island, Cartier had noted that the land was "wonderfully high with a great depth of water and the strongest possible tidal currents." He made no report on any previous settlement and found the island otherwise hardly worth mentioning. By mid-century Cape Breton held no interest to explorers except as the place that had already been discovered. Cape Breton was already old news.

While it was being ignored by explorers and adventurers, the eastern shore of Cape Breton was becoming a second home to generations of European fishermen. John Cabot's observations had proven true: "The sea is covered with fish which are caught not merely with nets but with baskets, a stone being attached to make the basket sink in the water." While Spain had already seized over 13,000 pounds of gold and twice as much silver from its conquest of the Inca Empire in Peru, the French were trying to make economic sense out of the cold northern lands. Codfish wasn't the golden treasure that had been found farther south, but it was what the northern coast offered, and, in the long run, the fisheries proved to be almost as valuable as plundered gold and slaves. Until the fifteenth century, the European cod industry had relied on the northern fishing grounds off the coast of Iceland, but these stocks had been depleted. The stringent dietary regulations imposed by the Roman Catholic Church continued to make dried codfish a valuable European commodity. Over the next several centuries, the waters off Cape Breton Island and Newfoundland were to provide most of Europe's fish needs.

By early in the sixteenth century, fishing vessels from England, Portugal, Spain and France would sail to the coasts of Newfoundland and Cape Breton in the spring of each year and then, after three months of fishing, return to their home ports with hulls full, their catch already prepared for European markets. As they fished off the coast, the fishermen for the most part lived on their ships, cleaning and salting the cod as it was caught. However, if the fish were slowly dried in the sun on shore and then cured using less salt, they would sell for a higher price back home. The crews therefore built camps on the coast where the catch was delivered daily. Each camp had a dock, a storage shed, a landing system built of logs, and drying racks close to the shore where the coastal breezes could transform the cod into this more valuable commodity. They were small enterprises at best, but these early fishing camps were built solidly enough to last from year to year. That was the case along the sandbar at the mouth of St. Anns Bay, across from what is now Englishtown, which French fishermen established as their harbour. The need to dry fish led to the first successful European seasonal settlements in North America.

These camps also provided the setting for the first interactions between Europeans and the Mi'kmaq, who remained the only people living permanently on the island. Visited in the summer fishing season, Cape Breton remained as it had been before any European incursions. Though they had no permanent settlements, Europeans had become so familiar with the island that, by late in the century, there were four seasonal ports along 150 kilometres of the eastern coast, one for each European nation that used it: English Harbour, Spanish Bay, the French port at St. Anns Bay and the Portuguese port at Niganish. There were two other seasonal harbours along the west coast of the island: St. Peters and Chéticamp (which would eventually become home to the Acadians in the eighteenth century), as well as Canso, another important harbour, on the mainland across from St. Peters. In total, there were seven well-known and well-established Cape Breton harbours in the earliest days of the European fishing industry. One of the most important mid-sixteenth-century map-makers was a Portuguese cartographer named Lope Homem, who was privileged to have access to the collection of New World maps and diagrams kept in the archives in Lisbon. Homem drew a map showing the recent discoveries in the Americas. He labelled Cape Breton as *C. des Bertois* — the Cape of the English — and marked six Mi'kmaq harbours. These are believed to be the first native names mapped to specific locations in the Americas. Such intense activity early in the island's history only added to the confusion over who had originally discovered the land and who had left what behind.

At first the Europeans traded peacefully with the natives. The Mi'kmaq valued metal utensils and cloth; the Europeans needed fish and had begun lusting after the northern Atlantic's newest commodity, furs. Cape Breton and Newfoundland, and now the interior of the continent newly discovered by Jacques Cartier, supplied fur to a market hungry for its luxury. Medieval Europe had depleted the source of its own best wildlife to supply centuries of fashionable linings and trimmings.

The beaver skins of New France became a favourite because this fur's unique barbed hairs made the best hats. Fox, squirrel, and deer were plentiful. To prove the financial good sense of maintaining a French claim in the colder northern lands of the New World, Cartier had returned to Paris after his first voyage in 1534 with a cargo of furs. By the mid-sixteenth century, New France had become an easy source to feed Europe's hunger for both fur and codfish.

During this time, European maps and records continued to make curious references to Cape Breton. A mid-sixteenth-century map labelled the island as "Terra de Muyta Gemte"—the Land of Many People—yet offered nothing to explain why it would have been more populated than anywhere else along the coast. In 1584 Richard Hakluyt, an English historian, recorded the discovery of "a townie of fourscore houses" on Cape Breton. But Cape Breton was home to the Mi'kmaq Nation, and they were the only people living along its shores. Neither report fits with what we know of them. They did not live in large settlements. They were nomadic, living in small camps of extended families. Their houses were pyramidal, tent-like wigwams built of thin poles overlain with sheets of birchbark. Once rolled into bundles, these components were carried by the women from camp to camp. The descriptions of "a land of many people" and a town of eighty houses are both surprising.

By the end of the sixteenth century, the legend of the Seven Cities had been extinguished by the Spanish army in New Mexico. Meanwhile, Cartier had discovered a larger and politically more valuable region in the interior of the continent.

The St. Lawrence River gave settlers access, and land ownership was becoming more important than fish. Nonetheless, a strategic gateway was needed for the effective administration of a North American empire, and Cape Breton could provide it. Hakluyt cautioned his government in 1584: "If we do procrastinate the planting [on Cape Breton], the French, the Normans, the Bretons or the Dutch, or some other nation, will not only prevent us of the mighty St. Lawrence, where they have gotten the start of us already, though we had the same revealed to us by books published and printed in English before them, but also deprive us of that good land which we have discovered [Newfoundland]."

Cape Breton looked as though it might be vital for defence: the island was to be a supplier of goods for European markets and a strategic coastline from which to aim a cannon. Political battles for overseas ownership and control took over the island's history. John Cabot's claim and the stories told by the early maps receded farther into the past.

In William Ganong's *Crucial Maps in the Early Cartography and Place-Nomenclature of the Atlantic Coast of Canada,* I found a document written by a French naval pilot, born Jean Fonteneau, who took the family name of his Portuguese wife and was known and published under the name of Jean Alfonce. Ganong's reference to Alfonce reminded me of a mention I had come across several months earlier in Morison's *European Discovery of America: The Northern Voyages A.D. 500–1600* (1971). Alfonce was a name I didn't recognize, but now it had come up twice, referenced by two respected scholars.

During the middle of the sixteenth century, acting as a navigator on ships venturing as far as the coasts of Africa, the Middle East and Japan, Alfonce had sailed the world. In 1542 he had been hired as navigator to accompany Jacques Cartier's last voyage to the New World. Alfonce had explored much of the northern continent on his own, becoming the first Frenchman to visit as far north as Baffin Island. He seemed to be a grand adventurer, and I warmed to his spirit. As a naval pilot he recorded the various reports of returning sailors. His first book, *Les voyages aventureux du Capitaine Jean Alfonce*, a collection of sailing directions for various places in the world, including New France, the newly discovered St. Lawrence River and the northern waters of the New World, was published in 1559.

In *Les voyages aventureux*, Alfonce suggested that there may have been a Portuguese settlement somewhere in the Gulf of St. Lawrence. He reports his understanding that "formerly the Portuguese sought to settle the land which lies the lowest, but the natives of the country put an end to the attempt and killed all of those who came there." This sentence again raised the notion of a Portuguese settlement, but at least his report suggested an end—an attempt destroyed. Alfonce also gave directions to the Island of Seven Cities: two hundred leagues—about 950 kilometres—out to sea, a large island that "it is said was once populated by people." This island would seem to be the place that Cabot had reported. By 1559 the legend had not yet completely faded.

Alfonce's third description was the most unusual. I had become almost immune to stories of Seven Cities and

Portuguese settlements, discounting mention of them as anomalies in the reports, bits of history that make little sense and so had been ignored by historians and scholars for good reason. But Alfonce called the third place *la Tarterie*, the Tartary. To sixteenth-century Europe the word meant "the region of the Chinese." I read the directions again and scaled his distances on a map. He navigated the reader back down the St. Lawrence River, along the coast of the Gulf of St. Lawrence and up the western coast of Cape Breton. There, "less than 400 leagues" from the farthest inland reaches of Cartier's discoveries, Alfonce reported a place called Tartary. Not China, but the region of the Chinese—a curious name. Alfonce had been to Asia and had travelled the world. He was a good navigator, and I trusted him. Having myself spent a winter in the far north of Canada as a young man, I respected anyone who had the strength of character not only to survive but to explore in the harsh cold and darkness of the Arctic, beautiful and dangerous. Sadly, I could no longer consider him a credible witness. The Portuguese, the Seven Cities, and a Chinese settlement—all within two pages! Alfonce's *Voyages aventureux* was simply unbelievable.

In 1569 the cartographer Gerardus Mercator published a map that promised a "New and Improved Description of the Lands of the World, amended and intended for the Use of Navigators." His revolutionary approach to map-making, with its grid of horizontal latitude markings and equally spaced longitudinal lines running in the opposite direction, allowed sailors to plot straight sailing courses around a curved world. Ocean exploration became easier, and the aspirations of European empires exploded. Forgotten was some strange land "discovered a long time ago." Cape Breton Island was about to be remade as a symbol of French ambition and pride.

CHAPTER SIX

THE FRENCH SETTLE IN

IT WAS A SIMPLE, if lengthy, exercise. I had started with a rugged, remote — and, most important, pristine — wilderness and was trudging patiently forward in time until I found the documentation left by the builders of the wall. I was getting warmer now, I felt, as the big players entered the field, but I hadn't found my builders yet, and I hadn't really expected to. But I also hadn't expected to unearth such a confused tapestry of claims and such multiple shards of incongruous evidence.

———

As the seventeenth century began, flotillas of ships—most of them from ports on the west coast of England or France—were fishing the Grand Banks.

The Grand Banks are a long series of shallow underwater plateaus located off the coast of Cape Breton and Newfoundland, where the warm, nutrient-rich water of the Gulf Stream meets the colder Labrador Current moving in the opposite direction. The Gulf Stream slows down and changes direction, flowing out into the open Atlantic. At this critical turning point, the nutrients collect in these shallow waters close to shore and provide an immense feeding ground for one of the largest concentrations of edible fish on the planet.

The Grand Banks fishery had become a relatively risk-free and lucrative business by the 1600s. A small ship with a crew of thirty men could return to port in the early fall laden with 200,000 dry, hard, salted cod. At the end of each summer, hundreds of these vessels would leave the coasts of Newfoundland and Cape Breton to make the short trip home, aided by the seasonal North Atlantic currents. Besides being a "fasting" mainstay of the Catholic population, cod provided a critical source of protein in countries where fresh meat was scarce. The population of France was eighteen million, an eager market for a readily available resource that needed only to be caught, cleaned, salted, dried and sold. Taxes were imposed on the catch and, though not gold or spices, salted fish was a dependable source of revenue for the French government. As the trade grew, Cape Breton became a focus of general European interest, particularly on the part of the French.

John Cabot claimed the coast for England, and Jacques Cartier planted those big crosses, so both England and France claimed rights of ownership to the lucrative new coastline. The French were quick to take an active interest in colonization, but that meant bringing settlers from Europe, providing for their well-being and visiting them each spring with supplies from home. Added to these obligations was the difficulty of successfully governing a new venture in a harsh wilderness from the quiet comforts of Paris. Even though royal charters were needed to support land claims, the first settlements in North America were not government-supported. An overseas project in seventeenth-century France was a private enterprise that needed individual investors and adventurers willing to take a risk. The history of Cape Breton at this time was the history of these small business adventures and, for the most part, the history of individuals who took it upon themselves to live a life for which they were not prepared.

In 1603 the French King, Henry IV, appointed Pierre du Gua de Monts as lieutenant-general of the New World, to preside over an area from 40° to 46° latitude, a territory stretching approximately from present-day Philadelphia to Montreal—or northeastern North America as far inland as the St. Lawrence. This region included Acadia—the land from Maine to Nova Scotia—and Cape Breton Island. Newfoundland was excluded from the royal grant because it was under the control of a joint stock company in London. The Portuguese were never in the picture.

De Monts and his partners were given a ten-year monopoly on the fur trade, a business that was proving more lucrative and easier than cod fishing. They knew from Cartier's reports that the long, harsh winters made settlement along the St. Lawrence River difficult. Hoping for more temperate weather, de Monts and his group of adventurer-investors chose to build their first colony on the Atlantic coast. For many of the participants, this was a land of opportunity. For others, it was simply a New France, a lucrative source of trade goods. And for a few, it was a place of pure wonder untouched by the sophistications of European society.

For a single winter, the colonists lived on St. Croix Island. Of the seventy-nine colonists, half died of scurvy. Those who were left in the spring moved to a settlement they called Port Royal, on the southern shores of the Bay of Fundy, the fertile tidal basin located on the Nova Scotian peninsula.

Port Royal was not simply another seasonal fishing camp; it was an intelligent experiment to see what kind of life was possible in this new land. A society developed among the Port Royal settlers, and ideas were exchanged. Two notable members of the company—Samuel de Champlain and Marc Lescarbot—wrote books that would eventually become popular in France. They reported their observations in maps and descriptions of the new territory, its geography, and its indigenous peoples. Champlain came from a military background, had served in the French army, and had been appointed Royal Geographer by the French King before he arrived in Acadia. Marc Lescarbot was a well-connected lawyer and writer who travelled to Port Royal to escape the urbanity of Paris. He wrote *Le Théâtre de Neptune,* and the settlers staged it—the first play written and performed in North America.

The colony lasted until 1607, when de Monts's fur monopoly was revoked. The forty settlers returned to France. These three short years were vital, however, because the temporary settlement at Port Royal proved that cereal grains and vegetables would flourish in the New World and that a self-sufficient settlement was possible.

The descriptions that Champlain and Lescarbot wrote of New France were published within a few years of their return home. They wrote very little of Cape Breton Island. On their maps, the island was shown off the northern tip of the peninsula of Acadia, with the central Bras d'Or Lake system predominant. The interior and exterior coastlines are drawn with craggy lines to indicate the bays, inlets and small islands off shore. Both men depicted the island as a group of smaller islands assembled around a large inland sea. It was Lescarbot's map that I had compared to the map Christopher Columbus had drawn of the Island of Seven Cities. Champlain's map was similar. Navigators were now able to give specific latitudes, and Champlain wrote that "l'isle du cap Breton qui est par la hauteur de 45. degrez trois quars de latitude"—45° 45' latitude. John Cabot had used the same latitude over a hundred years earlier when he gave his Bordeaux River equivalent for the Island of Seven Cities.

I found mention by both Champlain and Lescarbot of a past colony on Cape Breton. Champlain believed that it had been Portuguese. He wrote: "The Portuguese formerly attempted to settle upon this island, and passed a winter there: but the rigour of the season and the cold made them abandon their settlement." Champlain had seen or heard about something that was old and not Mi'kmaq, and he assumed it must have

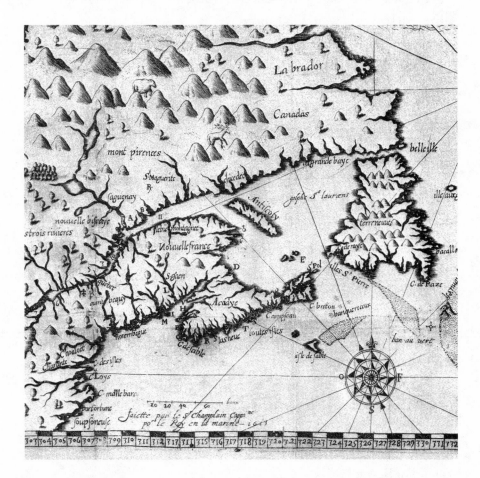

Champlain's map of France's holdings in the New World, which he drew after he spent a winter living in a settlement at Port Royal in the Bay of Fundy.

been left by the Portuguese. Lescarbot mentioned ruins on the island. He believed they had been left by the French in 1541. He wrote in *The History of New France* that Cartier and Jean-François de La Rocque de Roberval, the lieutenant-general who had been appointed to oversee Cartier's third voyage, had "fortified themselves on Cape Breton, where traces of their dwelling still remain."

Champlain and Lescarbot spent twelve months together at Port Royal in a wooden fortress, not much more than a small camp, with thirty-eight other men. It is not a stretch to imagine that they discussed Cape Breton. Like the explorers who had come before them, they likely agreed that there was something on the island, something abandoned in the not-too-distant past. Their reports disagreed over who was responsible for the "traces of the dwellings that still remain." They agreed that there had been some previous history, a notion consistent with those of the previous hundred years and with several generations of explorers. Someone had lived here recently enough to leave remains behind.

The disagreement between Champlain and Lescarbot continued the confusion about unusual settlements on Cape Breton—the tales of the early Portuguese fishermen, the Seven Cities legends, Nicolo Zeno's reports in Italy, the rumour of a failed Fagundes attempt, the Verrazano report, the notes made in the navigational directions of Jean Alfonce. Both men's books were read by people hungry for information about the new French holdings in New France. The seventeenth-century reader in Paris was left with an image of Cape Breton as a barren island on the edge of the ocean, a place of rugged mountains, forests and rivers. However, just as the first maps had done a century earlier, these early New France writings reinforced the belief that "this place was discovered"—that is, discovered already. They showed that, in the early years of the New World, Europeans believed that Cape Breton held the remains of a previous settlement but disagreed on whose settlement it was. Meanwhile, the coast was still attracting a multinational fleet, and claims to the island by the French and the English changed from decade to decade. Cape Breton was proving lucrative for almost every Western European nation. It was easy to ignore ruins. Who knew what undesirable claim they might prove?

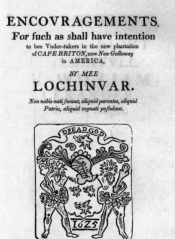

——

Just as the settlement at Port Royal was being abandoned, the English were planting a foothold on the continent in Virginia and, over the next several decades, control of various territories of the northeast coast, including Cape Breton Island, was to be assumed by the governments of either France or England. In 1621 King James I of England granted Sir William Alexander, a Scot, the area bounded on three sides by the St. Lawrence River, the Atlantic Ocean and, to the west, the St. Croix River. The land was christened Nova Scotia, or New Scotland, and was considered Alexander's kingdom, with service to be provided to the Crown in return. To assist in the colonizing effort, Alexander awarded Cape Breton Island to Sir John Gordon of Lochinvar, a young Scottish nobleman well known at court as a skilled swordsman. By 1626 England had named the island New Galloway, and Lochinvar had distributed an advertisement for his new colony, hoping to attract investors and colonists. He titled his publication "Encouragements for such as shall have intention to be under-takers in the new plantation of Cape Breton, now New Galloway in America, by me, Lochinvar." Before anything came of his enterprise, Lochinvar died, and his efforts to colonize New Galloway collapsed.

Two years after Lochinvar's death, another Scottish settlement scheme was launched by Alexander and his group of merchant venturers. Sir James Stewart of Killeith, Lord Ochiltree, was given royal authorization to borrow £500 for a planned colony on New Galloway. In the spring of 1629, in a single ship with sixty settlers, building materials and boxes of ammunition, Ochiltree sailed along with Alexander's fleet to

Nova Scotia. In July he landed the settlers at Baliene, a small cove on the east coast of Cape Breton in the area then known as English Harbour—the same wild, rocky shore as the site of the later Louisbourg. Within a few weeks the settlers had built a small wooden fort near the shore and begun to fish and trade along the coast. Trouble started only when they claimed the area as their own and began arresting French fishermen, demanding a ten percent tax on their catch. Ochiltree's aggression begged a response from the French.

In August, Ochiltree and his band of settlers had been living on the shore of Baliene Cove for just over two months when a group of French ships stopped along the coast to rest after making their Atlantic crossing. This French fleet, under the command of Charles Daniel, a naval captain from the northern French coastal city of Dieppe, anchored in St. Anns Bay on its way to Quebec "to bring assistance and provisions to the Sieur de Champlain and the French who were at the fort and habitation of Quebec in New France." After landing in St. Anns, Captain Daniel sent out a recognizance party. Ten men in a small boat sailed along the coast, questioning the seasonal fishermen on what they might know of the changing political situation in the interior of the country. The men returned with news of Ochiltree's incursion onto French territory and of the tax he levied against French fishermen. Lord Ochiltree was the first European to actually settle on the island, but for Daniel, Cape Breton was French. Daniel knew he had to act decisively, and he and his crew raided the Scottish settlement, taking Lord Ochiltree and his settlers prisoner and demolishing whatever fortifications they had built.

Captain Daniel was convinced the island needed a French presence. The destruction and looting of the Scottish settlement provided him and his men with enough building materials and ammunition to establish their own fortress. It was a quick, unplanned decision: the crew had been anchored for only three weeks when Daniel decided to build Fort St. Anne. He transferred the remains of the Scottish fort, the settlers, and all the ammunition to his camp on what is now St. Anns Bay, across from the sandbar on the shore where Englishtown currently stands.

Daniel organized a small garrison of soldiers to police the coasts of the island and maintain the French claim. He positioned his fort to command the narrow entrance to a large harbour: cannon fire from this key position could easily maintain control of the bay. In 1635 Father Julien Perrault, a visiting missionary, described its location this way: "On the summit of the shore that faces the Northwest, is built the fort of Sainte Anne, at the entrance of the harbour, opposite a little cove. The situation of the place is so advantageous, according to the report of those who are acquainted with it, that with ten or twelve pieces of cannon, all the hostile ships that might present themselves could be sent to the bottom." Voicing the sentiment of the sailors who had visited the bay over the past century, the missionary remarked on the unusually fine quality of the harbour: "Those who have grown old upon the sea protest that they have never seen a more desirable port, either in extent or for its facility of access." St. Anns Bay continued to be a critical point of arrival for ships sailing the northern Atlantic and, as the seventeenth century progressed, it became important to France's control of her empire.

———

At last I was getting closer to an answer, I thought. I was about to uncover real facts that would allow me to discount all that talk of previous colonies and strange ruins. Here was the point at which I would turn up a real building project. The road on Cape Dauphin could only be French, and the French regime began here, with Captain Daniel in 1629. No doubt, as the scale of the road suggested, the actual building took place during the Louisbourg period. But Daniel's saga, which produced the first solid building in the neighbourhood, was a wise place to start, since the road would have been planned and constructed some time after his first fort at St. Anne. Daniel himself did not have the means to build such a road, and, anyway, the road was on the opposite side of the cape.

A report filed in Paris by Champlain, *Narrative of the Voyage Made by Captain Daniel of Diepe to New France in the Present Year, 1629,* confirms that Daniel's crew, having "demolished and levelled" the Scottish fort at Baliene, salvaged the construction materials for their own buildings. Much like the earlier settlement at Port Royal, the fort at St. Anne was surrounded by a high wooden palisade. It had a wooden bunkhouse for fifty men, a chapel, and a storehouse for the considerable amount of arms and ammunition taken from the Scottish at Baliene. To provide the garrison with fresh produce, the French established and tended gardens outside the fortress walls. There are reports of an apple orchard nearby. This was the scale of the earliest settlements: small, not yet self-sufficient, located directly on the shore, and dependent on the spring fleets to bring supplies from the home ports. It was not yet the type of enterprise that could build a well-graded road up the side of a mountain.

In early November 1629, Captain Daniel sailed back to Europe, first to England with most of the Scottish settlers he had taken from Ochiltree's fort, and then to France with eighteen of the settlers he considered political prisoners, including Lord Ochiltree. Daniel left behind a small garrison of forty men to spend the winter on the island.

Other than the very brief Scottish settlement at Baliene, Fort St. Anne is the first permanent European settlement on the island—the first time that Europeans had stayed for more than the fishing season. Its scant remains are the earliest ruins on the island that can still be located and traced to their European roots. As to the road up Cape Dauphin, it would be easy for seasonal fishermen to overlook the strange stones on the hill, but these new settlers were not occasional visitors who concentrated all their energies on the catching and curing of cod. These were men who wrote, observers of life. The fort at St. Anne, a small piece of French society, was literally within the shadow of Cape Dauphin.

It also marked the site of a Jesuit mission, the first in New France. Among the group of men whom Daniel left at St. Anne in 1629 was a thirty-five-year-old priest, Father Barthélémy Vimont. Vimont was both well educated and well trained—he'd joined the order in France at nineteen—though he had no wilderness experience of any kind. A second Jesuit, Father Alexandre de Vieuxpont, arrived later in the year, after being shipwrecked en route to serve in Port Royal. Vieuxpont had been rescued by a Basque fishing vessel and had met a

Mi'kmaq man who told him of Daniel's fort and of the new mission there. He accompanied the man back to St. Anne, after receiving the blessing of his fellow shipwrecked Jesuit, the Reverend Father l'Allemand, who reported to his superiors in France that Vieuxpont wished to "remain with this Savage upon this coast, for he was one of the best Savages that could be found." Vieuxpont had been trained to do such work: to tend to a garrison of French soldiers and to teach and baptize new believers in the rituals of the Christian faith. I followed them in the records and reports, as the Jesuits became a vital force in the control of the French Empire, a force to be feared.

Before Captain Daniel left Fort St. Anne, he organized a small, well-ordered and adequately equipped armed garrison. The cache of arms and ammunition taken from Ochiltree included eight cannons. The soldiers constructed a chapel, and the new Jesuit mission began welcoming the Mi'kmaq. All this, unplanned as it was, with the wilderness on one side and the ocean on the other, Daniel left under the charge of a French aristocrat, Sieur Claude de Beauvais.

That winter at the fort saw the first murder in New France. The military commander, a Captain Gaude, fired three shots from his handgun into the chest of his second-in-command after the two men had eaten supper together. Gaude was imprisoned but escaped into the woods of Cape Breton. He was never heard of again, and he was never tried, but the story was reported in both military and Jesuit letters. The crime had the colour of passion: three shots, close range, a private dinner, a missing suspect. For both the French in Europe and those now in the territories of New France, Acadia and Cape Breton, these dramatic stories of murdered lieutenants and shipwrecked Jesuits must have made more interesting news than an old road on a hill. At any rate, I could find no mention of ruins in the reports and letters written during this early period. By 1629, if there was anything on Cape Dauphin, it appears to have been forgotten.

Soon after he arrived, Daniel had replaced the traditional Mi'kmaq name for the bay, Cibo, with the European name, St. Anne, in honour of Queen Anne of Austria, the wife of the French king, Louis XIII.[1] The name Cibo appears to have been in long use by the Mi'kmaq and was recorded by Europeans as early as 1597 in an English description of the area. In 1629, when Daniel and his men first arrived at St. Anns, they knew the bay as "the river called by the Indians the Grand Cibou." Early Jesuit letters referred to the area as Chibou, and the name is still used for Cibox Island, one of the two tiny dots of land off the tip of Cape Dauphin, unofficially referred to as the Bird Islands. Now I recalled that the term Cibo had turned up when I was researching the death of the Seven Cities legends.

When interest in the legend was rekindled by the Spanish in New Mexico forty years after John Cabot's initial discovery, a similar word—*Cibola*—made its way into the story. In the Spanish rendition, *Cibola* refers to the most important city in the legend. To the Spanish, who occupied themselves for almost a decade in their search for the Seven Cities, it was a mysterious place of untold riches. They had learned the name

1 Today it is officially called St. Anns Bay, and the inner bay is called St. Anns Harbour.

from the local people, who used *Cibola* to refer to an important city located "thirty days' journey to the north." The Mi'kmaq, then, who lived on what Cabot had identified as the Island of Seven Cities, spoke of Cibo; during the 1530s the Spanish, when referring to the Seven Cities, spoke of Cibola, a term they had learned from the Zuni. The connection was tenuous but tantalizing.

When Daniel changed the name from Cibo to St. Anne, it was part of the process by which he transformed the area into a European outpost with European norms, expectations and intrigues. Regular reports and descriptions of Cape Breton were sent back to Europe, mostly the work of the Jesuits, and the history of St. Anns Bay was recorded continuously for the next four centuries. But to this point, it seemed, no one had chosen to mention any building projects on Cape Dauphin.

CHAPTER SEVEN

MORE BROTHERS

NOW THAT THE FRENCH had their talons firmly set into the New World, I was looking forward to discovering an answer to the mystery of the road. I wasn't to be disappointed.

In 1627 Cardinal de Richelieu established the private Company of New France in Paris to exploit the fishing and fur trade in the overseas territories. In the spring of 1631, two years after Captain Charles Daniel had returned to France with the bumbling Lord Ochiltree, the directors of the company sent the captain back with supplies for the St. Anne garrison.

Champlain described Daniel's vessel as "laden and provided with everything that was necessary for the said place—which is in a very good situation, at the entrance of one of the best ports on those coasts." Along with food and ammunition for the garrison, Daniel's ship also carried new priests. They were to replace Fathers Vimont and Vieuxpont, who had spent the winter of 1629 nursing an outbreak of scurvy among the soldiers and had been recalled to France by their superior. Daniel's voyage brought Father Ambroise Davost and Father Antoine Daniel, the captain's brother, to St. Anne.

These young Jesuits were eventually followed by others dedicated to baptizing the indigenous population into the Christian faith. They made regular reports to France, and these *Jesuit Relations*, as they were called, were published in Paris every year from 1632 to 1673. Although their subject was primarily religious, they are valuable records of the history of New France, an area then understood to include the upper St. Lawrence River (referred to as Canada), the lands of Acadia, and the little island of Cape Breton at the easternmost tip. Written from tiny missions that were isolated in a cold and hostile wilderness and surrounded by the worst kind of difficulties, the letters give insight into the notion of religious commitment and the fearless intelligence and militaristic discipline these first missionaries brought to the New World. They were the product of energetic minds that were expected to report accurately to their superiors on conditions in the new land. News from the mission at St. Anne, one of the earliest, was included in the first years of these epistles. I read through them carefully, but none of the several priests who resided at St. Anne from 1629 until the mission closed a decade later recorded anything strange or unusual in the immediate area and nothing on the neighbouring Cape Dauphin.

After Father Vimont's single winter as leader of the St. Anne mission and his subsequent return to France, he rose quickly in the ranks of the Jesuits. In 1635, barely forty, he was appointed superior at the Jesuit residence in Dieppe, an important position for a young member of the order. He sailed back to New France in 1639 and stayed until 1659, participating in the founding of Montreal and becoming a respected administrator who moved among and influenced the powerful. However, like the missionaries who followed him at St. Anne, he made no mention of anything unusual beyond the small fort.

The Jesuit who replaced Vimont in 1632, Father Antoine Daniel, restarted the St. Anne mission but left after only a year. He went on to work with the Huron in the dangerous and often volatile wilderness up the St. Lawrence. In 1648, when he was forty-seven years old, he was attacked by an Iroquois raiding party, killed and dismembered, his body thrown into the fires of his burning chapel. His dramatic life is well documented. He became known as a martyr for his faith and was canonized as Saint Anthony Daniel in 1930. Yet I could not turn up anything written on his life—and the life of a saint is a well-documented thing—that gives any insight into what he or his Jesuit companions had come to know of Cape Dauphin, the place the Mi'kmaq called Cibo, once the home of Kluscap, their most important cultural hero.

In the spring of 1634 Father Julien Perrault, another Jesuit missionary living at Captain Daniel's fort, described St. Anns Bay and the mission at St. Anne in a Jesuit report titled "Relation of certain details regarding the Island of Cape Breton and its inhabitants." Written primarily to keep French Catholics informed about the success of their overseas missions, Perrault gave a detailed description of their work in the area still known as Chibou. The report was one of the first that tried to communicate some understanding of the unique culture of the Mi'kmaq people: how they lived in harmony with the seasons, what they looked like, and how they dressed and behaved. Perrault's ability to be objective failed him when he spoke of religious matters. Describing the honesty, decency, diligence and "attentiveness to instruction" of these primitive people, or "savages," his report is less about truthful observation and more about winning increased revenues from wealthy French patrons. When Perrault reported that "what they do lack is the knowledge of God and of the services that they ought to render to him," he implied that the Jesuits were the appropriate vessel for the transmission of such knowledge.

Perrault's belief that he lived in the "midst of ignorance and barbarism" during his year at the St. Anne mission gives an indication of how little interested the Jesuits were in life beyond their chapel walls. He, like the others, left no insight into the new land. If the Mi'kmaq had recorded anything significant about the area before the Europeans arrived, such knowledge had been absorbed into Mi'kmaq ancestry, legends and beliefs — matters of little interest to European missionaries.

The Jesuit letters mentioned the mission at St. Anne several times. The relationship between the French and the Mi'kmaq was deemed to be good, and the mission became popular with the local people: at one time there were seven Jesuits at St. Anne. However, by 1641 the native population had dwindled to the point where the mission was no longer seen as useful. The Mi'kmaq Nation covered most of the territory of Acadia, and Cape Breton was located at its eastern extremity, far removed from the main population of Mi'kmaq. The Jesuit administrators decided that Cape Breton was not a productive location for teaching and conversion. The mission was closed, the Jesuits were sent farther inland, and the tiny military garrison was transferred to Newfoundland, where a French military presence was becoming necessary to counter English claims to the island's rich fishing grounds. Daniel's little wooden fort at St. Anne was left to decay, adding another layer to the "remains of a past settlement." The more reports and descriptions I read, the more I discovered how these various stories had become interwoven. Here was another failed settlement and another layer of evidence that the next generation would interpret. I had to focus on my own objective to keep the stories clear.

I looked back through my notes on the Jesuit era on Cape Breton. There was certainly evidence that men of this calibre—intelligent, energetic young missionaries, among the best educated in the Western world—were so focused on their official religious task that they had no time for any ruins in the wilderness or the stories of the Mi'kmaq. But the evidence I now had was pointing to a simpler conclusion: the road I had

found did not exist in the early seventeenth century. It was in
none of the records. The French regime, probably at the time
of the construction of Louisbourg, was emerging as the likely
builder. But before that great enterprise got underway, one
more player was to appear on Cape Breton's stage.

During the years that the St. Anne mission had been in operation, the political events determining Cape Breton's future
were in a state of turmoil. Much of Acadia had been given to
the English, but by the 1632 Treaty of Saint Germain, the
English left Port Royal and returned Acadia to the French.
The Company of New France appointed Isaac de Razilly
to supervise the trading and fishing enterprises, but after
de Razilly's death a bitter rivalry arose between his successors,
Charles Menou de Charnisay, Sieur d'Aulnay, and Charles de
La Tour, great names in the history of early industry in New
France. To settle the conflict, in 1638 the King of France
divided Acadia between the two men. For reasons that remain
unrecorded, the King wanted Cape Breton Island made a
separate territory. Its position within European politics and
history became even more ambivalent. Around this time, the
island came under the control of Nicolas Denys, a fisherman
and part-time fur trader who had been one of the original
leaders in the Acadian enterprise under Razilly.

Denys, a businessman, had been in Acadia since 1632. He
had made plans for a trading post on Cape Breton but had
been frustrated by the struggle for power between d'Aulnay
and La Tour. He made attempts to establish a colony, but
settlers never came and he was forced out twice by his rivals.

Denys travelled to Paris and succeeded in buying from the Company of New France the specific territories along the south shore of the St. Lawrence, Newfoundland and Cape Breton. Cape Breton was French, to be played with by the French Crown, but in official decision-making it was not considered Acadia. In 1653 Louis XIV appointed Nicolas Denys governor and lieutenant-general of his newly acquired territory. The island of Cape Breton, being neither part of Acadia nor close enough to Quebec for any direct control by the French government, became Denys's personal fiefdom for the next twenty years.

During his rule there were almost constant conflicts between the French and the English throughout the rest of Acadia. This was the time when the earliest Acadians were beginning to settle, when my ancestor Guyon Chiasson first arrived on the shores of the Bay of Fundy. This is the time, too, when the English began to notice the quality of the flat agricultural land that the Acadians were cultivating along these tidal shores. Acadia became of economic and political value, but Cape Breton was left undisturbed, and Denys was able to continue his seasonal fur-trading and fishing ventures. He and his brother Simon attempted to establish settlements, Simon at Captain Daniel's abandoned fort on the Bay of St. Anns, and Nicolas at St. Peters on the far southern coast, closer to the new communities along the Acadian shore than to St. Anne. Denys located his trading post at the narrowest stretch of land between the inland lakes of Cape Breton and the open water of the North Atlantic. St. Peters became important as Denys's main trading station—where fish and furs were the commodities.

Denys lived there on and off for fifteen years, as he built a small wooden fort on the shoreline next to St. Peters Harbour. In an 1885 article entitled "Lost Colonies of Northmen and Portuguese" by Robert Haliburton, the son of Nova Scotia's first historian, Thomas Chandler Haliburton, I found this intriguing comment: "Tradition as to an early settlement still linger among the Micmac, who aver that certain earth-mounds at St. Peter's, Cape Breton, were built by white men before the arrival of the French . . . My knowledge of this circumstance is derived from [my father], who for more than twenty years was on circuit in Cape Breton once, if not twice, a year."

And stone ruins—a long, thin, rectangular barracks-like structure on top of a hill overlooking the harbour—puzzled historians and local authorities because they appeared to predate the small wooden fort that Denys built along the water's edge. Oddest of all, Denys reported that he had eighty arpents of land—about eighty acres—cleared and under cultivation on top of this hill. For a seventeenth-century European to have more than a garden plot under cultivation was unusual, and, on an island almost entirely covered by dense forest, a single acre represented a considerable piece of farmland. If Denys overstated his claim by a factor of ten, even eight arpents was vast.

St. Peters was one of that small group of well-known local ports—Chéticamp, Niganish, St. Anns, Spanish Bay, English Harbour and Canso, along the opposite shore on the mainland across a narrow strait. St. Peters had become a crucial centre for trade between the Mi'kmaq and the ships arriving from Europe on their way either to the Acadian shore at Port Royal or through the strait that separates the island from the mainland and thence up the St. Lawrence River to the growing French settlement of Quebec. St. Peters was an excellent port and a success for the Denys brothers. At St. Anne, Simon Denys was noted for his stand of apple trees, famous among fishermen because fruit was rare along this coast.

Nicolas Denys left one of the earliest records of the area of Acadia, including Cape Breton, in a two-volume book he called *The Description and Natural History of the Coasts of North America.* The book, published in 1672 during one of Denys's several trips back to France, gave an account of Cape Breton Island as it was seen by Europeans in the middle of the seventeenth century. Denys devoted half of his thirty-six chapters to the fishing industry. The business remained his primary focus, and his descriptions created the best early account of the cod-fishing enterprise in the New World. Denys also wrote five chapters on the daily lives of the Mi'kmaq. He described everything from the way they dressed and ornamented themselves to their methods of marriage, building and burial. He also wrote on the geography of Acadia. For each area of the coast he described the "the goodness of the land, of the quality of the woods, of the birds, fishes, animals and other objects contained in all the extent of the coasts." I was delighted to discover that Denys devoted an entire chapter to Cape Breton Island. The chapter summary reads: "The Island of Cap Breton, its ports, harbours, its rivers and islands which are dependencies of it; the nature of the land; of the kinds of woods, of the fishing, of the hunting and of all it contains." I searched this chapter for mention of the

road. Perhaps the French had noticed that the cape would provide a good military defence and therefore planned a road to
the summit. Possibly Denys had mentioned it.

Denys started his description of Cape Breton at St. Peters,
the fishing and trading post where he was supposed to have
eighty arpents under cultivation. He guided the reader around
the outer coast of the island to all the primary ports. He gave
the impression that the island was well visited but still desolate
and wild. He paid little attention to the interior, which he
called Labrador, or to the Bras d'Or Lakes, which he described
as bordered with mountains. The land, he wrote, was poor. He
devoted the bulk of his descriptions to the ocean coast, where
the fishing was good, and pointed out the places where cod

DESCRIPTION
GEOGRAPHIQUE
ET HISTORIQUE
DES COSTES
DE L'AMERIQVE
SEPTENTRIONALE.
Avec l'Hiftoire naturelle du Païs.

Par Monfieur DENYS, Gouverneur Lieutenant
General pour le Roy, & proprietaire de toutes
les Terres & Ifles qui font depuis le Cap de
Campfeaux, jufques au Cap des Roziers.

TOME I.

A PARIS,

Chez CLAUDE BARBIN, au Palais,
fur le Perron de la fainte Chapelle.

M. DC. LXXII.
Avec Privilege du Roy.

was abundant and where the inlets were known to be safe harbours. He referred to the entrance to St. Anns Bay as the Grand Chibou. His first impression, much like the first impressions of others who had gone before him, was of an excellent harbour, the anchorage good enough to hold a thousand ships. He described the abundance of salmon, mackerel and shellfish, the freshwater streams and the rivers that emptied into the bay, and how "wild geese, ducks, and all other kinds of game" could be easily had.

But Denys made no mention of the hill overlooking the mouth of the bay. He described no roads, no stone walls. Cape Dauphin he simply referred to as the beginning of "a great bay which extends to Niganiche"—present-day Ingonish. Denys's description of the area was not very different from the several other harbours he noted along the island's eastern coast, naming each for the European country that had been using the harbour for its summer fishing fleet since the early 1500s. He reported what he knew and what interested him: fish. This preoccupation—like the Jesuits' preoccupation before him— might account for his overlooking ruins and roads. But, on balance, I was prepared to accept that the road had not been built yet and certainly not during Denys's time. It would have to turn up in the Louisbourg records from the next century.

I did take note of Denys's reference to two minerals in his description of St. Anns Bay, because these minerals were to play an important role in the twentieth-century economy of the island. He described a gypsum cliff at the southern end of the harbour, "a mountain of rock, white as milk, which is also as hard as marble." Ground as plaster, gypsum is valuable as a building material. More important, he reported coal. In the introduction to his first volume, he wrote that "there are mines of coal within the limits of my concession and upon the border of the sea."

He made specific reference to the abundant source of coal in the area of Petit Chibou, the coast in the neighbourhood of Cape Dauphin. It was to become known as one of the most important exposed coal seams along the eastern coast of North America. Though the oily blackness of coal comes to the surface along many of the cliffs in the area, in his book written fifty years earlier, Champlain had ignored the coal and perhaps did not recognize it. It was not then an important fuel in Europe. In Denys's day, however, coal was just becoming useful to European industry. To Denys, it was worth money. He believed that these black cliffs, along with the neighbouring cliffs of pure white gypsum, were within his jurisdiction. In 1677 he obtained an ordinance from the intendant at Quebec, Jacques Duchesneau, that "no person shall take coal and plaster that may be found on those said lands" without Denys's permission and without paying him a tax on both commodities. Aside from fish, it was clear from the documents that Denys's primary concern was the economic value of his mineral resources.

Perhaps the mineral-rich cliffs, along with the well-protected harbours, helped explain the emphasis placed on this little point of land. St. Anns Bay may not have been what aristocratic French adventurers were looking for, but Denys's description was of a land perfectly suited for an overseas colony, especially for colonists who understood the value of coal.

———

The Denys trading post at St. Peters burned to the ground during the winter of 1668 and was never rebuilt. Denys had failed to provide settlers, so the destruction of St. Peters represented the loss of a business establishment only, not the loss of a colony. His had been a small affair, more wild west than French court.

Denys's failure to establish a viable long-term colony on his land was in violation of an important term of his royal charter. During his time in Cape Breton, Denys had remained primarily a fisherman. His lack of interest in bringing over settlers from France led to large sections of his territory being given away to other businessmen. His rights and claims over the land were revoked in 1688 when he was almost ninety years old and still living in Acadia. He died the same year. In all the records, I could find no reason to believe that he had built a road—or had any reason to build a road—up Cape Dauphin.

There were no further European settlements on Cape Breton Island until the beginning of the next century. The land of Acadia was played like a pawn in European struggles for control of North America, but the territory of Cape Breton, considered an independent holding, meant very little to that struggle. Seasonal vessels from Western Europe and now ships from the New England colonies to the south used the fishing stations set up along the coast, safe harbours that supplied wood and water. Daniel's fort at St. Anne was never resettled after the Jesuits left and the French garrison moved to Newfoundland in 1641. The island was all but empty of Europeans. Even most of the Mi'kmaq had left.

Beginning in 1671, accurate census figures were kept for the Acadian population. It is at about this point that Guyon Chiasson, having been married for the second time, began appearing on official ledgers with his twelve children. Among those early censuses, one in 1687 was the first to include Cape Breton Island. A government accountant named Gargas, an *ecrivan principal* from the French court, was sent to Port Royal to enumerate the sparsely populated territory, which consisted of not much more than small settlements scattered throughout the coastal wilderness. It was also his job to inspect and pay the soldiers and to supervise the unloading of the guns and ammunition delivered to the fort. After all the soldiers were paid and the bullets accounted for, Gargas, in the fine, even handwriting of a dedicated civil servant, not only counted the number of men, women and children but listed their ages, the number of religious households, enlisted men, Mi'kmaq, and the number and types of buildings—from hospitals (there were none) to wigwams. He counted the animals kept: horses, colts and both horned and wool-bearing cattle. He included the extent and type of acreage under cultivation, and each gun, sword and pistol he found. All this was listed for forty-eight different tiny settlements throughout Acadia. For the entire island of Cape Breton, the Gargas census listed six Europeans, just over fifty Mi'kmaq, one house, ten wigwams, no farms or animals or acres under cultivation, and a total of nine guns. With six Frenchmen and only one house on the island, it is clear that neither Nicolas Denys's trading post at St. Peters nor the St. Anne mission still existed.

That all changed in 1713, when the European treaty known as the Peace of Utrecht rearranged the territories in North America between England and France. France gave the land of Acadia, with its still-undetermined borders, back to England again, and England gave permission to the French Acadians to remain on their farmland. These so-called French Neutrals promised not to fight for either the French or the English and to abide by English law as long as they could keep their French language and their Catholic religion. Paris agreed to evacuate the French military base in Newfoundland and, in return, was given both the Island of St. Jean—the present-day Prince Edward Island—and Cape Breton.

England was now in possession of Nova Scotia and Newfoundland. Cape Breton was the only remaining French territory at the opening to the St. Lawrence River, a critical connection to the centre of the continent. At the same time, Cape Breton became the only location from which France could protect her interests along the coast of North America. The 1713 treaty brought Cape Breton to the centre of French foreign policy. The island was renamed Île Royale. Denys's trading post at St. Peters became Port Toulouse, English Harbour became Louisbourg in honour of Louis XIV, and Daniel's old fort at St. Anne was renamed Port Dauphin, in honour of the eldest son of the French king.

By the time of this renewed French interest, there had already been two hundred years of European exploration and settlement on the island: first the English, then stories of the Portuguese, then the English again, and now the French— and there had always been fishermen. Cape Breton had so many separate stories of beginnings and endings layered in its history that, like an old house renovated every generation to a new style, the original framework and the subsequent changes had become impossible to distinguish. Cape Breton was soon to become the most important fortress of the French naval authority in the North Atlantic. At the same time, the island would act as a highly lucrative, cosmopolitan and busy international trade link between Europe and the West Indies. I was confident now: here is where I would find my builders.

CHAPTER EIGHT

A PUZZLING CHANGE OF MIND

IT WAS A THURSDAY in February 2003 and my friend Beth and I had just sat down at our regular place at the bar of Zelda's. She's a lawyer with the Ontario Ministry of Health, a sharp critic who lets me get away with nothing. She spotted my black binder while she was still shaking snowflakes out of her hair, and asked, "What've you got tonight?"

"The Coronelli Map."

"Sounds like another Italian."

"You're going to like this. It's evidence."

"I love evidence."

I'd come to the Coronelli maps while investigating the work of Giovanni Cassini, the official astronomer to the Pope in the 1660s. While navigators could determine latitude well enough by sighting the North Star, longitude—the observer's position east or west on the globe—was a thornier problem. Cassini had devised a brilliant method for determining longitude by using a set of tables based on the position of Jupiter's moons, only fairly recently observable through telescopes. Astronomers eventually honoured Cassini by naming a gap in the rings of Saturn after him—if having a gap named after you is indeed an honour! Meanwhile, an Italian friar, Brother Vincenzo Coronelli, an internationally respected cartographer, a compiler of encyclopedias, a founder of the first European geographical society and a cosmographer to the Republic of Venice, was quick to see the significance of Cassini's work. Right away, the correct measurement of longitude gave Brother Coronelli's cartography a level of exactitude that more closely resembles present-day maps than the rough, unsure outlines of earlier European efforts. As a result, Coronelli's work was noticed in Paris, where he was presented to King Louis XIV in 1669. Louis commissioned him to construct two globes, one of the earth and one of the heavens, and it is for these globes that Coronelli is best known.

But years later, in 1692, he also produced an atlas of maps representing the best cartographic information available in the Western world. The map he called "Canada Orientale nell'America Settentrionale," which depicted the northeast coast of North America, appears in this *Corso geografico universale.* It represented two centuries of information from returning sailors and navigators.

I took a map from the binder and brought her up to speed on Coronelli.

"It's not perfect," I explained. "He made mistakes through oversimplification."

"Okay, but it's recognizable. I can see what's what."

"Exactly. And his mapping of Cape Breton Island was the best to date. Now remember Christopher Columbus's map of the Island of Seven Cities? Remember how he drew it?"

"The little islands."

"Right. You can see that Coronelli also drew a group of one large and two smaller islands — in the same proportion, configuration and orientation. But he was basing his work on information brought back by men like Jean Alfonce, Champlain, Lescarbot, Captain Daniel and Nicolas Denys."

"Okay. So this is how Cape Breton looked to Europeans — when?"

"About 1692. Just before the French arrived in force in the New World."

"Well. It's a very nice map, Paul."

"Thank you, Beth. But I want you to look closely at it."

"I thought you would."

"When Coronelli was drawing maps, there was no established set of rules. A smart cartographer would draw images to indicate this or that. For example, a little rectangle might mean a simple fort had been located in a certain place. The cartographer had to trust the reader to understand what the

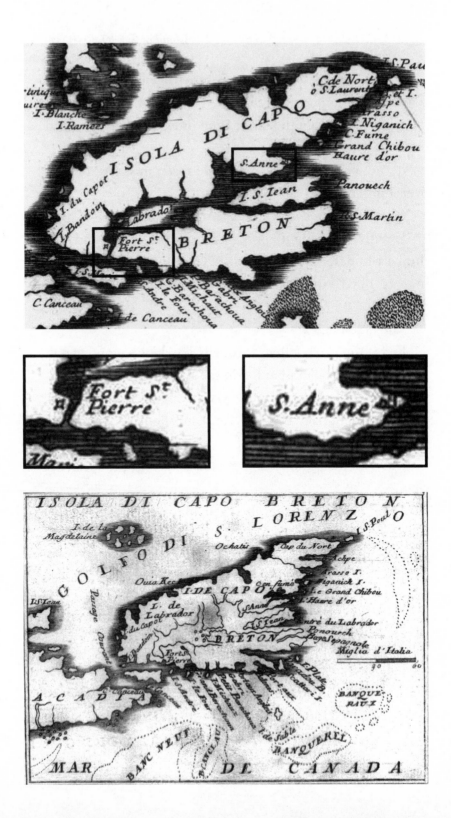

icons meant. On Coronelli's map of Cape Breton, *Isola di Capo Breton,* you can see two such symbols. See them?"

"Certainly."

"At the area he calls Fort St. Pierre, on the site of Nicolas Denys's trading post, he draws a tiny square—a small fortress."

"Makes sense."

"Right. His symbolism works. Now out here, on Cape Dauphin, he draws another symbol. Right on the tip of the peninsula, he draws a building with an attached tower. It's not a plan drawing, like this other one he uses to designate Fort St. Pierre? It's a front elevation."

"Yeah, yeah. Right. It's a tower."

"It reminds me of San Gimingnano."

"That's that little fortified Italian town in Tuscany?"

"Exactly."

"The one overrun by tourists."

I'd spent a year in Florence and didn't like to imagine San Gimingnano overrun with tourists. But thinking of the old towns of Italy I'd seen, I could identify the single tall tower attached to a rectangular building as an Italian's reference to a fortification. It was a shorthand that would have made sense to an Italian cartographer. Coronelli labels the cape as *S. Anne,* a name Captain Daniel had given to the area in the early part of the seventeenth century.

OPPOSITE: *The Coronelli map from 1692 (top) shows two small icons at "St. Anne" (Cape Dauphin) and at "Fort St. Pierre" (St. Peters). Only five years later, in 1697, Coronelli drew a map (bottom) on which he removed the icons.*

"So it's probably a reference to Daniel's fort," Beth said.

"No, it's not. That was way farther down the bay and it had disappeared half a century before."

"Well, maybe it's a reference to that other French guy, you know, the fisherman."

"Nicolas Denys. Actually his brother Simon had the house on the peninsula. But that had been no more than a log cabin and a few apple trees. I mean, it seems inconceivable that a fine cartographer like Coronelli would draw an atlas of the world and label some obscure log cabin as a fortification."

"Okay, okay. Good point. Deserves another glass of wine."

"No, let's stay focused. This is the tricky part."

She pointed to what we now call St. Anns Bay. "What's this here?"

"He's written 'Grand Chibou.' That was the Mi'kmaq name for St. Anns. Under that name he's written 'Havre d'or.'"

"Harbour of Gold?"

"Right. They're always talking about gold, these guys. Bras d'or, Havre d'or. But Coronelli would have reported only those things he believed he knew."

"So what did he know?"

"That's the problem. I don't know what he knew."

"Hmm."

"But Beth, look at this. This is the funny thing about it all. Coronelli published two versions of his Cape Breton map. This one and"—I took out the second map—"this one in an atlas called *Atlante Veneto,* published several years later. In *Atlante Veneto* he gives Cape Breton its own short chapter and a larger-scale map."

"So the place was sort of important."

"The funny thing is that the fortress shown on the Corso map—the little tower on Cape Dauphin near St. Anne and l'Havre d'Or—has disappeared from the larger-scale map. There doesn't seem to be a fort shown at Fort St. Pierre either."

"Maybe he just forgot it, Paul. It doesn't do to oversignify this stuff."

"Oh yeah? Let's say your client is accused of giving his buddy forty whacks with an axe, but during your interview you notice he has no arms. Would you forget to mention that to the judge?"

"Okay, Paul. I get it."

"Why would you not forget?"

"Because good lawyers don't forget their clients have no arms."

"Right. And good cartographers don't forget their forts. Coronelli knew there was something on Cape Breton, and he made a conscious effort first to report and then *not* to report it."

"A puzzle."

"I'd say so."

With the Peace of Utrecht in 1713, the French agreed to evacuate their base in Newfoundland and relocate to Cape Breton. The military establishment immediately began making extensive surveys and plans of the island, and French settlers from Newfoundland—116 men, 10 women and 23 children—landed at Louisbourg in the fall of that year. Over the next seven years France evaluated proposed sites for fortifications at Port

Toulouse (Denys's St. Peters), Port Dauphin (Daniel's St. Anne) and Louisbourg (English Harbour to the fishermen). In 1720 France decided to direct all its energies to the fortifications of the new town of Louisbourg. It became one of the most planned building projects in the eighteenth-century world and, an admittedly minor note, it was among these vast ruins that I played as a child.

Brother Coronelli and his generation of map-makers helped introduce accuracy into this planning. A hill drawn here was an actual hill, a river was an actual river, a coastline an actual coastline. Using these maps, an engineer in Paris could design battlements, buildings and new town layouts in the correct place, size and scale and be confident that they would be built where and how they were drawn. Ideas produced in one place could now be realized in another location. It represented a monumental achievement in engineering, architecture and foreign policy. So was born the great French professions of engineer, naval architect and designer of battlements. And no place in the New World benefited more from these new professions than Cape Breton Island.

At the same time that the French fortress of Louisbourg was being built, the Acadians living along the shores of the Bay of Fundy and in Newfoundland came under British rule. Some Acadians, still hoping to leave British-occupied Acadia, scouted Cape Breton as a possible area for resettlement. They reported: "There is not in all the island land suitable for the maintenance of our families, since there are no meadows sufficient to feed our cattle, which are our principal means of subsistence . . . To leave our residences and our cleared lands to take new waste lands, which must be cleared without assistance or subsidy, would expose us to die of starvation."

The Acadians were eventually removed forcibly from their homes, their settlements burned so they would not return and their property redistributed among the English, who at the same time placed a bounty on Mi'kmaq scalps. Many Acadians went into hiding, and my own family escaped to Île St. Jean in 1750. Jacques Chiasson, son of Guyon, had lived in the Acadian town of Beaubassin on the Fundy side of the isthmus of Chignecto. Beaubassin was an important trading centre on the narrow stretch of land separating the Bay of Fundy from the Northumberland Strait and the St. Lawrence River. Produce from the farmlands of Acadia was shipped fifteen kilometres overland to the bay on the opposite side of the isthmus, where vessels from England, New England and France would trade manufactured goods for food. Beaubassin was a great success, but by 1750 it had become the site of a major British garrison. Life was becoming unsafe in an environment of arbitrary rule and British hatred for the Acadians, their language and their religion. No longer a young man, Jacques moved his entire family to Île St. Jean, the French-owned island across the Northumberland Strait. Cape Breton Island was the only other French territory in the region but, with no cleared land along the shore for livestock and farming, it was the last place the Acadians wanted to resettle. Finally, pushed out again by the British from Île St. Jean, my family would scatter around Atlantic Canada.

Meanwhile, the French military hoped that the Acadians would come to the island to provide food for the thousands of soldiers who would live in Louisbourg. In their search for places of interest, the French produced over five hundred surveys, drawings and maps during their occupation. They documented everything from barren wilderness to proposed street layouts for small settlements to designs for the grand royal bastion. Every metre of Louisbourg and its surroundings was drawn, often in great detail.

Various published histories carried a few of the more important drawings of the fortifications. I found reproductions of historical maps of Louisbourg and of Cape Breton in general in the map section at the library, but I needed to see what had been built at the time in Cape Dauphin. The French surveys included Port Toulouse (St. Peters) and Port Dauphin (St. Anns Bay), with proposals for fortifications at both. At Port Toulouse a fort was planned for the shore near Nicolas Denys's earlier trading post, but the various plans were never realized. By March 2003 I knew I needed to see these maps, but they were difficult to find. My only hope was an article, "Beyond the Bastions of French Mapping of Cape Breton Island, 1713–1758," published in a 1990 edition of the *Nova Scotia Historical Review*. The title was promising. It was shelved behind closed doors in the reference library and, like most seldom-used magazines and reports, it had to be ordered from the fourth-floor periodical desk. As usual, I was anxious—the librarians had become used to my pacing as I waited for my requests to be delivered. If the Cape Dauphin plans were not illustrated here, I would have to make special arrangements to visit the collection kept in the archives at the fortress of Louisbourg, in Ottawa or in Paris. The French

must have built the road, but I needed to see the actual drawings made by the Paris engineers. As an architect, I needed to
know how and when they had planned it, why they had built
it and where it went.

I knew that plans for the area must have been made sometime between 1713 and 1720, the years it was being considered
for the location of the fortress. When the *Nova Scotia
Historical Review* finally arrived from storage, the first thing
I noticed was the short quotation on the cover page, "More
delicate than the historians' are the map-makers' colours."
I was hoping that was true, for the histories of the area I
had read had told me very little of Cape Dauphin or why the
road had been built. It was the "map-makers' colours" that
could be revelatory. As I quickly scanned the illustrations,
I felt I'd stumbled on a gold mine. The report included many
of the Louisbourg drawings and there, on page after page —
and as clear and black and white as a well-surveyed and carefully rendered drawing can be — were proposals for both Port
Toulouse and Port Dauphin. I was breathing heavily when
I sat down at a library table to look at the issue carefully.

Nothing. Nothing had been built on Cape Dauphin, nothing at all. I spent several days with my eye to a magnifying glass,
trying to see if there was something in the drawings I had
missed. Cape Dauphin was indeed shown, clearly and cor-
rectly, but there was no road. The cape, with its hilly slope and
its craggy coastline, matched almost exactly its depiction on
present-day maps, but it was rendered as nothing more than a
mountain of forested wilderness. There were several proposals
for the area, but all the fortifications of St. Anns Bay were

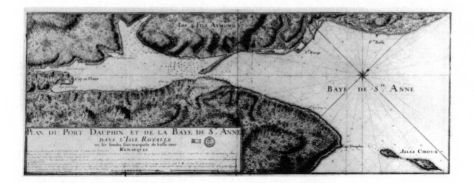

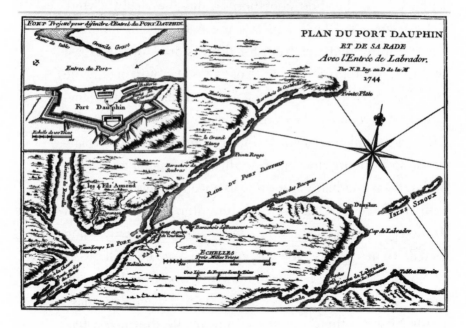

TOP: *Map of the St. Anns area from 1733 during the French regime at Louisbourg, showing no construction on Cape Dauphin.*

ABOVE: *Map from 1744, when the French were firmly established at Louisbourg, showing plans (inset) for a fortress across from the sandbar. The fortress was never built. Again, there is no construction indicated on Cape Dauphin.*

planned on the same spot where Captain Daniel had built his earlier fort, across from the sandbar.

From all the surveys and maps of the area, it was clear that this spot had been considered very seriously by the new governor of the island, Philippe Pastour de Costebelle. He wanted to do what was best for his settlers: they were Frenchmen, not Acadians. He had been their governor in Newfoundland and resumed that position after moving to Cape Breton. It was he who commissioned the first surveys of sites for the new fortress. In 1713 he assigned a French engineer, Major Jacques L'Hermitte, to make a report on the various options offered by the island. L'Hermitte, who had been third in command of the settlers' original Newfoundland outpost at Placentia, wrote that St. Anns Bay "is one of the finest harbours to be seen for wood and land. There is also plaster and coal. Not only is it preferable from a mercantile point of view, but a single fort would command the entrance, while owing to the precipitous hills, by which it is surrounded, there is no danger to be anticipated from a land attack."

L'Hermitte's first reports and maps of the island, sent to Paris in 1713, showed that the proposed fortifications would be located across from the sandbar that helped block the inner harbour. His survey showed there was almost nothing left in the area other than the sandbar on which the seasonal fishermen still prepared their catch. The surveyors had ignored the "precipitous hills."

Another of the early Cape Breton surveys, made in 1714 by the Quebec naval pilot Joseph Guyon, urged that "the bay of Ste. Anne's was the locality that combined the greatest advantages:

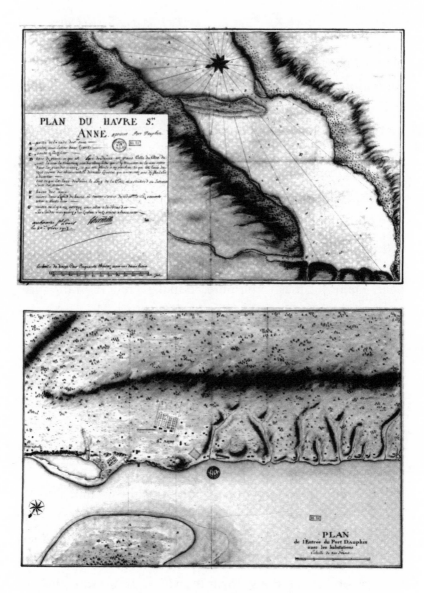

TOP: *A 1713 map of St. Anns harbour, drawn by Jacques L'Hermitte,*
the engineer responsible for the establishment of the
new French colony on the island.

ABOVE: *Map of the tiny settlement of Port Dauphin, at the time it*
was being considered for the site of the French fortress.

> [The bay] has a narrow entrance, not much wider than the range of a musket shot, and could be easily fortified. There were very fine beaches of gravel so large that thirty or forty vessels could use them for dry- ing fish. Codfish were caught there more plentifully than in any other part of the island. The whole extent of the land around was level and suitable for the growth of all sorts of grain. That place had been formerly inhabited by Mr. Denys, and that they now gathered there a large quantity of apples, from trees planted in that period.

Guyon described the bay much as earlier explorers had. His only addition to the description was the possibility of farming along the far southern end of the bay, land that the Acadians had rejected but that a group of Scottish Protestants would set- tle a hundred years later.

About the same time that these two reports appeared, the grandson of Nicolas Denys, who had been living at the Acadian settlement of Port Royal, wrote to the French government to support St. Anns as "the finest harbour in the world." Buttressed by these positive reports, both Philippe Pastour de Costbelle, governor of Cape Breton Island, and Philippe de Rigaud de Vaudreuil, the governor general of New France, recommended that the new French fortress be built at Port Dauphin. A small settlement began to establish itself there. Several houses, a lime kiln, forge, powder magazine, barracks and small gardens were built, but no road. There were additional proposals for the building of defences at Port Dauphin, but a 1733 map called

"Plan du Port Dauphin et de la Baye de Ste Anne dans l'Isle Royal" shows nothing other than the few small buildings that made up the tiny settlement. No major buildings were ever built.

Cape Dauphin appeared on several of these maps, but none of them showed roads or stone walls on the hill — in fact, they showed nothing at all. To the French during the eighteenth century, Cape Dauphin was a row of steep cliffs leading up to a barren, forested plateau.

I looked up from these maps baffled and disappointed. The road I'd found was a project neither planned nor built. The French, as it turned out, had built very little on Cape Dauphin, and what they did build was located only at the site across from the sandbar.

As the spring of 2003 wore on, I fell into a bit of a slump. After the shock of discovering nothing in the French survey, I thought I should give the whole thing a rest. Then Gerard and Debra invited me to design and oversee the renovation of a floor of their house on Willard Gardens. Here was an opportunity to see the family more often and do something I was good at. The first few weekends, when everyone was home, I tried not to mention my research at all. I helped my niece Laura with a school project, a scale model of the ancient Milvian Bridge that spans the Tiber. I cut out small blocks of wood, scaled to size and the shape of the actual stone blocks. It was Laura's job to glue them together into the arches that spanned the river, to form a model the size of a school desk. I love teaching, and although I didn't understand why it was necessary for a class of ten-year-olds to build scale models of Roman bridges, at least she could learn how arches were constructed and what a keystone was. For those weekends, I was Uncle Paul, the architect.

But despite every effort, my mind returned to the road. I helped Laura build the miniature scaffolding supporting the wooden arches and as the glue dried to hold it all in place, Gerard came to look over my shoulder.

"Gerard? You know the road I found on Cape Dauphin? It's not French."

"Your road? Not French? So who made it then?"

"That's what I'm trying to figure out. That road's old—it's centuries old. I was pretty sure it had to be French. But I've been looking at official documents that say the road didn't exist. Why didn't those French surveyors talk about it? These people were trained to observe and report things like that. So now I'm starting to wonder if it might be *older* than the French regime. I'm wondering if that's possible. If that's the case, the thing is older than John Cabot because I *know* nothing was built between the late fifteenth and the late eighteenth centuries. I've looked at everything."

As I watched my niece walk her fingers over our newly constructed bridge, I blurted, "I'm lucky to have climbed over those stones that day and felt their cut edges. I'm lucky because, right now, I'm facing mounting proof that they don't exist."

I made copies of all the important French material and spread it out in my apartment. It was clear that the French eventually ignored Port Dauphin. The final decision to choose

Louisbourg came down to the cod-fishing industry, since the French had been forced to desert their fishing base in Placentia. Louisbourg was closer by twenty kilometres to the best fishing grounds, and fish was where the money was. Once built, the harbour traffic at Louisbourg increased and Cape Breton became a vital centre for international trade in the North Atlantic, which included ships from Europe, New France, Acadia and New England. The Gulf Stream provided ships with a direct and constant connection to the French territories in the Caribbean.

Along with New France, several Caribbean islands made up the French overseas empire. These were slave islands, populated by a workforce taken from Africa. Slaves were big business. By the end of the seventeenth century the population of slaves in the French Caribbean islands was 27,000, more than the number of free French citizens. Fifty years later, the number of slaves had multiplied to over 250,000. These Caribbean islands supplied most of the sugar and rum to France, products that were then traded throughout Europe. The islands became a source for cotton, tobacco, indigo, cocoa and even coffee. These goods had to be shipped back to France, and ships from the Caribbean would use the Gulf Stream to sail easily up to Cape Breton. The stream— one of the fastest ocean currents in the world—made for a strong natural connection between the two places, a connection that mariners exploited. For centuries Cape Breton acted as a pivot point to the Gulf Stream. Ships would dock in Cape Breton before using the current and the west winds to cross the Atlantic.

For the first time I understood clearly that currents determined ocean traffic and that the Gulf Stream had made Cape Breton Island both a crucial centre for trade in the North Atlantic and a port of international importance in the eighteenth century. Finally, I realized that these currents might also have played a role in the island's curious earlier importance.

At Louisbourg, the French hoped to create a self-sufficient European town, the seat of a successful colonial government and an unrivalled naval stronghold. In almost all ways, they failed. The fortress of Louisbourg was a vast enterprise, but in spite of its urban scale and elaborate walled fortifications, it proved ineffective. It fell to the British both times it was attacked, in 1745 and in 1758. Weak as it was as a French sentinel on the St. Lawrence, it did succeed as a major commercial port, growing rich from trading and fishing. By 1752, with a population of close to five thousand, Louisbourg was considered one of the largest, best-supplied and most cosmopolitan of Atlantic communities. Its streets included commercial, military and residential districts, with inns, shops, bakeries and taverns, lots of taverns. There were warehouses and workshops, mansions and fishermen's shacks, a large modern hospital, the elaborate King's Bastion, and a stone lighthouse, all constructed in the French neo-classical style of the mid-eighteenth century. It was well built and sophisticated, and its streets and buildings were regulated by the French civil code, which described the rights and obligations of urban property owners.

Grand though it was, after a seven-week siege in the summer of 1758 Louisbourg was captured by the English. With the

French outnumbered ten to one, the English were able to take
the garrison from the weak landward side. Two weeks later, a
detachment of English soldiers took possession of the tiny
hamlet of Port Dauphin without resistance.

By the mid-eighteenth century, most of Cape Breton was
densely mapped, surveyed and recorded but still sparsely populated. By the 1730s Port Dauphin was a small French hamlet
whose inhabitants fished, built small ships and quarried lime-
stone. In 1744 there was a new proposal to fortify the port, but
nothing came of it. The town was burnt in 1745 by a force
from New England during the island's first conquest by the
English. By the time Cape Breton was captured for the final
time in 1758, Port Dauphin was once again of little importance to anyone. A census in 1752 listed fewer than twenty
people living there.

The only other French structures in the area were built
south of Cape Dauphin, across the narrow strait of water that
enters the Bras d'Or Lakes, the strait that Nicolas Denys had
referred to as Petit Cibou. The long, narrow island along
the south of this strait was known by the French as L'Isle
Verdronne, now called Boularderie Island after a French soldier with an imposing name, Sieur Louis Simon de St. Aubin,
Poupet, Chevalier de La Boularderie. Boularderie was an
Acadian who had been in the French military at both Port
Royal and Louisbourg. In 1719, in a rare private land grant, he
had been given this small but fertile island that still bears his
name. After Boularderie's death in 1748, the land passed to
his son. In a 1755 disposition made at Louisbourg, the younger
Boularderie declared that he had improved the land, had hired

artisans and farm workers, and had enlarged the property to include a manor house, farm buildings, a wind and water mill and an orchard. Boularderie's small island settlement was deserted by its occupants and then burned by the English after Louisbourg fell in 1758. They also left no records of any road built up the side of the mountain on the opposite shore.

After the English captured the fortress of Louisbourg, they used it briefly as a base for their attack on Quebec. Having already established themselves at the port of Halifax, the English finally decided to destroy the French fort. It was decreed that "the said Fortress, together with all the works, and Defences of the Harbour, be most effectually and most entirely demolished." The fortifications and main fortress walls were blown up, but the town buildings were saved. Following the English conquest, Île Royal was renamed Cape Breton and formally annexed to Nova Scotia by the Treaty of Paris in 1763. Along with most of the French colonies in North America, it became part of the British Empire. The little harbour across from the sandbar that had first been called St. Anne, then Port Dauphin, was now renamed St. Anns.

With the bulk of British naval fortifications centred in Halifax, Cape Breton Island lost the strategic importance it had held since the early 1500s. The French and Acadian inhabitants had been dispersed or deported. The English government invested very little public money in the region and had no development policy for the island. A census of Nova Scotia taken in 1766 gave the population of the island as just over seven hundred, exclusive of Mi'kmaq. Eight years later, in 1774, an Englishman named Samuel Holland, the surveyor general of the Northern District of America, made a survey of the island. Like the European explorers who came before him, Holland also claimed that "no part of North America can boast of a more advantageous Situation for Commerce and Fishing, than the Island of Cape Breton." Of Louisbourg and the French fortress that had recently been destroyed, Holland wrote that "the Crown of France hath squandered away such immense Sums on one of the worst Spots in the Island." Holland described Port Dauphin, which he named Conway Harbour, as "the best harbour in this Island but few are equal to it on the Continent of North America." He reported that the French had had a stockaded fort and barracks at Port Dauphin and that there were still the remains of houses and orchards in the area. The soil was good, and the meadow land that had grown wild would be easy to reclaim for farming. Holland recommended the place for a small town. For the first time in an official written survey, Cape Dauphin was mentioned by name. In describing the outer coast of the bay, Holland wrote that "the Lands are very high, of which Cape Dauphine or Cape Hertford is the most remarkable; but none are fit for Improvement." The English survey made no mention of anything on the hill.

CHAPTER NINE

ISLAND OF THE DISPOSSESSED

CAPE DAUPHIN, the name Samuel Holland used in 1774, was an English adaptation of the French and demonstrates just how densely layered the history of Cape Breton had become. The Acadians appear to have weathered these changing tides, even though it is difficult to view their lot as anything other than miserable.

In 1763 many of my family fled Prince Edward Island for the neighbouring French-owned islands of St. Pierre and Miquelon in the Gulf of St. Lawrence. About this time, Chéticamp on Cape Breton had become the site of a new fishing enterprise set up by the Robin family, a group of Huguenots from Jersey, an English-owned island offshore from the French city of St. Malo.

The Robins settled an area already known by the Mi'kmaq and visited by the Europeans, but whose location on the west side of the island had delayed its settlement until the Acadians arrived to occupy whatever had been left by other, more favoured, peoples. In his 1672 book, Nicolas Denys had made note of it: "Le Chadye is a great cove which has about two leagues of depth. In its extremity is a beach of sand intermingled with gravel which the sea has made, behind which is a pond of salt water. This cove is bordered with rocks on both shores. The Cod is very abundant in this bay, and this attracts vessels there, although they are often lost because of the little shelter it affords." The name Chéticamp may derive from an earlier Mi'kmaq name, Chady, which appears on seventeenth-century maps.

As Protestants, the French-speaking Robins had rights among the British of Nova Scotia that few others enjoyed. The leader of the family empire, Charles Robin, built fishing sheds and wharves along the Chéticamp shore and enticed a small group of Acadian and French families to come to work for him. The composition of that first group of fourteen families, "les Quatorze Vieux" as they are now known in local history, shows just how unusual a sociological mix these pioneers were.

St. Malo, near the headquarters of Charles Robin, had become the home of several displaced Acadian families, many of whom had arrived in France after being refused entry by the New England states and after spending time in English prisons. The close connection between the Isle of Jersey and St. Malo, along with the desire of the Acadians to return to their homeland, led to the partnership with Robin. By agreeing to work for Robin, several families left France to return not only to their homes but to their extended families. When they settled in Chéticamp, several generations of Acadians were reunited.

Three of the first families were Chiassons: Paul, Basil and Jean. Two of those men had married Boudreau women — the Boudreau family having been separated for over a decade, with some members in Acadia and some in St. Malo. Isabelle Boudreau, whose parents had spent five years in an English prison, moved from St. Malo to Chéticamp and married Jean Chiasson. Her sister also married a Chiasson. Their mother's sister was Paul's wife. The connections become quickly confusing, a web of family relationships woven over many decades and across several different countries. Throughout it all, the Acadians had been consistently loyal to their family connections. The size and the closeness of Acadian families was one of the things that the British found remarkable. It was these families from St. Malo, original Acadians who had been deported and eventually found their way back to the homeland they had known for over five generations, who joined with my own ancestors to become "les Quatorze Vieux," the fourteen founding families of Chéticamp. Over the next fifty years, Acadian families continued to arrive from various parts of the Maritimes and from France. By the middle of the nineteenth century, a stretch of some of the most beautiful and rugged coastline of western Cape Breton was settled by this uniquely French community, speaking eighteenth-century French and following eighteenth-century habits. In their origins and their isolation, these people were similar to the Acadians who settled in Louisiana and became known as the Cajuns.

The Acadians had depended on the Mi'kmaq during the early period of French occupation, but, following the deportation, the Acadian and Mi'kmaq peoples suffered different fates, forced as they were into different areas. The Acadians of Chéticamp now lived in isolation, and the Mi'kmaq who were left went back to the forest. Ninety percent of their nation had died in the early years of European contact. Before Europeans arrived, the Mi'kmaq population has been estimated at just over 35,000. By the time French accounts were published in the early seventeenth century, their numbers were estimated to be fewer than 3,500. This decline is clear in one of the first reports from New France, written in 1611 by a Jesuit missionary, Father Pierre Biard. He quoted a prominent Mi'kmaq leader, Chief Membertou, as witness. Membertou claimed that, in his youth, there had been people "as thickly planted there as the hairs upon his head." He explained to Biard, and to other missionaries who followed him, that this decline in native population was due to the Europeans. According to Membertou, the Mi'kmaq had begun declining in the mid-sixteenth century, when this area of New France saw the beginning of the lucrative European trade in fish and furs. Today, it is usual to attribute aboriginal mortality to European microbes, but I could find no references to European sicknesses among the Mi'kmaq. The records left by both Nicolas

Denys in 1672 and by a missionary, Father Pierre Maillard, in 1755, claim that the unlimited introduction of alcohol by European fishermen as payment for trade goods was responsible for the decline. Fuelled by alcohol and a surplus of unfamiliar goods, the Mi'kmaq lost their sense of family cohesion and stopped taking care of themselves. The men of this previously peaceful society began to turn against one another.

By the time of the fall of Louisbourg, the remaining Mi'kmaq had moved to the mainland. By the end of the eighteenth century, Cape Breton, now English, was all but deserted except for Acadians. In 1778 a half-dozen English families settled in Port Dauphin, renaming it Englishtown. It remained no more than a tiny hamlet. In 1784, hoping to attract Quebec loyalists, the British colonial authorities separated the island of Cape Breton from mainland Nova Scotia, established its own government and appointed a local lieutenant-governor. They hoped to create a self-sufficient colony, but of the five thousand settlers they expected, only 140 actually came. The area originally known as Spanish Harbour was renamed Sydney and designated as the administrative centre of the island, the primary settlement on Cape Breton. It was a "town of about 50 hovels . . . with not the smallest trace of industry as the inhabitants live by selling rum to the soldiers."

The area around St. Anns Bay did not see settlers again until the early nineteenth century, when Scottish immigrants, banished from their homes in the Highlands, found Nova Scotia—New Scotland—to be much like the land they had been forced to leave.

In 1817, under the leadership of the Reverend Norman McLeod, a group of these religious Scots settled in Pictou on the mainland of Nova Scotia. Shortly afterwards, McLeod moved his flock to St. Anns Bay to escape what he believed to be the unhealthy influence of other Scottish ministers already established on the mainland. Records and letters from his community leave a sadly comic impression of this vain, self-righteous man. His original plan had been to take his followers from Pictou to Ohio in the American Midwest by sailing down the eastern seaboard to the Gulf of Mexico and up the Mississippi River as far as he could get. However, during a temporary stop in St. Anns Bay, McLeod and his advance party fell under the spell of those charms that had attracted generations of previous settlers: meadows, fish, woodland and one of the best natural harbours in the world. This place, he decided, would be their new home. He added a Scottish layer to the scattered but complex history of Cape Dauphin's ruins.

McLeod was my last chance for a clue to the history of the road. The Acadians were isolated and self-sufficient on the other side of the island, and the Mi'kmaq had all but left. The Scottish group was small, but this group made the final significant influx of settlers to Cape Breton. If it wasn't this Scottish church group who had built the road, my research would end with the native community, who, to my knowledge, built neither monuments nor roads. I had an awful premonition of ending my project with fewer answers than when I started.

When I discovered that McLeod had brought only two hundred settlers with him, including women and children, I knew he didn't have a large enough workforce. The men would have had enough on their hands to provide even the barest shelter and the simplest provisions for their families. They survived primarily on potatoes and fish, and stayed close to the shore where the fishing was good. When they had to travel at all, it was along the narrow paths across their fields that connected their few wooden farm buildings. The grandest scheme and proudest achievement recorded during their entire stay on the island was a single church. They arrived in the spring of 1820 in boats they had built themselves. They were interested in only one area: the shore along the coves at the west end of the bay, as far away from Cape Dauphin as the bay allowed. They built simple farmhouses of spruce logs with sod roofs and rough fieldstone chimneys, much as they had built in Scotland. After a few years, they built sawmills and added sawn boards and shingles to the houses. In the town of Sydney—then the only place of business and exchange on the island—they traded their harvest for whatever they could not produce themselves. Under McLeod's leadership, St. Anns became "the most sober, industrious, and orderly settlement on the island." Their farms, built along the edge of the bay, were productive; fish was readily available and the community prospered.

But McLeod was a tyrant. The records describe how, in 1823, he had himself made magistrate of the community. In 1827 he was appointed the only schoolmaster. In 1830 he had a large three-storey house built for himself, and by 1840 the congregation had built him the church, known simply as the "Big Church"—the only structure of note in the area, indeed on the entire island, built during the nineteenth century. It was twenty metres long and thirteen metres wide, about the size of a tennis court. By Cape Breton standards, that was a massive undertaking; by comparison to any other buildings around the bay, it was palatial. Like the farms of McLeod's community, the Big Church, his private residence and his school were all built on the south and west shores of St. Anns, at the opposite end of the bay from Cape Dauphin.

For these people, Cape Dauphin could hardly have been more than the barren tip of land at the head of their beautiful bay. Any old roads there, if they were discussed at all, were ignored and forgotten.

The abundance of forests surrounding the new settlers supplied wood for a small shipbuilding industry, and the settlers were able to launch large boats and even a small schooner from a shipyard in a cove down from the Big Church. By the 1840s the success of the enterprise was such that McLeod's son Donald was able to sail back to Scotland in one of the locally built ships.

This account was the second mention I'd come across of the area's ability to provide for the construction of world-class sailing ships. The first had been the French map from 1733, which noted that a ship for the King had been built in the bay. But it was, in fact, uncommon to find wood suitable for shipbuilding on Cape Breton. It is a rocky island of low softwood, its timber too small for serious construction work. It was a rock with a shallow covering of soil, a place that was home to very few maples, oaks and lofty pines. Shipbuilding required hardwoods of this kind as well as tall timbers. Why would such trees grow here and only here, in this one specific bay? I might have ignored the shipbuilding records were it not for that road up the mountain. Was it conceivable that the trees had been planted sometime in the distant past, before the French? Had the bay been chosen for some sort of large shipbuilding enterprise, another grand project?

Eventually the Reverend McLeod's son Donald travelled to Australia, perhaps to get as far away as possible from his father. Then he wrote back to the Cape Breton community with an account of the climate, soil and general wealth in that part of the Antipodes. His letter arrived just as the potato crop had failed in St. Anns and the community was occupied with thoughts of famine and hardship. The Reverend McLeod decided to lead his congregation out of the unforeseen hardships of Cape Breton to the promise of a better life in Australia. In October 1851 a group of settlers who had farmed the shores of St. Anns since 1820 departed on the *Margaret*, a ship they had built themselves, to sail halfway around the world to settle in New Zealand. Over the next eight years, five similar voyages left St. Anns carrying settlers away to join the Reverend's flock. Between McLeod's first voyage on the *Margaret* and the last voyage in 1859, almost nine hundred people left Cape Breton for New Zealand. The population of St. Anns had never risen above a thousand.

The farms that McLeod's people had vacated were soon occupied by other settlers, all Scots from the Highland clans, and, by the late nineteenth century, the shores of St. Anns had become a small Gaelic-speaking farm community, sparsely populated by a mixture of the descendants of McLeod's early settlers and new immigrants from Scotland. By this time the village of Englishtown, built on the ruins of the earlier Port Dauphin, had grown to twenty-three households. My mother's family was among them.

The shipbuilding industry started by McLeod's settlers continued to expand and, for a short time, St. Anns became a centre of Nova Scotia's world-famous handcrafted ships. But with the coming of the railway in the late 1890s, the age of wooden-hulled shipbuilding in St. Anns Bay passed. The last wooden sailing vessel was built there in 1894, its glory supplanted by the new steam-powered ships. The ruins of that enterprise still remain at Shipyard Point on the south shore of the bay, far removed from Cape Dauphin.

I grasped at a few final straws. In 1862 a small coal mine was opened on the opposite side of Cape Dauphin, on the east coast facing the narrow island that the French soldier Antoine Boularderie had settled a century earlier. The mine was close to the shore, next to a small but deep harbour that was used to transport the coal overseas or south to the American markets. A Scotsman named Campbell started mining from two coal seams, and the settlement that grew up there came to be called New Campbellton. A land survey of 1864 showed the mine to be situated on the side of the high eastern face of the cape, facing the Bras d'Or Lakes. The operation was successful enough to justify the building of a tiny train track leading down to the nearby cove. Cape Breton coal was famous and, by this time, there were dozens of other mines along its coast.

I examined the mining records to see if they could have any link to the road I had found some kilometres distant, but they were quite unrelated. The miners lived around the mine, and the only road they needed was between the rock face and the shore. They and their goods and supplies would have arrived and left through the harbour. Between the little mines and the road were miles of pathless coast. Between the mines and the summit was a precipitous slope.

In 1864 a professional surveyor conducted a highly detailed survey of Cape Breton Island. Around the shores of St. Anns Bay as well as along the harbour, he recorded the location, the plot size and the name of each landowner. Almost every shore in the area was lined with Scottish names, except for the northern tip: Cape Dauphin. The coastal roads on either side of the peninsula stopped short of the northern tip, as they still do. There has never been a road along this short stretch of coastline because it has never been settled. The 1864 survey, like the earlier French surveys, showed the tip of the peninsula as an empty plateau: no roads, settlers, farm sites or buildings, just empty land "not fit for improvement." Cape Dauphin has been left alone to face the North Atlantic—yet I knew I had seen that road.

A 1901 census gave the population of Englishtown as 359. The population of New Campbellton was 391. During the course of the twentieth century those population figures did not vary much. The area around Cape Dauphin is still predominantly Scottish, and many people can trace their ancestry back to McLeod's congregation. The land is still farmed, and the Bay of St. Anns is known for its spectacular scenery.

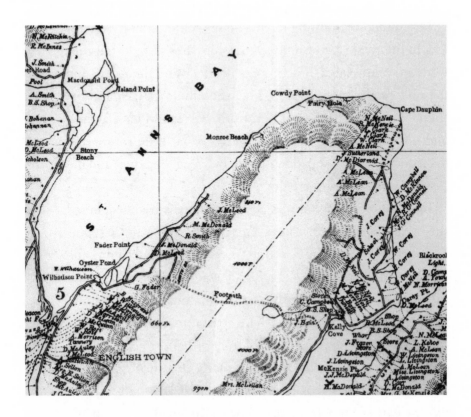

This land ownership map, surveyed and drawn in the mid-nineteenth century, shows Cape Dauphin as a barren hilltop.

Chéticamp is still an Acadian village. The Mi'kmaq live in small settlements throughout Cape Breton and Nova Scotia, integrated into the local economy. The Mi'kmaq and the elders maintain their legends.

Those legends were the one piece of this puzzle I had yet to consider.

CHAPTER TEN

Mysteries of the Mi'kmaq

As I had been digging methodically through the histor-ical record, amassing more and more research about settle-ment on Cape Breton in order to unmask the builders of the road, the AIDS virus was multiplying in my blood. By the sum-mer of 2003 I had hit a stable, if not desirable, plateau. Determined to ignore what I could not change, I pressed onward as best I could to answer the question that was now obsessing me. If it wasn't the Portuguese, the French, the English or the Scots who engineered the road, then who could it be? I was not well enough to go back to Cape Dauphin and climb to the top to hunt for clues, but I had one last research avenue I could explore on paper, one last nation on the list of candidates: the Mi'kmaq, the people native to the Atlantic coast. Certain elements of Mi'kmaq culture, reported very early in the records of the New World, are unique among the aboriginal peoples of North America. They had inhabited much of the east coast of what is now Canada for hundreds of years before European explorers arrived. Early European visitors wrote a great deal about the Mi'kmaq. Among the most detailed observations were those published in Paris in 1691 by a French Roman Catholic missionary, Father Chrestien Le Clercq. He was a Recollet, a member of a small sect of the Franciscan Brothers who hoped to live a life of extreme austerity. Austerity and hardship were important to these men: they saw Christianity as a difficult and dangerous task, and their missionaries as its advance soldiers. Le Clercq had joined the order in 1668 when he was twenty-seven. He was sent to the territories of New France seven years later and given the lonely job of teaching the Christian gospel to the Mi'kmaq, who lived in small seasonal communities along the coast. Le Clercq spent twelve years living among the Mi'kmaq and travelling throughout Acadia, in areas now called New Brunswick and the Gaspé peninsula, Prince Edward Island, Nova Scotia and Cape Breton. He called these people the Gaspésians. They had been called the Souriquois by other early writers, and more recently by variations on the term Mi'kmaq.

Father Le Clercq's book, *Nouvelle Relation de la Gaspésie*, was not the only description of the Mi'kmaq published in France. Samuel de Champlain and Marc Lescarbot had both

NOUVELLE
RELATION
DE LA
GASPESIE,
QUI CONTIENT

Les Mœurs & la Religion des Sau-
vages Gafpefiens Porte - Croix,
adorateurs du Soleil, & d'autres
Peuples de l'Amerique Septentrionale, dite le Canada.

DEDIE'E A MADAME LA
PRINCESSE D'EPINOY,

Par le Pere CHRESTIEN LE CLERCQ,
*Miffionnaire Recollet de la Province de
Saint Antoine de Pade en Artois , &,
Gardien du Convent de Lens.*

A PARIS,
Chez AMABLE AUROY, ruë Saint
Jacques, à l'Image S. Jerôme, attenant
la Fontaine S. Severin.

M. DC. XCI.
AVEC PRIVILEGE DU ROY.

written reports in the early part of the century, and Jesuit missionaries had sent their letters back to their French superiors.
Lescarbot's *Histoire de la Nouvelle-France* had been the earliest of all. Written in 1609 after a year spent in the tiny pal-
isaded fortress of Port Royal in the heart of Mi'kmaq land,
Lescarbot's book set up the framework by which this native

society was described by most later French writers. Trained as a lawyer, Lescarbot organized his observations into more than twenty chapters, each describing a specific aspect of their customs. The chapter titles ranged from "Of Marriage," "Of the Feeding of Their Children," "Of Their Love Towards Their Children" and "Of Their Funerals" to the more physical descriptions "Of Their Language" and "Of Their Clothing and Wearing of Their Hairs" to the more subtle observations "Of Their Virtues and Vices" and "Of Their Civility." Lescarbot was followed by other reporters, resulting in an amazingly rich source of documentation on the Mi'kmaq, one of the earliest collections of such knowledge in North America. The account that Father Le Clercq wrote at the end of the century is important in this group of writings because he had learned the Mi'kmaq language, an accomplishment that gave him an unusual advantage. He wrote what he saw and heard, and reported the sometimes strange things that surrounded him in the wilderness. His account is the most authentic early evidence about the daily lives of the Mi'kmaq.

The native people told Le Clercq their history before the coming of Europeans. They described how their nation had been settled long before by visitors from overseas. Reading Le Clercq, it was impossible not to remember the map drawn by Christopher Columbus and John Cabot's report of Seven Cities. Le Clercq recorded what the Mi'kmaq told him of these visitors. He wrote:

> This new world has been peopled by certain indi-
> viduals who, having embarked upon the sea for the

purpose of establishing a colony in foreign parts, were surprised by storm and tempest, which threw them upon the coasts of North America. Here they were unfortunately shipwrecked, and, with their ships, they lost everything which they must have had with them of property, and of the things which they valued most in the world. Affairs were such that this shipwreck having left them wholly without hope of ever returning into their own country, they resolved to set to work in earnest at the preservation of their lives by applying themselves to hunting and fishing, which have always been very good in those parts, while, in default of their clothes, necessity, which is the mother of inventions, gave them the ingenuity to clothe themselves with skins of beaver, of moose, and of other animals which they killed in hunting.

This story—ships, foreign visitors, the founding of a new settlement—appeared similar in outline and specifics to the fifteenth-century European legend of Seven Cities. It echoed explorers' reports that there had been a much earlier Portuguese, or English, or French settlement on Cape Breton.

One of the most puzzling elements in Le Clercq's account was the section covering Mi'kmaq religious practices. He was able to be specific, for he spoke the language and observed carefully:

They hold, further, that it could well have been a fact that these individuals were instructed in the sacred mysteries of our holy Religion, and that they had even

a knowledge and the use of letters, since, in the establishment of colonies, it is customary to send there men
who are alike learned and pious, in order that they may
teach to the peoples, along with purely human knowledge, the most solid maxims of Christian wisdom and
piety. Nobody, however, having followed them in these
glorious employments, the knowledge which they had
of the true God, of letters, and of their origin, was
thus gradually lost and effaced from the minds of their
unfortunate posterity by the lapse of time.

The Mi'kmaq were a people living alone, surrounded by
water on three sides, on the edge of the wilderness. Outside
influences were minimal, and yet Le Clercq found not only
that Christian doctrine had already been planted among them
but that "they had even a knowledge of letters." Still, this
claim was typical among missionaries, and the same thought
had been expressed by others in different countries: the
Christian faith had miraculously preceded them.

Then, to my surprise, I found that Le Clercq had documented a unique community living among the Mi'kmaq,
whom he called the *Porte-Croix*, the Cross-Bearers. I had
taught a course on religious architecture at the Catholic
University of America and knew something about the topic of
iconography. An understanding of how and why we use visual
images to describe our faith involves many interrelated and
fundamental disciplines: theology, architecture, communication. Le Clercq described the Cross-Bearers as people who
"held the ancient worship and religious use of the Cross." For

their important assemblies they would raise a large wooden cross, around which they would form a circle. They wore the cross as an ornament on their bodies and on their clothes. Images of the cross accompanied them on voyages. They used their fingers to form a cross when making important oaths, and crosses marked their burial places. They placed crosses both outside and inside their homes in order to "distinguish them from the other nations of Canada." It was clear that they used the image in ways familiar to Christians: during assemblies, for oaths, on burial places. Le Clercq believed that this group was so devout in its veneration of the cross that its faith could have been based only on the Christian gospels. From a purely iconographic and theological point of view, I had to agree with him. Le Clercq was reporting anthropological fact, not myth. But who could have introduced these images of Christianity to the Mi'kmaq before the French missionaries?

Le Clercq's belief that the Mi'kmaq had lost the specific knowledge of the gospels "through the negligence and the licentiousness of their ancestors" is the usual way by which the history of an icon evolves. People retain the symbolism of an image, using it on their tombs or as a mark of oath-taking long after they have forgotten the fundamental teachings of the faith from which the image was born. That is what happens to iconography: the stories fade as the visuals become stronger references for a community of believers.

Some curious thread was running through these reports.

It turned out that Le Clercq was not the only person to report that Christianity had been planted among the Mi'kmaq. This early connection to Christianity has been substantiated by recent Mi'kmaq scholars and remains central to the Mi'kmaq culture. I found a 1997 copy of the *Mi'kmaq Concordat with the Vatican*, published by the Mi'kmaq to help unravel the complicated relationship that has existed since the early 1600s between them and the Roman Catholic Church and to outline for the Vatican their most fundamental beliefs. Like Le Clercq's book, *Nouvelle Relation de la Gaspésie*, the *Mi'kmaq Concordat* also claimed that there had been a settlement of Cross-Bearers among them before the arrival of Europeans. They believe that these foreign visitors had travelled from Central America to Atlantic Canada by sea "under the vision of three crosses." These visitors had been "enriched in their knowledge, language and culture by their travels and their meeting with other peoples." They were known as harvesters of the land and sea who enshrined their "language of symbols" within the Mi'kmaq Nation. This reference to the three crosses was another specifically Christian image, one apparently deeply rooted in Mi'kmaq history.

Three centuries separated the two documents, but both Le Clercq's 1691 book and the 1997 concordat relate the belief that a Christian people had settled among the Mi'kmaq along the eastern coast of North America before the arrival of European missionaries. Both books reported specific and unique ways in which the cross imagery had been used. I knew that, by the time of Le Clercq's writing, the European presence would not have been strong enough to instill such devotion. The Jesuit missionaries had been uneven, and the Recollets had just started to arrive. Le Clercq himself had reported that the source was pre-European.

Historians have largely ignored Le Clercq's report of the Cross-Bearers, just as I was prepared to do until I realized that he could only be describing something real. Several Catholic writers have maintained that Le Clercq observed nothing more than the image of a bird with wings spread open, an aboriginal totem that identified a specific group or family. Could a bird icon be mistaken for a cross? I was not convinced. The Mi'kmaq used the cross in ways that were specific to traditional Christian iconography, small enough to be worn around the neck and large enough to be the centre of community meetings. The Mi'kmaq even erected crosses to mark their graves. As Le Clercq reported, "their cemeteries, distinguished by this sign of salvation, appear more like those of Christians than of Indians." To explain the Mi'kmaq cross as a tribal totem of a bird did not explain their employment of the cross as an element in a well-articulated belief system. For over three centuries the source of that imagery has been a mystery. Now I shared that sense of mystery. Who had taught the Mi'kmaq the iconography of the cross?

The legend of the Great Kluscap, the most important among a variety of tales that have been passed down by the Mi'kmaq from pre-European history to the present, tells the story of a great teacher who lived among the Mi'kmaq before any Europeans came. As a child, I heard the legends of Kluscap in school and accepted them as pure myth.

In the written narratives of the legends, reported by both Europeans and Mi'kmaq, several important elements consistently emerge. Kluscap was not a god. He was a man who arrived by sea from far away, sailing up from the southwest. He lived among the Mi'kmaq before Europeans had discovered the New World, and he left just before the first explorers arrived at the end of the fifteenth century.

I read the Kluscap stories again, remembering certain ones from when I was a schoolboy. In "Kluscap and His Four Visitors," a group of Mi'kmaq men visit Kluscap's home and describe their reception. After following "a path marked by blazed trees" and coming to the top of a hill overlooking a broad, beautiful lake, they found his "well-constructed wig-wam." The men met Kluscap, whom they described as "a man apparently about forty years old, who looked healthy and hale," and who lived with two family members, an old woman and a young man. After the men had taken time to look around the area where Kluscap lived, they described it as "delightful in the extreme." "Tall trees with luxuriant foliage, and covered with beautiful, fragrant blossoms, extend in all directions; they are so free from limbs and underbrush, and they stand in rows so straight and so far apart, that the visitors can see a long distance in every direction. The air is balmy and sweet, and everything wears the impress of health, repose, and happiness."

The description reminded me of the accounts of the Island of Seven Cities. I looked at the map that had been published in the *Journal of American Folklore* article, "Beothuk and MicMac," written in 1915 by an American ethnographer named Frank Speck. The map's title was "Hunting Territories of the Micmac Indians in Nova Scotia," but Speck also used the map to chart the traditional travels of Kluscap. His final home was Cape Dauphin, the summit reached by the stone-walled road in the forest.

Early writers often chose to describe the Mi'kmaq as a nation of dirty savages. Europeans wrote that the Mi'kmaq were a lazy, gluttonous, barbarous people who lived like animals and didn't wash themselves when they ate. Lescarbot, the romantic socialite from Paris, was shocked that the Mi'kmaq saw no need for table linen. Their wigwams had none of the substance of a good European home. To many Europeans, the Mi'kmaq were beasts. However, when you strip away the prejudices from the observations, physical descriptions left by the Europeans bear witness to something quite different.

One of the most insightful observations was made by Father Le Clercq himself. He described the Mi'kmaq as a noble race who kept themselves free from all that was bad and who lived peacefully in their "land of friendship." According to Le Clercq, their nation had a highly organized government, a ritualized family structure and a culture that honoured trust and equality. Father Pierre Biard, another French Jesuit, left a telling description of the Mi'kmaq: "Generally speaking, they are lighter built than we are, but handsome and well-shaped, just as we would be if we continued in the same condition in which we were at the age of twenty-five . . . They love justice and hate violence and robbery, a thing really remarkable in men who have neither laws nor magistrates; for, among them, each man is his own master and his own protector."

As I read more deeply about the Mi'kmaq, I became more and more aware of the many traits and practices that set them apart from other North American aboriginal cultures. In Le Clercq's chapter on the Cross-Bearers, he wrote of the Mi'kmaq having "knowledge of letters"—they knew how to read. At first, I dismissed this sentence as confusion on his part or misunderstanding on mine. As far as I knew, no native people of North America had a "knowledge of letters" when Europeans first arrived in the New World. Later in his book, however, he supports his claim with specific eyewitness accounts. I found others who claimed the same thing: the Mi'kmaq, unique among all North American native nations, were reading and writing before Europeans arrived.

In Le Clercq's chapter "On the Ignorance of the Gaspesians," I found a very specific reference to Mi'kmaq writing: "I noticed that some children were making marks with charcoal upon birchbark, and were counting these with the finger very accurately at each word of prayers which they pronounced." He wanted, perhaps, to impress upon his readers the devotion he was able to instill with his teachings. Instead, he discovered that the Mi'kmaq could write down what they were hearing and then read it back.

This skill was unprecedented among native groups in North America, but so was Christianity among the Mi'kmaq before the Europeans arrived, or an island with seven cities, or a map drawn by Christopher Columbus before his voyages that showed an island uncannily like Cape Breton, or centuries of early reports of strange ruins. And standing behind this mountain of information I had accumulated was that other mountain and the very real road that ran up its steep side—the starting point of my quest.

I was no longer prepared to ignore information that didn't fit in comfortably—indeed, that seemed to be the only sort of information I was collecting. The basic facts I had been able to accumulate on the early Mi'kmaq were straightforward: these people were not a large nation. When the first Europeans arrived, the Mi'kmaq lived in small seasonal camps on the coast, usually in family groups. These small groups would relocate for purposes of hunting and fishing. According to their folklore, Kluscap had organized them into the seven separate political districts that made up the Mi'kmaq Nation. Chiefs of the seven districts were responsible for allotting hunting rights to the members of their areas, with no single chief having hierarchy over the others. The common concerns of the settlements were addressed to these district chiefs. Ultimately, it was a council of these seven elders that decided the affairs of the Mi'kmaq. Council meetings were called by the grand chief, who acted as the nominal head of the nation, and the seat of the government was traditionally on Cape Breton Island. It was a tiny nation of disparate parts, mostly cut off from its neighbours, surrounded by a barren coastland and without the possibility of ongoing communication with any other culture, except visitors who might arrive by sea. The Mi'kmaq had no villages, towns or cities. They governed themselves and were self-sufficient. However, in spite of the nation's small size and nomadic traditions, the Mi'kmaq had a language, both written and spoken, unlike any other native nation in the Americas. Difficult as that was to believe, it was impossible for me to ignore.

When Father Le Clercq arrived in 1675, he developed his own system of writing based on the characters the Mi'kmaq were using. He tried to use these characters as a way of instructing the Mi'kmaq in the Christian gospels, but his attempts to develop a new alphabet were utterly unsuccessful. The Mi'kmaq were able to transcribe Le Clercq's teachings using their own language, writing with charcoal on bark and reading it back to themselves. Le Clercq then introduced individual characters as abstractions from the text he saw the Mi'kmaq writing, but that didn't work.

Unfortunately, the pictograph language that Le Clercq invented, while relying on the Mi'kmaq practice of using simply drawn single characters in their script, was an unwise adaptation. It was neither Mi'kmaq nor even a useful script. It had few rules and no grammar and was arbitrary in its expressions. The characters that Le Clercq invented—stars, crosses, a variety of Roman letters, and miscellaneous, unrelated lines—appear to have acted only as memory devices for the Mi'kmaq.

In every case, the subject was religion. The characters were used only to teach the Catholic catechism and only to

OPPOSITE: *A page from Maillard's Mi'kmaq text. The details (above) compare five of the Mi'kmaq quarters with five Chinese characters.*

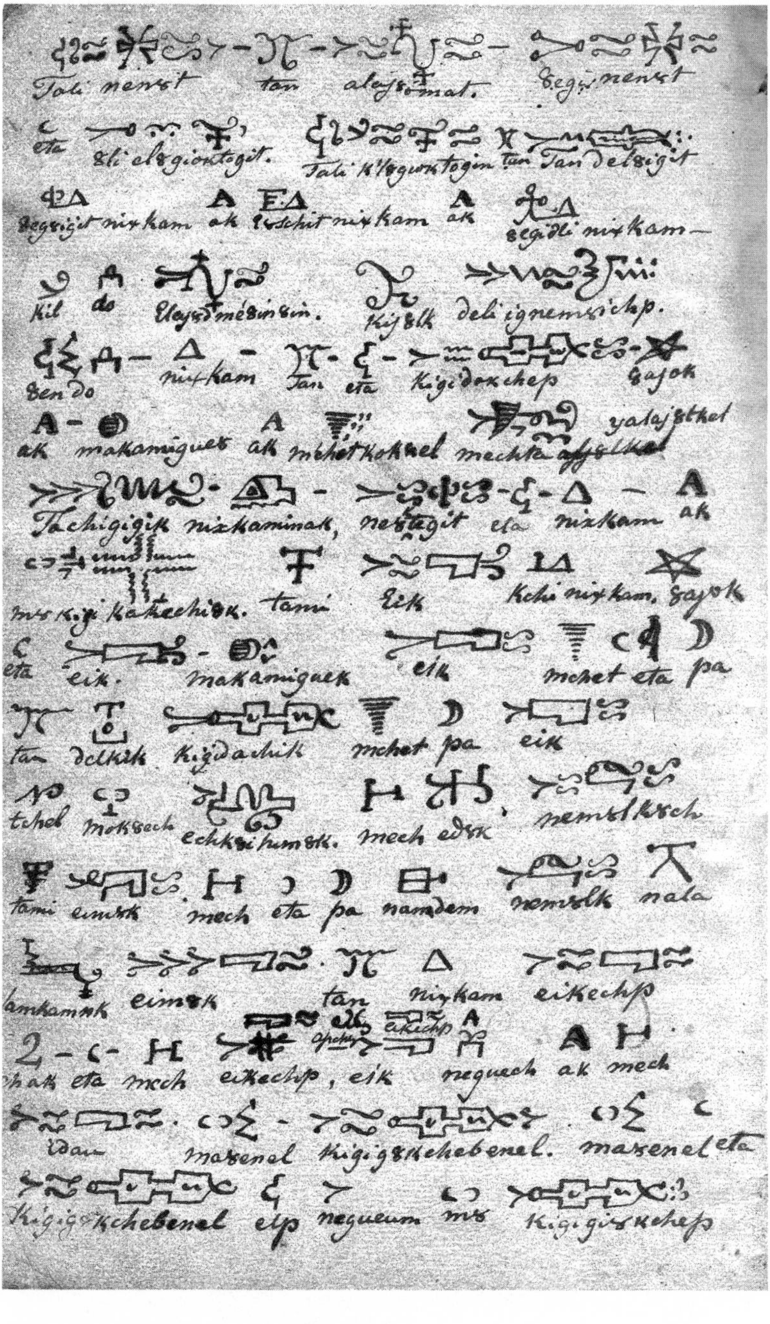

the Mi'kmaq. European missionaries later introduced much simpler pictograph alphabets to the Cherokee and the Cree nations, and they failed as well. According to a later writer, Silas Rand, who was a theologian and missionary himself, Le Clercq's system, "so far as use is concerned, to say nothing of its theological errors, it is one of the grossest literary blunders that was ever perpetrated." During the winter of 1737 Le Clercq's characters were revised in a similar system invented for the Mi'kmaq by another missionary, Pierre Maillard. The characters were again revised by Catholic missionaries and published in Vienna in an 1866 German edition. In each of these instances the characters were based on the ones Le Clercq first discovered among the Mi'kmaq. That an earlier writing system existed for the Mi'kmaq and that it was based on a text of simply written square characters seems irrefutable.

The writer who pointed out Le Clercq's "theological errors" and "literary blunders"—the Reverend Silas Tertius Rand— was a Baptist clergyman, an expert on the Mi'kmaq and their language. Born in 1810, he was the eighth of twenty-two children of an English family that had moved to Nova Scotia after the French Acadians had been expelled from their homes. Rand was married with twelve children of his own. Besides being a missionary, he was also a seemingly inexhaustible writer and an internationally respected scholar of languages. He died when he was almost eighty within a few miles of the small Nova Scotian town where he had been born. He was known as one of the leading scholars of the Mi'kmaq language: he compiled the first Mi'kmaq dictionary, a work of over forty thousand words, and produced scores of scriptural translations in both Mi'kmaq and Maliseet, the Mi'kmaq's closest neighbours. He mastered Latin, Greek, French, Italian, German and Spanish, as well as Mi'kmaq, Maliseet and Mohawk. Of the cultures he studied, Rand said he was most fascinated by Mi'kmaq customs, folklore and language. He was the first to translate into English the Mi'kmaq legends told to him by the nation's elders, and it was Rand's translations that made the tales of Kluscap available to the public for the first time, during the nineteenth century.

Silas Tertius Rand, missionary, language scholar and champion of the "Micmacs."

Rand was critical of what Europeans, particularly the early missionaries, had done to the Mi'kmaq. He wrote that the level of poverty to which the Mi'kmaq had been driven could be attributed to "the darkness, superstition and bigotry of Romanism." He blamed many of the problems on the Roman Catholic missionaries who had controlled much of native society since early in the seventeenth century. It was then that the Mi'kmaq social fabric began to break down with the introduction of alcohol by European traders. In spite of this deterioration in their traditional ways, Rand saw that the Mi'kmaq language had maintained its strength and beauty, and he decided to concentrate on it. Of all the languages Rand had mastered, he held Mi'kmaq in the highest esteem. He reported that, throughout the centuries of European settlement, the Mi'kmaq women had kept the traditions of their language alive. The women were critical when it was spoken poorly, and they praised those who could use it most beautifully. To Rand, "it is one of the most marvellous of all languages, ancient or modern — marvellous in its construction, in its regularity, in its fullness."

I learned from Olive Dickason, a twentieth-century scholar who has studied the native peoples of eastern North America, that the Mi'kmaq believed their unique language separated them from their nearest neighbours, the Maliseet. The languages spoken by both nations were derived from the same language group and had developed from the same base. At one time the Mi'kmaq and the Maliseet would have had one language and been one people. However, by the time the French missionaries arrived, the Mi'kmaq had separated themselves from their Maliseet neighbours in what is now

New Brunswick and the Gaspé, and felt superior and better educated. The French called the Maliseet the Etchemin or Eteminquois, but the Mi'kmaq preferred "Maliseet," a pejorative term meaning "they don't talk as we do," "corrupted speech" or "broken talk." To the Mi'kmaq, language was the characteristic that distinguished them; they believed that they spoke well, but the Maliseet did not. The Mi'kmaq derided their neighbours because they did not come up to the standard the Mi'kmaq had set.

I searched through more reports and books in an attempt to find the source of the Christian icons and the written language among the Mi'kmaq. Even their spoken language was sufficiently unusual to have been a subject of continued interest to many early observers. The eighteenth-century missionary Pierre Maillard, a well-educated man with a remarkable facility for languages, wrote that "nothing enchants those people more than a style of metaphors and allegories, in which even their common conversation abounds." The most unusual aspect of this claim is that, unlike most other elements of native culture reported through European eyes, Maillard's impression of the Mi'kmaq language was all positive. Maillard described how their usual prose "runs into poetry," how they used rhyming patterns at the ends of their sentences and employed a "thousand similes" when they spoke. His compliments were effusive, in a reserved, priestly way. Silas Rand made the same observation when, in 1888, he wrote that the Mi'kmaq language "is remarkable for its copiousness, its regularity of declension and conjunction, its expressiveness, its simplicity of vocables, and its mellifluousness."

———

In these early reports I also found more than a few observations about the remarkable technical knowledge of the Mi'kmaq. They did not have metal tools and lived as nomads by hunting and gathering. Yet Europeans observed that the Mi'kmaq already knew aspects of astronomy, map-making and navigation that appeared advanced even by Western standards. The Mi'kmaq could sail in open water, charting their direction by the stars, and, after listening to them explain the night sky, Rand believed they must have studied astronomy in the past. They knew the North Star as a stationary point of reference in the sky, recognized the constellations and even referred to the Milky Way by a similar phrase in Mi'kmaq. They had their own legends about the stars and the constellations. In 1691 Le Clercq had observed that "they have some knowledge of the Great and Little Bears [and] they say that the three guards of the North Star is a canoe in which three Indians are embarked to overtake this bear, but that, unfortunately, they have not been able to catch it." These were not skills they had learned from European fishermen.

The Mi'kmaq were map-makers at a time when most Europeans had not seen a map, when the sciences of cartography and surveying were still in their infancy. Le Clercq observed how the Mi'kmaq had "much ingenuity in drawing upon bark a kind of map which marks exactly all the rivers and streams of a country of which they wish to make a representation. They mark all the places thereon exactly and so well that they make use of them successfully, and an Indian who possesses one makes long voyages without going astray."

Those trips included voyages across open water in canoes fitted with sails. The Mi'kmaq reached Newfoundland before Europeans arrived in the New World and were accustomed to making trips to the Magdalen Islands, a distance of more than three hundred kilometres. According to Father Biard, after Europeans arrived, the Mi'kmaq were known to buy small vessels from the French and "handle them as skilfully as our most courageous and active sailors." They were considered among the most accomplished sailors in native North America. The neighbours of the Mi'kmaq were not reported as sailors, nor were they able to make maps or read the stars: these traditions appeared to be specific to the Mi'kmaq. Moreover, each of these unusual aspects of their culture impressed me as possibly having been adapted from a visiting culture: the Christian iconography, the character-based language, the navigational and cartographic skills.

Even aspects of Mi'kmaq life as traditional as the way they fished showed signs of an outside influence. Local shore fishing and seasonal hunting gave the Mi'kmaq an almost unlimited supply of food. Nonetheless, an account written in 1593 by Richard Strong, the captain of an English ship, the *Marigold*, which was fishing off the coast of Cape Breton, observed that the Mi'kmaq raised fish in artificial ponds. For a moment, I put the book down in disbelief. Strong wrote that he and his crew had "sailed farther four leagues to the west of Cape Breton, where we saw many seals. And here, having need of fresh water, we went again on shore, and, passing somewhat more into the land, we found certain round ponds artificially made by the Savages to keep fish in, with weirs in them to take fish." The Mi'kmaq were farming fish in 1593.

I had seen modern fish farms as a child during my weekly trips with my grandparents along the back roads of the island. Much of Cape Breton Island is a fisherman's paradise, and I was fascinated by the many small-scale fish-farming operations that raised trout and salmon in small round ponds to maintain the island's fish stocks. Strong's description is unmistakable in what it implied. During the sixteenth century the Mi'kmaq farmed and harvested fish in artificially constructed ponds. They were surrounded by such a rich source of wild fish that the techniques of artificial fish culture would not have grown out of necessity. This practice was not well established among the Mi'kmaq—Strong's mention was the only one. It appears to have been borrowed and newly learned, and was not found among any other native people along the coast of North America. Towards the end of the sixteenth century, the practice appears to have been lost by the Mi'kmaq. How, why and when the Mi'kmaq had developed the technology were unclear.

When I turned to discussions of Mi'kmaq medicine, I discovered that physicians among the Mi'kmaq had sufficient medical knowledge to surprise early Europeans. They could cure diseases even the French deemed incurable. They were skilled at blood letting, performed abortions on women too weak to carry another child, had an "infallible remedy" for epilepsy, could heal burns and wounds, and were adept at the treatment and setting of broken bones. According to observers, they were physicians and apothecaries by nature, with a knowledge of herbs and roots unknown to Europeans. In 1708 the French surgeon Sieur de Dièreville published *Relation du voyage du Port Royal de l'Acadie, ou de la Nouvelle France,* in which he wrote that Mi'kmaq doctors were so adept it seemed they could cure themselves of death itself. From all the observations during the seventeenth century, the Mi'kmaq appeared to know a great deal more about medicine than Europe did. It may not be surprising that Mi'kmaq doctors knew more than the Europeans about medicinal herbs and local remedies, but the degree to which they understood and followed a wide range of medical practices makes these observations of particular note.

Like so many other characteristics of this small nation, Mi'kmaq fish farming and medical practices were remarkable but inexplicable. There were early observations—too many to be ignored—that clearly implied the Mi'kmaq had technologies far in advance of their immediate neighbours and impressive even by European standards. As I organized these different observations and eyewitness accounts, I had to admit there was a possible explanation, though it made no sense to me. Had a Western nation visited the New World before the first recorded Europeans had arrived but left no record in European history of that visit?

CHAPTER ELEVEN

A LIGHT IN THE EAST

As the summer of 2003 came to an end I realized that many of the facts I had collected led to nothing except a new list of questions. Much evidence failed to fit into the mainstream history of the New World.

More and more I felt that the Mi'kmaq were the key. They were unlike other native peoples in North America. They were able to read and write. Their society included highly skilled navigators, sailors, cartographers and physicians. And there was evidence that a foreign community, probably with a small group of Christians among its members, had held some place within the Mi'kmaq Nation. The Mi'kmaq laid much of this knowledge at the door of Kluscap, their cultural hero, who had lived among them before Europeans arrived and had transformed their nation.

Each of these elements might be simple misrepresentation or coincidence: the memories of witnesses are often faulty. But I had come across so many unusual and curiously complementary facts about the Mi'kmaq that I felt compelled to think back over the research. I could not avoid the impression that someone else had lived with the Mi'kmaq, someone from a society technically advanced and literate enough to know and understand navigation, cartography, medicine and even fish cultivation. Mi'kmaq legends suggested that the home of that someone—represented as Kluscap—was on Cape Dauphin.

There was the Island of Seven Cities, apparently identified with Cape Breton during the fifteenth century. Christopher Columbus had drawn it, and John Cabot located it with specific coordinates. The Seven Cities legend and the Zeno family stories both described a major city. According to the Zenos, the few Europeans who visited the island noted that the community had lost its knowledge of the Latin books in its library, although it kept its understanding of its "language and letters." A century and a half later the Frenchman Le Clercq provided an eyewitness account of the Mi'kmaq that mirrored the Zeno stories: the Mi'kmaq's knowledge and use of letters had been "gradually lost and effaced from the minds of their unfortunate posterity by the lapse of time."

Then there were the ruins reported by the earliest explorers. After Cabot's discovery, the island was rumoured to hold the remains of a previous settlement, but no one knew exactly what they were. The records suggested Portuguese or possibly English origins, but, however vague the attribution, it was apparent that the observers believed there had been something there. Yet, as I had worked my way document by document through the entire history of the island, I could discover no mention of anything larger than a few small, wooden fishing sheds along the shore and a single stone church at the end of the bay.

The only mention of the road was in James Lamb's local history, written in 1975. Lamb saw "the traces of wide and well-built roadways deep in these wooded hills," and he wrote of "ancient clearings, old stone fences, the outlines of forgotten foundations." He had thought they might be French, and so had I. But the records did not support that theory. Lamb had died some years earlier, but I knew for certain the road was there.

I began to wonder if whatever was atop Cape Dauphin might be large enough to be seen from the air. More aerial photographs were only a phone call away. I ordered coverage of the entire tip of Cape Dauphin, photographs from different seasons, different years, at different scales and of different areas.

From the air, a landscape resembles an architectural drawing at a much larger scale. Buildings, even ruins, make a recognizable geometry in the organic pattern of natural wilderness. If there were ruins up there, I was determined to see them.

I set up a sort of on-screen air-intelligence lab in the apartment and superimposed all the photographs onto a detailed topographic map I scanned into Photoshop. This process allowed me to cover the site in great detail and to pinpoint the location of anything that seemed unusual. It was as though I was looking at kilometres of hillside with a magnifying glass.

But when you spend days staring at aerial photographs of forested hills veined by jagged mountain streams, your eyes get tired, trees and rivers dance into weird patterns, and the shades and shadows of nature begin to make imagined and unnatural shapes. After a few days my eyes were physically sore.

Then finally I found it: a tiny line etched faintly into the side of the slope. When I saw the road on the computer screen I remembered its contours from having walked down it. I was able to find the point where, just before it led down the last section of the slope, it turned at almost a right angle. When I was actually on the road, it seemed like such an odd turn on a path of shallow curves. With the road now visible to me on the side of the hill, I was able to trace the line farther up the slope. It was overgrown in many sections, but parts of it were visible in photographs taken during different seasons and over most of the last century. Using the topographic map as a guide, I followed it as it climbed. And there, just before the summit, I saw the ruins for the first time.

On the north side of the slope, facing the northern coast and the open Atlantic, was a roughly rectangular enclosure, massive enough to be seen from the air. It was a wall of some sort, and it was big. From the underlying map I could determine that the width of the wall was about six or seven metres at its thickest point and that the wall enclosed an area roughly similar in size to that of the fortified town of Louisbourg. The wall had been a major construction project when it was built. It was much broader than the tiny line made by the road I had followed initially. This was a wall joined only to itself, and it enclosed an area roughly rectangular in shape with broad curved corners and jagged edges. The upper wall followed the slope, just shy of the summit. Along this wall I could see wide openings, as if parts of the wall had disappeared or had once been broken by gates. However, along the slopes on

It was on this aerial photograph of Cape Dauphin, taken in August 1929, that I spotted the ruins for the first time.

both the shorter east and the west sides and along the long, lower, northern edge, I could see that the line was distinctly man-made.

I was struck by its size. I could imagine from the photos that it was built of stone, but the scale was enormous. Louisbourg had taken the French forty years to build, and its construction had left a long trail of documents on both continents and in several countries. What I was looking at here had left no documents at all.

All I could see from the photographs was that the enclosure was big, about a kilometre long and half as wide. It was located northwest of the summit, and its lower wall followed the curve of a small river along the far northern border. The road I had originally discovered led up to the enclosure from the east. The enclosure appeared cradled by the low rise of the summit and the shallow valley made by the river. Yet the geometry was clear: its long north and south walls were parallel to each other, as were those that climbed the incline from the river along the far eastern and western ends. I didn't need to be an architect to see that the building of an enormous walled enclosure over difficult, hilly terrain would have required a major workforce and years of organization and planning. This construction wasn't Acadian; it wasn't Mi'kmaq. I kept thinking of Louisbourg.

Though computer programs allowed me to look at the photographs in extreme close-up, it was difficult to make out exactly what I was seeing. I kept scanning the photographs of the area around the enclosure, photographs taken in different years and different seasons, and saw other consistently

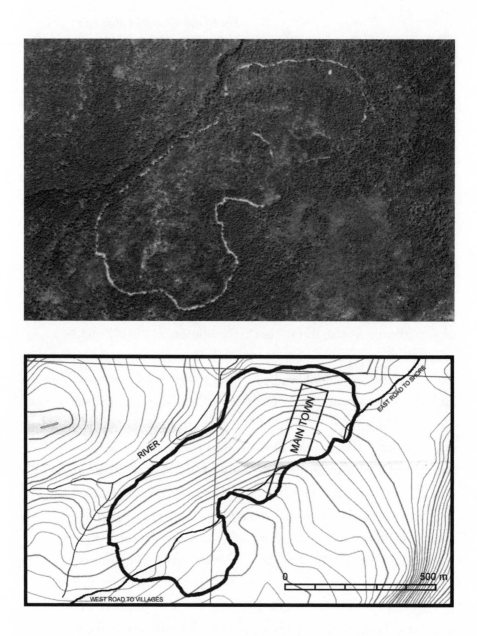

Detail (top) of the 1929 aerial photograph enlarged to show the site of the ruins. At bottom, the author's illustration of the wall and town site based on the photograph.

visible man-made geometry. In the eastern section of the enclosure, a narrow rectangular clearing ran down the slope. It was not aligned to compass north but to true north—the North Star. It looked like an area where something, or a group of things, had been organized and built around a central spine. The lower end of this rectangular area stopped just short of the eastern wall of the enclosure. From the very specific way in which it was configured, with defined edges and a clear axis, it, too, appeared to have been planned and built on an impressive scale. The long axis of the large enclosure was oriented along the magnetic compass, while the axis of the rectangular clearing within the wall was oriented along the axis of the North Star, an almost 25° difference in this part of the world.

This plateau, running along the summit, had been the site of a great deal of construction. The aerial photographs showed that the road I had walked, after disappearing along the southern length of the enclosure, reappeared on the west side of the wall and continued along the crest of the cape to a relatively flat area dotted by tiny lakes. I could make out more geometry in this area. Overall, the evidence pointed to a construction project that would have required government participation on a scale large enough to leave significant documentation. Yet I could find no record that anything had been built on this land. The French and the English had considered it barren, not worth cultivation. All I knew was what I had learned from the Mi'kmaq legends: I was looking at the home of Kluscap.

—

For several days I carried on studying the photographs, and finally accepted the fact that what I was seeing was big, but not European. Louisbourg, even though it was considered France's most important fortification in the North Atlantic arena, was not surrounded by walls on all sides but was fortified only at the most important defensive positions. It was built on flat terrain, directly on the shore, and incorporated an easily available harbour. This enclosure on Cape Dauphin was built on a mountain but not right on the summit; it was near the coast but separated from it by a long, steep road; it followed the hilly site rather than levelling the terrain; the overall geometry was relaxed and somewhat natural rather than rigid and angular; and the scale was clearly not Western. This was a wall that might have been intended primarily for enclosure and definition, not defence.

I began to mull and take long walks. I set out my notes on the large table and began again to pore over them. One sheet I reserved for general observations. At its bottom were three names—Maillard, Rand, and Alfonce—written as the apexes of a triangle. In the middle of the triangle I'd doodled a question mark.

Just before I went to bed one night in early September the spark leapt across the gap. The common elements abruptly fused together the reports of Father Maillard, Silas Rand and Jean Alfonce—three different observers, one writing at the end of the nineteenth century, one in 1755, and the remaining one in 1559. The sixteenth-century French navigator Jean Alfonce described the territory as *la Tarterie*, the region of the Tartars. Silas Rand reported that the Mi'kmaq wrote "after the manner of the Chinese." Father Maillard, questioning the origin of their writing, suggested that "possibly some light might be got into it, by discovering whether there was any affinity or not between their language, and that of the Orientalists, as the Chinese or Tartars."

I've got to tell Gerard, I thought. I looked at the clock. It was 12:45 a.m. I winced, imagining his reaction. I went back and peered at the photographs, and the ghostly geometry on that mountain top I had never visited stared back at me.

Architecturally there was every reason to believe that these ruins were not of Western origin. The walled towns of China were often located along small rivers and built into the sides of hills. These were not the remains of a small European outpost built on a mountaintop as a position of strength. Rather, this walled town nestled among the hills in the way the Chinese had built for centuries. Impossible! I better keep this interpretation to myself, I thought.

I came back to the apartment one afternoon a week or two later, turned on the TV and heard a discussion of old maps. It was the very end of a television interview with a British mariner and writer named Gavin Menzies. He had apparently just published a book entitled 1421. I didn't know the subject, but the title stuck with me. That date, 1421, was around the time when the earliest European maps began to appear. It was also just about the time that the Island of Seven Cities legend had started to circulate in Europe, and it was also the period when the age of discovery was getting underway.

I was doing my accustomed wandering around a bookstore that evening when I saw Menzies's book. Toronto is fortunate in having a few small bookstores among the giants, and these bookstores are pleasant places to be. By choosing fewer books to sell and playing a more editorial role in what they carry, these dedicated booksellers make choices for those of us who like to browse. The full title of Menzies's book was 1421: *The Year China Discovered the World*. I would normally consider such titles to be in the New Age domain of legends of Lost Atlantis or the Holy Grail. The book's photographs—the underwater stone formations of the Bimini Road in the Caribbean and an illustration of the Rhode Island Tower, a round stone structure of unresolved origins located on the east coast of the United States—did not inspire further confidence. Both stories have traditionally attracted seekers of things bewildering.

But Menzies was talking about China, and China was very much on my mind. He showed maps: old ones, well-respected ones, maps I recognized from studying the history of North America. I have a soft spot for maps. And the author had been a naval commander, so would know the oceans. I had some inkling that ocean currents had played a crucial role in Cape Breton history, and I wanted to read more about them. The island had been important primarily because of the Gulf Stream. But this Gulf Stream, which regulated the trade between the Caribbean and Cape Breton during the eighteenth century, was only one current among many. Perhaps at the very least Menzies could give me some insight into how the ocean currents flowed throughout the entire Atlantic, where they came from and where they went. I took 1421 home, ready to read about the sea.

From Menzies and other writers and historians I learned that China had ruled the Indian Ocean during the early fifteenth century. If her ships had rounded the Cape of Good Hope off the southern tip of Africa, Cape Breton Island would have been reached easily via the ocean currents. The Benguela Current flows up the west coast of Africa, out towards the mid-Atlantic and into the North Equatorial Current, where it ends up skimming northward along the outer edge of the Caribbean. The numerous warm-water currents of the Caribbean collect into the Gulf Stream, which flows up the east coast of North America. In the waters off Cape Breton the warm current of the Gulf Stream hits the colder Labrador Current flowing down from the north. Here the powerful Gulf Stream loses its strength and is deflected back out into the Atlantic. The change is so great that the majority of the water-borne nutrients fall out of the solution, making the shallow banks off the coast of Cape Breton and Newfoundland the feeding ground for much of the world's cold-water marine life. In simple terms, because of the way the ocean flows, there is a good chance that a beach ball that slipped into the surf off the coast of South Africa would end up on the shores of Cape Breton Island. Once mariners reached the eastern side of the island, finding Cape Dauphin would be as easy as finding that place where the coast curves to the north.

The Chinese trading fleets, along with those of the Arabs, had controlled most of the Indian Ocean for centuries. It was compelling to consider that they may have reached the Cape of Good Hope at the southern tip of Africa in the first years of the fifteenth century. The natural ocean currents would have done much of the rest. If the Chinese had managed a settlement on Cape Breton, that would explain its being seen as an island of grand cities. It would explain the reports of mysterious ruins, the Mi'kmaq legends, Jean Alfonce's reference to *la Tarterie*, the written language, and the road I had found, well made and lined with stone walls.

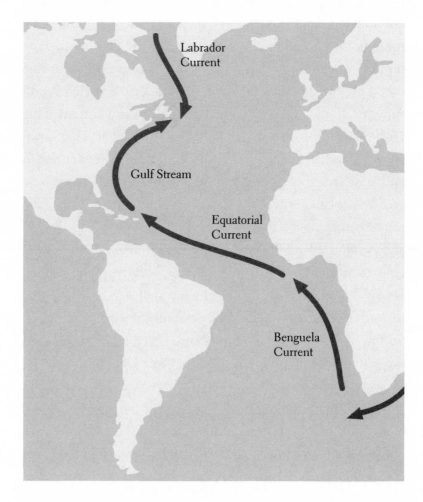

———

Five hundred years of maps, records and eyewitness accounts powerfully suggested that what I was seeing on the top of Cape Dauphin had not been built by a European government or by European settlers. Nor had it been built in the centuries since John Cabot first discovered the island in 1497. It was obvious that the discovery of significant non-European North American ruins built before the end of the fifteenth century would be important, but if what I was looking at was indeed Chinese, then this site was a major discovery. I could not even imagine the magnitude.

Surprisingly, my own first thoughts on facing the Chinese hypothesis were about change—change at every level. Perhaps it was my training that made such change seem difficult. Change for an architect means beginnings and endings, surfaces and materials coming together, lines that transform from one shape into another or forces that change direction. Change means that energy must be expended. Where once lines and surfaces were simple, beginnings and endings require passion, patience and much thought. When I finished reading 1421, I took its implications in a personal way. The simple story of old ruins on a hill threatened to reveal a much more complicated structure. I wondered if I was really prepared to deal with the magnitude of what I now confronted. In a purely personal and selfish way, it made no sense to continue

OPPOSITE: *Could the Chinese ships have made it to Cape Dauphin? If you dropped a beach ball into the sea at the Cape of Good Hope, ocean currents would carry it to Cape Breton Island.*

this search if it led where I feared it might. Wasn't my life more important than old ruins on a mountaintop? At what should have been a thrilling juncture in my work, I was enveloped by gloom. I couldn't continue. I wanted out.

During the days after I finished 1421, I considered the possible enormity of the ruins' significance but, with an immune system running close to empty, I dwelt only on its potential for change and stress. What if this road *was* built by the Chinese? What if I *had* come across something monumental?

But by this time—the early autumn of 2003—I had passed the point of no return. Perhaps there's a link between curiosity and spiritual redemption, and now, for me, curiosity intervened. The single Chinese connection rose in my mind in the way a Gothic cathedral explains in perfect logic all its disparate elements. Soon I would need to see the summit of Cape Dauphin and test the foundations of that cathedral.

CHAPTER TWELVE

LEARNING ANEW

AFTER THE INITIAL astonishment had passed, I became somewhat uncomfortable with the Menzies thesis. Did the Chinese actually have a navy large enough to navigate the Atlantic Ocean? And how could an enterprise of that scale and importance be erased from history?

I began to read Chinese history of the period. It quickly became clear how little I knew. Most of my historical knowledge had come on the coattails of architectural history, and, at the several universities I had attended and in the few where I had taught, the history of China was little appreciated. I knew a bit about classical Greece because of the Parthenon. I'd read Renaissance philosophy only because of its impact on the work of its architects. But Chinese architecture never loomed large for me, and I would call myself typical in that respect. Architectural history in the West generally stops at the city limits of Istanbul. Chinese history in any form is not part of the curriculum or even the background of Western history, architectural or otherwise. It was shocking to discover how much of the world I had been ignoring. Large Chinese ships were in fact sailing throughout Southeast Asia, Arabia and the west coast of Africa while Europe was still in its infancy. Chinese ships had sailed the full extent of the Indian Ocean well before the early fifteenth century.

The Chinese court maintained smooth and lucrative business relationships with a vast array of foreign countries through clever political means. Ambassadors and emissaries from around the Indian Ocean visited China during the early fifteenth century, exchanged valuable gifts and were treated royally. In response to their allegiance, they were given a nominal position in the vast empire and a preferential trade status. That part of the history is beyond dispute. One of the clearest and most telling witnesses to that trade is an early fifteenth-century Chinese painted illustration of an African giraffe sent as a tribute to the emperor. China tried to make these ambassadorial visits grand affairs. Giraffes and other exotic African beasts were delivered to the Chinese emperor during some of these exchanges and, in return, the foreign dignitaries returned home with Chinese gifts. That single illustration of one healthy giraffe in the Chinese court shows how normal it

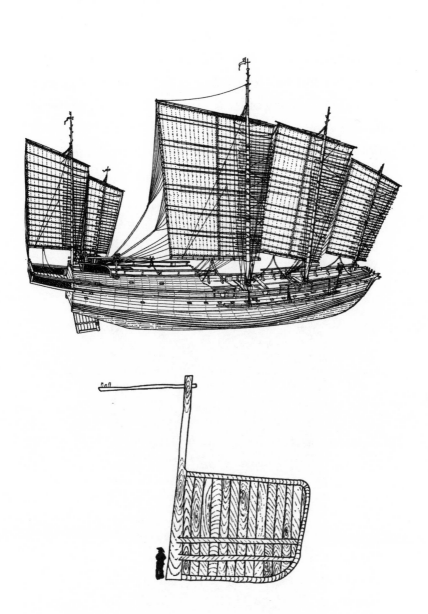

A five-masted Chinese freighter (top) similar to the ships used by Zheng He during the voyages of the Treasure Ships, along with an illustration of a rudder discovered in Nanking in the twentieth century, which is believed to be from one of Zheng He's ships.

was for Chinese ships to sail between coasts at the farthest edges of the Indian Ocean. In the early fifteenth century, China, more than any other country in the world, controlled the seas. In the history of later Western expansion and the European age of discovery, there is little record of that fact.

A Chinese painting done in 1414 showing a giraffe sent from the east coast of Africa in tribute to the emperor.

The more I read, the clearer it became that, early in its history, China had established a vast shipping industry. That industry had evolved initially to navigate a system of inland waterways and artificial canals, the longest in the world. China's canals connected rivers, lakes and coasts throughout the entire country, improving communication and commerce along with the skills of both shipbuilders and sailors. Sailing, shipbuilding, navigation and cartography had long been important businesses in China, vital to the country's prosperity and far in advance of anything that was happening in Europe at the time. By the late thirteenth century, Marco Polo reported to Europe that the river and canal system of China "goes so far and through so many regions, and there are so many cities upon it that I tell you truly that more boats loaded with more dear things and of greater value go and come by this river than go by all the rivers of Christians together or by all their seas." The trade carried on these waterways led to the construction and maintenance of vast fleets of vessels of different sizes and shapes for a variety of sailing conditions. Technical solutions were developed, tested and incorporated. As early as the tenth and eleventh centuries, the ships built by the Chinese had watertight compartments and multiple decks and masts, and they could carry hundreds of sailors. The Chinese invention of the compass helped lead to the construction of a vast and powerful navy. By the twelfth century China had displaced other Arabian, Asian and South Sea nations in her command of ocean travel. China was so far ahead of European shipping that, until the nineteenth century, there was no adequate comparison. Throughout the changes in governments over the centuries, the growth of a vast Chinese navy was never interrupted. The Mongols, for instance, using experienced Chinese sailors, were able to muster thousands of ships in 1274 and 1281 in unsuccessful attempts to conquer Japan. There was no need to search deeply into Chinese history to find examples of large ships that could have sailed beyond small local ports. The early naval history of China is clear in its technical achievements, and remarkable for the range of its adventures.

Aside from clocks, cartography and paper money, the Chinese had invented many technologies that, only much later, would be used in Europe. The Chinese were using a rudder as early as the first century to allow large vessels to steer properly and to go where they needed to go—a technical advance that was invaluable for long ocean voyages and one not adopted by Europeans until the twelfth century. Some of these ships' rudders were up to ten metres tall and designed to be raised and lowered from the deck according to the depth of the water. Their sails were efficiently designed using thin bamboo battens, sewn into a series of horizontal pockets, that allowed the sails to be raised and lowered from the deck and easily adjusted to use the available wind. In contrast, European sailors had to climb the ship's mast to unfurl their full sails from the yardarms when the wind changed. The bamboo battens helped keep the Chinese sails taut and better able to maintain their efficiency, even when sections were damaged. By the early part of the fifteenth century, technical advances, which would only much later be incorporated into European ocean-going vessels, had been made in every aspect of Chinese shipbuilding.

Chinese ships, with their battened sails and multiple masts, were trading regularly across large expanses of open water early in history. I found a description of ships from the tenth and eleventh centuries with six masts that could hold a thousand men. Six masts in the tenth century! All the canals, rivers and waterways of China were fully mapped as early as 1040. A description written in 1178 reported: "The ships which sail the southern sea and south of it are like houses. When their sails are spread they are like great clouds in the sky. Their rudders are several tens of feet long. A single ship carries several hundred men, and has in the stores a year's supply of grain. Pigs are fed and wine fermented on board." By 1281 the Chinese were able to assemble an armada of 4,400 ships and, by the beginning of the Ming Dynasty, with the planning and construction of the large fleets of the early fifteenth century, the Chinese navy was in a class far in advance of any other nation in the world.

In the many reports of Chinese fleets landing at the various ports around the Indian Ocean, one in particular caught my attention. I had studied Christian theology and was aware of the significant community of Nestorian Christians living in China as early as the seventh century, one large enough to leave behind icons from that period. Remarkable as it seems, Christianity established itself in China before it made much of an inroad in Europe. By the fifteenth century China had Christian bishops, large churches and an open channel to Rome. Now I read an observation, made in 1499 in the port of Calicut, which unexpectedly connected Chinese sailors and a small Christian community among them.

The city of Calicut is located on the southwest coast of India and was one of the most important ports in the Indian Ocean for much of the Middle Ages. A report written from Calicut in 1499 described the large Chinese ships that had visited the port earlier in the century: "It is now about 80 years since there arrived in this city of Calicut certain vessels of white Christians, who wore their hair long like Germans and had no beards, except round the mouth." The date of that visit—about 1420—belongs to the era of the large Chinese fleets. The Calicut report included a description of weapons. To historian Joseph Needham, writing in his multivolume work *Science and Civilisation in China*, it was evident that "the 'white Christians' were Chinese, if only from the description of their characteristic hand weapon." We know, then, that there was Christian iconography in China, and this Calicut report claims there were Christians on the Chinese fleets.

The Calicut report could explain why a small group of Cross-Bearers had been found among the Mi'kmaq. The iconography of the cross was known and used among that Chinese community in the same ways that Le Clercq had observed it being used among some of the Mi'kmaq. Genghis Khan's mother was a Nestorian Christian. Strange as I found the facts and difficult as they were to accept, the Mi'kmaq iconography makes most sense if its pre-European use had been learned from the Chinese, perhaps before the fifteenth century.

Certainly by the early fifteenth century the Chinese were in a position to send their best and brightest out onto the oceans, whether those oceans were known and navigated or not. They had the technical knowledge, the sailors and the ships. They had navigated to the farthest edges of the Indian Ocean. The ships were huge, though just how huge has been a central issue for critics of Gavin Menzies. Skeptics claim that the Chinese ships described by Menzies could not have been as large as he suggests.

Menzies estimates that the largest of these ships, called Treasure Ships by the Chinese because they were being used to carry ambassadors and rich trade goods, had been 160 metres long. He arrives at that length by employing the Chinese measurement of 444 *chi*, the length traditionally quoted in Chinese records and a number used by scholars of Chinese naval technology, and adopting the accepted ratio of 1 *chi* to just over 12 inches. However, several authors have questioned the original Chinese measurement, and they may have a valid point. One of the issues is a physical one: How big could such a wooden-hulled ship be and still survive the high seas without splitting up under the stress? Among Menzies's critics there is little unanimity, except that a 160-metre wooden hull would seem almost impossible to keep together in rough water.

Recent scholarship has suggested that it would be safer to accept a measurement closer to half of Menzies's claim for the largest of the Chinese vessels. The remains of a rudderpost from one of these early ships has been found and its size, although massive, points to an estimate lower than Menzies's original. However, even if the Chinese ships sailing the Indian Ocean in the early fifteenth century were no larger than eighty metres, half of what Menzies estimated, that would still put them in the same league as any large wooden-hulled European vessel proven able to cross the ocean. All of Columbus's ships were less than one-third that size; the *Mayflower* was only thirty metres long. Both James Cook and Charles Darwin sailed into the Pacific Ocean on ships of little more than thirty metres; Lord Horatio Nelson won the Battle of Trafalgar in 1805 aboard a massive wooden-hulled ship, the HMS *Victory*, that measured not quite ninety metres long and carried a full complement of 850 men. The Chinese were building ships in the early part of the fifteenth century that were at least as large and probably larger than any of these examples.

What is clear is that the Chinese navy was the largest in the world and had the technology, the navigational expertise and the centuries of cartographic skills necessary to sail anywhere they wanted. By early in the century, the records—including the giraffes in Peking—establish that the Chinese had reached the southwestern tip of Africa. It was almost a century later before Europeans—in much smaller ships and with minimal crews—met that challenge.

Nonetheless, the Chinese rounding of the Cape of Good Hope in the early fifteenth century is a point of controversy. A Chinese map from 1402, the Kangnido Map, clearly shows both sides of the African continent, a map that could have been drawn only from surveys of the western coast. What this map proves is that China had enough interest in the far side of Africa to have mapped it with a high degree of accuracy. Chinese mariners had to have rounded the southern tip to do their surveying. The issue is not whether China could have rounded the tip of Africa and sailed across the Atlantic—that ability is widely accepted—or even why they might have wanted to do so. To get to the other side has, throughout history, proven itself a consistent human motivator. The real issue is, if the Chinese did what they likely did, how did the construction of a large settlement on Cape Dauphin on the opposite side of the globe disappear so completely from history?

I knew the ruins existed and I knew Europeans had failed to notice them in surveys or to report them. Alternatively, if someone did report them, the people in power ignored the reports. I had walked on the road, and I could see clearly from the aerial photographs that there were ruins on this site, ruins that would be difficult for anyone surveying the area to miss. Yet they had been ignored. I gained some insight into this anomaly from Le Clercq's book. When the Mi'kmaq tried to explain the origin of their Christian images to Le Clercq, he observed only that "they also add certain other wholly ridiculous circumstances, which I purposefully omit, because they do not bear at all upon a secret which is unknown to men, and reserved to God alone." We see from this remark how easy it is for people to suppress, forget or purposefully omit the unusual, the misunderstood or the uncomfortable. I had seen the same habits of mind in commentary made by historians trying to explain the Zeno stories. The island settlement described by Zeno *did* not exist because it *could* not exist. It was simply unimaginable.

I could see from the documents sitting on my desk that my own ancestry bore the same mark of officially sponsored invisibility. By the time of the Acadian deportation in 1755, the

British had decided to remove any memory of the Acadians. The most effective way of doing that was "to destroy all these settlements by burning down all their houses, cutting the dikes, and destroying all the grain." The British plan was to "destroy the country, because that would make it very difficult for the French to re-establish themselves," with the goal of "good Protestant subjects transplanted in their room." Acadian place names were changed to English, farms were destroyed and the land was redistributed. With horses, sheep and cattle given to the British military, the Acadian communities and families were separated, loaded onto transports in small groups and sent to various New England colonies, prisons in England, or back to French-speaking settlements in the Caribbean or on the Continent. The goal was to divide them so "they cannot easily collect themselves together again." The land was cleansed of Acadians. However, in spite of the magnitude of this venture, in the following century Thomas Chandler Haliburton, Nova Scotia's first official historian, noted: "It is very remarkable that there are no traces of this important event to be found among the records. I could not discover that the correspondence had been preserved, or that the orders, returns, and memorials, had ever been filed there." In Haliburton's well-studied and well-respected view, "the particulars of this affair seem to have been carefully concealed, although it is not now easy to assign the reason, unless the parties were, as in truth they might be, ashamed of the transaction." The British had made every attempt not only to erase the memory of the Acadians but also to wipe out the stigma of the event. As I started to review the evidence for the Chinese erasing the memory of Cape Dauphin, I had many reasons to believe it was not only possible but a relatively easy thing for a government to do.

The Chinese overseas adventures appear to have begun in earnest at the beginning of the Ming Dynasty in the latter fourteenth century. Before the Ming, the foreign Mongol Dynasty had maintained much of Chinese culture and even improved the infrastructure of the country, but it was not liked. Mongol control of China collapsed in 1368 because of internal rebellions by local peasant groups eager to return to true Chinese rule. As Marco Polo had reported at the end of the previous century: "You should know that all the Cathians [the Chinese] detested the Great Khan's rule because he set over them governors who were Tartars [the Mongols], or still more frequently Saracens [the Arabs], and these they could not endure, for they were treated by them just like slaves."

Marco Polo used the word Tartar, a term that would come to be used to refer to the land of the Chinese in general, the same reference used by Jean Alfonce several centuries later when he referred to the territory of Cape Breton as *la Tarterie*. When the first Ming emperor came to power in 1368, one of his early projects was to improve the Chinese navy. In 1391 fifty million trees to be used for shipbuilding were planted around Nanking, in type and scale a uniquely Chinese project. I thought of the large tracts of various woods in the vicinity of Cape Dauphin which were used for shipbuilding, particularly masts, and remarked on by early European visitors. In the mid-eighteenth century the Englishman Samuel Holland reported that the woods in the vicinity of Cape Dauphin were "of the best Sort, as Oak, Birch, Maple, Beech, &c, with Pines of all Kinds, & of a Growth fit for Masts of all Sorts." Yet this in a land whose forests predominantly consisted of modest conifers.

In July 1405, just a few years after a new and aggressive emperor had taken the throne, the first large-scale Ming-sponsored fleets set out. Like the dimensions of the ships, the size and composition of this first major armada is a subject of dispute among scholars. All agree, however, that it was massive by any measure and equipped to handle the wildest oceans. The ships numbered at least in the hundreds, with a total complement in the many thousands. Between 1405 and 1421, in addition to the regular smaller trade missions, five more of these enormous fleets left China. More and more states around the Indian Ocean were sending envoys, ambassadors and exotic tribute back to the Chinese court. The voyage to Africa was soon familiar to a whole generation of Chinese sailors.

By this time the navy had gained such mastery that commanders felt secure enough to send out smaller groups of ships, detached from the main core of the large armada, with the mandate and the means to explore more distant lands. All these expeditions were meant to be great adventures, but the fleet sailing in 1421 was one of the most important and provided Gavin Menzies with the title of his book. That fleet is believed to have been the largest and most ambitious. A 1432 memorial to the fleet's commander, Zheng He, recorded that, because of what the Chinese navy had accomplished, "the countries beyond the horizon and at the ends of the earth have all become subjects, and to the most westerly western, or to the most northerly northern countries, however far they may be, the distances and routes may be calculated."

That memorial, carved in stone, stands as testimony to the magnitude of these voyages. Yet the issue that plagues Chinese history is this: What happened to the records of the voyages that went beyond the confines of the Indian Ocean? Why did the Chinese not want their history to record that they had been such far-reaching adventurers?

There are several plausible answers.

By the time the emperor died in 1424, the state's costs had begun to exceed its income by two or three times, and the amount of government money spent on these large-scale voyages came under criticism. The first place to cut the budget was the navy. Its grand adventures were seen to be disposable in the light of growing anti-maritime feelings within the empire.

Additionally, the commanders of these fleets were often eunuchs chosen for their loyalty to the emperor but hated by the civil administration. Zheng He was a eunuch. The official class, always hostile to eunuchs and merchants, was only too glad to see the foreign fleets disbanded, the eunuchs reduced to their former subservient position in court politics and the wealthy merchants humbled. Government officials trained in Confucianism were against foreign trade, even contact, as a simple matter of principle.

Now a bad omen intervened. A fire destroyed much of the Forbidden City immediately following the launch of the great fleet of 1421. The heavens were said to be angry with the emperor's excess. Demands grew to bring the navy home.

After 1424 the anti-maritime bureaucrats started to assert greater control of government policy. A new emperor ascended the throne and issued an edict stopping the further sailing of any of these large fleets and putting an end not only to construction of the largest of these ships but to repair and maintenance as well. Visiting dignitaries still living in China were taken back to their homes aboard smaller ships, and Chinese officials in foreign cities were also instructed to return immediately. Any interests beyond the Chinese border were discontinued and, not surprisingly, trade suffered. In response, a final fleet was ordered in 1430 by the fifth Ming emperor to re-establish the foreign links lost over the nine years since the previous voyage. That mission was apparently successful, and new giraffes and elephants arrived from Africa.

By 1433 the treasury of the Ming Dynasty had been depleted, and there was trouble along the northern border with the Mongols. The Ming began the process of protecting those borders. As John King Fairbank and Merle Goldman put it in *China: A New History*, "anticommercialism and xeno-phobia won out, and China retired from the world scene." By 1436 the construction of any large ship at all was prohibited in China. By the end of the century, ships that had been damaged at sea were not repaired, and, by the sixteenth century, an imperial edict stopped all further construction of sea-going vessels. Chinese ships now sailed only the internal waterways or between ports along the coast. The construction plans and archives of the early Ming navy were burnt by the anti-maritime interests in the government, presumably to assure the irreversibility of the new edicts. This policy, more than any other factor, erased the memory of the navy, its technologies and the foreign settlements in its service.

Anxious to keep the country both protected and isolated, later politicians completed the destruction of records. Within a generation of these great overseas adventures, China had turned in on herself. The remaining references to these early-fifteenth-century naval exploits are now fragmentary. What governments wish to forget for a variety of reasons can be erased in a variety of ways.

The Chinese hypothesis held up against a multitude of reasonable objections. But the most compelling pieces of evidence were those aerial photographs and the four hundred years of history that failed to explain them. Now, certainly, I had to get back up the mountain.

And *that*, as the autumn of 2003 wore on, was the challenge I thought I faced.

CHAPTER THIRTEEN

AN UNEXPECTED DISCOVERY

IN THE FALL OF 2003, I felt increasingly unwell and tired even more quickly. I stopped doing the simple things I had always done. I no longer went on long walks. I stopped my daily swim. I found it increasingly difficult to focus as I once had. It was not a painful process or a difficult one: but this I knew was the beginning of the inevitable end.

As a young man living in various cities throughout the world, I saw both fame and fortune up close and learned that the rewards of both are often shallow and short-lived. The lives I witnessed in some of the loveliest houses in Manhattan were sometimes laced with anguish, ugly and debilitating. The difficulties inherent in a life of material success often unbalance any rewards. Perhaps as a consequence of those experiences, a simple life always made most sense to me. Even before getting sick, I had made a conscious effort to live simply, with as few things and cares as possible. Then, as my health failed during earlier HIV crises, I felt myself lucky to have found peace and to enjoy health that was at least consistent and predictable.

Now all that was changing. By February 2004, tests revealed that the virus was growing without opposition, clearly ready to exploit any moment of weakness in my immune system. I was not afraid, but I was not willing to make dying the focus of my life. My main concern was the research stacked in piles on my desk, my main worry that I'd never be able to climb the road except in my imagination.

I had come to know a great deal about a very small piece of land. I knew that during the fifteenth century a city had been reported on an island in the North Atlantic, a city visited by both Portuguese and Italian fishermen blown off course and shipwrecked. I knew the shallow rocky ledges along its coastline have given Cape Breton the grim title of Graveyard of the Atlantic, with hundreds of wrecks in the waters off its eastern shores. In Europe this distant island came to be called the Island of Seven Cities, and the visiting sailors reported that it was large enough to have a library and that its people used metal implements, even gold, and had their own written language. I knew Christopher Columbus had drawn a map of the island; and I knew John Cabot had later located it, claimed it, and described the brazil wood and silk he found there. The Corte-Real brothers had also found silver and gold.

I knew that the first European map of the Americas, drawn in 1500, described the area as the "cape that was discovered." Fifty years later it was labelled the "land of many people." I knew that Jean Alfonce had described the island as *la Tarterie* in 1559 and that he gave sailing directions to it. I knew that Cape Breton had been named, surveyed and mapped before any other location along the coast of North America. In the early years of the seventeenth century Samuel de Champlain and Marc Lescarbot, the first Europeans to live in the land that would soon be called Acadia, reported strange ruins on the island. Even after living in the territory for a year, they were still confused as to what the ruins represented. Champlain thought they were Portuguese, and Lescarbot believed they might be French, left over from one of Cartier's early voyages.

I knew that in 1691 Chrestien Le Clercq met witnesses to earlier visitors and that a community of people employing Christian symbolism lived among the Mi'kmaq. Le Clercq described how the Mi'kmaq could read and write, and his observation was substantiated by others. I knew that, in the nineteenth century, Silas Rand had studied the origin of the Mi'kmaq language and believed it pointed to China. In the Mi'kmaq's own history I had found clear references to visitors who had come in ships from the southwest long before Cabot and Cartier. Their cultural hero, Kluscap, came to them by ship. He had lived among them and had made a positive impact on their society. His home was on Cape Dauphin, and I knew Cape Dauphin was the site of ruins.

I turned again to my thick file on the Mi'kmaq, where I had spent so much time in recent months.

The Mi'kmaq remember Kluscap because he changed them. He introduced a new form of government and organized their nation's political structure. He is remembered as a transformer, not a god, but a man whose wisdom and leadership gave rise to his legend. The Mi'kmaq believe that, after living among them on Cape Dauphin, Kluscap predicted the coming of European settlers, told the Mi'kmaq that this land would soon no longer be their own and then left with his family. He sailed back down the coast towards the southwest, "going to the other side of the North Pole."

As I read about the cultural practices of the Mi'kmaq and the Chinese, I came to see the close similarities between their two worlds, similarities that seemed to go far beyond coincidence. According to early observers, the Mi'kmaq took every opportunity to recite their ancestry and to glorify their families. Age was respected, and the person who had the greatest number of children was held in highest esteem. Ancestor worship was a central aspect of Mi'kmaq spiritual life: they believed that the dead had influence over the living and that ancestors needed to be respected and cared for after death. In the preparation for the death of a family member, in the funeral rites and the grave building, and in the length and process of grieving, both the Mi'kmaq and the Chinese shared attitudes and similar ritualized practices. Extended family members were present for the death rituals, during which the dying person was washed and dressed for death. After death, the body was placed in a coffin and buried in the ground, surrounded by valuable gifts. The process was the same, with differences a matter of scale.

Throughout history, Chinese tombs have been the depository of stores of precious and utilitarian objects meant to aid and accompany the dead. The same practice was witnessed among the Mi'kmaq by early French missionaries. "After they have brought the dead to his rest, every one maketh him a present of the best thing he hath. Some do cover him with many skins of beavers, of otters, and other beasts." Nicolas Denys observed, during the ceremony surrounding the dead, that "all his relatives and friends threw bows, arrows, snowshoes, spears, robes of Moose, Otter and Beaver, stockings, moccasins, and everything that was needful for him in hunting and in clothing himself . . . There have been dead men in my time who have taken away more than two thousand pounds of peltries."

The periods and rituals of mourning following death and burial were also much the same in both cultures. In China, widows were required to be in deep mourning for prescribed lengths of time. Mourners allowed their finger nails and their hair to grow while they remained dirty and dishevelled. The immediate family was required to wear coarse sackcloth to indicate their status as mourners. Among the Mi'kmaq, widows painted their faces black and kept defined periods of mourning. According to one French account, "when these relatives die they wear mourning for a full year. This mourning consists of the men cutting their hair, while the women allow theirs to remain unkempt and dishevelled." Both cultures buried the dead in a grave dug in the ground, in a coffin and surrounded by all that was rich and good and useful in the world of shadows. In both cultures, these graves were round tumuli, grouped together in areas beyond any main settlement. Among the Mi'kmaq, Le Clercq reported that their graves are "quite round, of the form of a well, and four to five feet deep." The body was buried wrapped in birchbark, and on top of the tomb was sometimes built "very substantial and rainproof wigwams in order to preserve them" and "a quantity of logs, elevated three or four feet in the form of a mausoleum." Another French missionary was one of many who seemed to find the Mi'kmaq rituals surrounding death to be great curiosities: "On account of the depth of the grave, they arch the grave over with sticks, so that the earth will not fall back into it, and thus they cover up the tomb. If it is some illustrious personage they build a Pyramid or monument of interlacing poles: as eager in that for glory as we are in our marble and porphyry."

The Chinese grave marker was also round, but usually of stone, built on top of a grave in which a wooden casket had been buried. As with the Mi'kmaq, the grave site was elaborated, in China often with attached temple buildings, depending on the status and wealth of the family.

Rituals of dying, burial and tomb construction among other aboriginal peoples of the Northeast were significantly different from those of the Mi'kmaq, just as Chinese burial practices differed from European practices. The Huron, for example, held funeral feasts and gave funeral gifts, but the gifts were given to the relatives, not to the dead themselves. The body was exposed on a scaffold, and the bones were eventually buried in a common grave, with a communal burial service held once every decade. European graves have traditionally been rectangular, not circular. The differences between the Chinese and Mi'kmaq cultures often amounted to variations on the same practice, and the similarities I was finding far out-numbered those differences. Where the Chinese built their tombs in stone, the Mi'kmaq built with logs from the forest. The Chinese left jade in the tombs of their ancestors; the Mi'kmaq left their best furs. I could not escape the conclusion that the Chinese culture had left its effect on the Mi'kmaq, though I couldn't determine how important that effect was. When cultural elements such as religious iconography, mourning rituals and language are involved, the process of assimilation of those elements usually occurs over a long and gradual period.

I was now certain there had been a Chinese settlement on Cape Dauphin—but how long had it been there?

CHAPTER FOURTEEN

A FAMILY GATHERING

IN FEBRUARY 2004 most of my family converged on Toronto. The fact that my mother and father, along with two of my brothers and their families, would all be in town on the same weekend was presented to me as a happy coincidence, but I knew that everyone had actually come to take subtle stock of how I was coping. On a bitterly cold Saturday night, we all descended on my brother Robert's condominium for dinner—everyone in the family except my sister and her husband. I was determined to take advantage of the gathering to lay my pressing new theory on the table. Piece by piece I would walk them through the evidence that had led me to the Chinese.

I had hauled a huge pile of papers and maps with me, which for a time I left in the front hall. After the usual storm of catching up with each other over dinner had passed, and the plates were cleared away, my brother Bernie was the one who turned to me to ask how my search for the builders of the road was going.

First I had to disappoint my mother and reveal that the road had nothing to do with Louisbourg or any other French initiative. "And it wasn't the work of the Scots, the English, the Portuguese or the Mi'kmaq," I said.

I didn't know how to break the next bit to them, so I simply confessed that I'd been dragged by the evidence to one supposition: "It was the Chinese."

There was a silence.

"That's a pretty oddball idea," Gregory said. "How'd you arrive at that?"

And so I laid it out. I told them how I had worked my way through the recorded history of the northern New World from the earliest records onwards and failed to find the builder. This was a large construction project on the side and the summit of a mountain—not a stone wall around a farmer's field—and its planning and construction should have left a paper trail. It hadn't. But I did find a whole series of seemingly unrelated pieces of evidence pointing to some sort of settlement—not native—that predated Cabot and Cartier. When I was reviewing that work, I noticed a series of references that linked

Cape Breton to China or Chinese culture. Shortly afterwards, I saw the evidence of Chinese culture with my own eyes.

All of them knew I hadn't been able to climb Cape Dauphin again, and there was troubled skepticism in their expressions. I decided to retreat a little, and lead them slowly to my point.

The idea of Chinese ships reaching the Americas before Europeans isn't such a bizarre or revolutionary theory, I said. "The fact is, we can establish that the Chinese were actually able to make the voyage: they had the ships, the sailors and the technical ability. The ships were big—really big—and they had highly efficient sail technology and large rudders that would allow them to go anywhere they wanted. Even the most conservative estimates allow that Chinese ships by the early fifteenth century—no later—were at least as big as the largest wooden-hulled European vessels built over the next four hundred years. Now, of course, the Chinese navy had already reached the coast of Africa, and there's every reason to believe that they had rounded its southern tip."

My father was frowning. "The Chinese? I've never heard that."

"That's because our ideas of history are so culture-bound we aren't even aware of established historical fact—stuff our own historians agree on," I responded. "Most of us were never taught that while we poor Europeans were running around in the dark and still babbling about Jerusalem and falling off the world, the fifteenth-century Chinese were already great map-makers and had a good idea where they were on the planet. Their map-making and their geographical records go way back. And the Chinese didn't lose their traditions and technologies the way Europeans did. They tested and refined them. The Romans had been map-makers, but cartography pretty much disappeared during the Dark Ages. The Chinese established a science of cartography and, by the second century, they even had an accurate grid system to establish geographic locations."

I opened my map folder and took out a photocopy of the Kangnido Chart, a Chinese/Korean map from the early fifteenth century, a copy of which is now in the Ryukoku University in Kyoto. I spread it out on the table.

"Now this is the Kangnido Map. The year is 1403, maybe a bit later. And there's the east coast of Africa." I repeated the year again, so it would sink in. "By 267 the Chinese had rules for the correct construction of maps, and these rules acted as basic principles and drove the growth of the science. They were a sort of professional code. Chinese geographers, navigators and map-makers knew better than anyone else their position in the world. They'd established astronomical observatories, and they were able to make precise astronomical calculations. They invented the magnetic compass, and they incorporated Arab advances in navigation and cartography and picked up on knowledge of the Middle East and Africa. By the time of the Ming Dynasty in the fifteenth century, the Chinese had an array of maps, atlases and encyclopedias that could guide them throughout the known world."

My sister-in-law JoAnn interjected: "I remember reading a book review last year about a guy who said the Chinese discovered America."

"That's right. His name is Gavin Menzies and he's a retired British submarine commander who started looking carefully

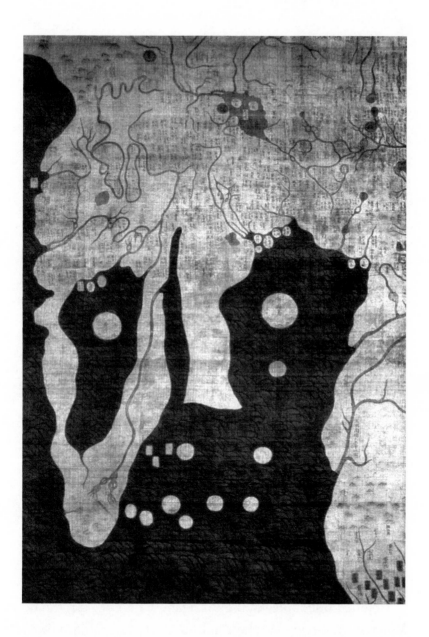

The Kangnido Map, presented to the Chinese emperor in 1403, showing both the east and west coasts of Africa.

at old maps. The critics tore him up something fierce. But Menzies started serious scholars thinking again about this stuff, and he's looking a lot less silly now. I came across Menzies by accident. When I read his book I realized that he was an expert on ocean currents, and those currents are a serious part of the picture. They were a missing piece."

"But," Bernie said, "even if the Chinese could get across the Atlantic, why would they try?"

I told them what I'd learned. During the early part of the fifteenth century, the Ming Dynasty had left behind the memory of their Mongol overlords and had entered an era of great prosperity. It was the time of major canal building and road reconstruction throughout China. The Great Wall was rebuilt and extended. The capital was moved to Peking, and the Forbidden City was built. Education and learning were elevated to new levels of importance. Books and encyclopedias were published. It was a time of renaissance, of stretching outward. Considering that spirit, it wasn't so surprising to think that the Chinese navy would have reached out to the farthest shores, to make known the greatness of the empire. Not only did China have the ability and the power to travel the oceans, but it also had the desire.

One of the biggest hints that the Chinese knew the coast of North America before Columbus and Cabot came from the biggest cartographic puzzle I'd found.

I hauled out copies of the Pizzigano Chart of 1424, the de Virga Map of 1410, and the Cantino Map of 1502 and showed them just how sketchy these early European maps are and how difficult to read. Then I laid out the Waldseemueller Map from 1507 and the Piri Reis Map of 1513, and pointed to what was clearly the coast of South America.

"It's the very sophistication of certain *parts* of these maps that's the puzzle. Historians and scholars of cartography have commented on it over and over again. Mostly, the areas these early explorers actually visited are shown on early maps as very vague and unsure lines. That's what you'd expect on maps made from the reports of sailors who didn't have the time or the tools or the training to survey the new coastlines. But vast areas are shown on these early maps, areas that had either never been visited by Europeans or had been seen once or twice, but almost no information had been recorded and returned to cartographers in Europe about them. Look at this area on the Cantino Map. This is Florida. But nobody from Europe had been there when this map was drawn. Where did the information come from?

"The facts suggest that European map-makers had too much information too early. They *had* to have gotten it from somewhere. The coasts they were drawing *had* to have been navigated and surveyed earlier, and copies of those maps had to have found their way into European hands. Here, look at this one. This is what they call the Columbus Map of 1490, one of the Island of Seven Cities maps. The date is early — before Europeans officially discovered North America, well before any major surveying of the coasts. And the map was certainly in the hands of Columbus. But it's not just the early date: it's the detail of some parts. Europeans were still getting over their flat-world theories with Jerusalem at the centre. They hadn't even visited the New World yet. Yet here is an island that is astonishingly like Cape Breton, and it's in the right place. From this map alone, we're entitled to believe that Cape Breton Island had been surveyed and mapped before the Columbus voyages, and the result had found its way to Columbus. See what it says there?"

Everyone craned harder.

"All that faint writing there under the island identifies it as the Island of Seven Cities."

"It is sort of unbelievable," Gerard said.

"It is. But by the time I studied the Columbus Map, I'd looked at enough early European maps to know that this drawing was exceptional. It was clear and precise and so specific. It seemed too far in advance of the other European maps of the time. And anyone who has looked at years of Cape Breton maps will see the resemblance immediately. The orientation, the composition, the layout of the interior waterways, the coastline, the scale of the parts, and the location all match. When I compared the Columbus map to *this* map—the Coronelli Map of Cape Breton drawn two hundred years later—there wasn't much that didn't match. The reality is that Cape Breton Island had been surveyed and mapped before any Europeans except for a few fishermen had even visited it. All Europeans knew the legend of the Island of Seven Cities, and I found lots of evidence to connect that legend to Cape Breton. They knew this place existed, that it had cities on it, and that this map was what it looked like—indeed, almost precisely what it looked like."

Gregory wanted it plainly stated. "So you're saying that somebody tipped off Columbus—and that somebody was the Chinese."

"Such a map may have found its way into Columbus's hands through John Cabot's trips to the Middle East. Cabot would have met with Arab cartographers who had worked with the Chinese earlier in the century. Really, it's the simplest explanation."

I pulled out my modern *Encyclopedia of Ocean and Atmospheric Sciences'* chart of the world's currents.

"You see, we know the Chinese were all over the west coast of Africa. And we've got pretty good evidence they may have rounded the Cape with their huge ships. Why wouldn't they? And if they did, the southern currents and the Gulf Stream would sweep them north to the east coast of North America. It's that simple: it's like a gift to sailors. It's an express lane that connects the two coasts. Just off Cape Breton's east coast, there are two strong ocean currents going in opposite directions. The Gulf Stream comes up from the south and the Labrador Current comes part way down the coast from the north. It's like a two-lane highway with the exit here—at Cape Breton. From my point of view, it's no longer a case of *if* the Chinese settled on the island—it's *why*."

The assumption everyone in the room but me still shared was that the Chinese were isolationists, and always had been. I set out to challenge that assumption: "The simple fact is, the Chinese were serious map-makers actively embarked on voyages of discovery. They had vast fleets of truly big vessels. Naturally they'd want to map the east coast of the Americas, and it was probably those maps that eventually found their way into European hands. But they'd need a base and, from everything we know about the mechanics of the Atlantic Ocean, that base would most conveniently be Cape Breton. You could get there from Africa with almost no effort; the harbours were simply the best; it was easy to find; and currents ran in both directions along the coast. Once it was properly mapped and you'd located the dangerous shoals, the island would have made an ideal North Atlantic outpost, just as it did for the French Empire in the eighteenth century."

There was a long pensive silence, which I broke by bringing it all even closer to home. I reminded them that our grandfathers on both sides of the family worked in coal. One was a miner, the other an engineer. Cape Breton has been called the Newcastle of North America because it sits on an enormous shoal of black bituminous coal, and most Cape Bretoners have grown up with its dust in their veins. Underground mines riddle the coastline, and the eastern shore of the island has the largest exposed coal seam on the North American seaboard, a seam that begins just south of Cape Dauphin. Many of the cliffs facing the ocean are composed of this shiny black stone, and the shoreline beaches in the area are lined with a filigree of fine black crystalline dust washed up by the tide. The mines are closed now, but it's still impossible to escape coal's presence.

Though it did escape the earliest European reports. Neither Cabot nor Champlain mentioned it, and probably did not recognize it. But during the sixteenth century, coal became the new fuel in Europe, at first used almost exclusively for industry. By the time Nicolas Denys was petitioning for rights to the island, he wanted the coal included, particularly in the area of Petit Chibou. Coal had become a commodity. When Europeans finally understood coal, a coal industry sprang up. Denys saw its potential in the seventeenth century, the French used it in Louisbourg in the eighteenth century, and the island became an international supplier in the nineteenth and early twentieth centuries.

The Chinese, of course, were long acquainted with coal. Marco Polo described coal to most Europeans for the first time in the late thirteenth century. Throughout China, he wrote, "there is found a sort of black stone, which they dig out of the mountains, where it runs in veins. When lighted, it burns like charcoal, and retains the fire much better than wood; insomuch that it may be preserved during the night, and in the morning be found still burning. These stones do not flame, excepting a little when first lighted, but during their ignition give out a considerable heat."

Coal was important in China and the Chinese would have recognized it immediately wherever they went. Cape Breton offered easy coal, the easiest in the Americas, an inexhaustible source of energy, an irresistible magnet to settlement. Today, we take it for granted that nations will go to any length in their search for energy—energy and information. The Chinese of the fourteenth and fifteenth centuries are unlikely to have been an exception.

Now I was ready to show them what I had meant when I said I had seen evidence of a Chinese presence on Cape Breton with my own eyes. From the thinnest folder of all, I took the high-definition enlargements of the aerial photographs of the summit of Cape Dauphin.

"This photo is an enlargement of the eastern slope of the mountain, the slope I climbed in 2002. I burned my eyes out trying to see traces of the road. Fortunately, the aerial image series includes photos taken in all seasons. And here, in this even-closer photo, you can just make out the road."

"I see it."

"So do I."

Next I laid out a photo of the summit, which looked like a rocky hilltop of scrubby spruce, followed by a very high-resolution image of the north slope showing where the road crested the summit.

The whole family pushed in.

Bernie said, "Hey, there's a field on top of the bloody mountain, a field with a wall around it."

"And just here," I said, "to the east you can see another narrow enclosure running down the slope. You can just make out signs of construction of some sort along a narrow spine."

I set out another photo. "Here, on the other side of the enclosure, the road continues to the west and passes through an area of little ponds. You can just make out something—some sort of man-made geometry."

"I can see it!" Bernie said.

"Here's another photo. It's enlarged to the point that the resolution is coming apart. But here are the roads and here . . ."

"My God!" Bernie said, and he is not a man for overstatement. "My God! They're little . . . rectangular . . . things."

"The whole mountain top is covered in some sort of construction," Gregory said, "connected by . . . roads."

"It's some sort of huge fort," JoAnn said. "I can see it. Or . . . or a town."

Most of the family was on their feet now, and several were staring at me rather than the pictures.

"Look at the hairs on my arm," Robert said. "Look at them. They're standing up."

I could not escape the logic that kept bringing me back to the Chinese. But what did it mean that a person in my condition had found himself in possession of such knowledge? I couldn't climb the mountain myself, but the least I could do was organize and write up the material in the best fashion I could manage. Then someone—perhaps one of my brothers—could carry on.

That was the limit of my ambition. My drug regimen had stopped working, and the only medical hope in the offing was a treatment of last resort, a combination of five drugs including one called tenofovir that was only available in Canada on "compassionate release." During the four weeks I waited for a supply of tenofovir, I turned to my desk and the stacks full of research.

I thought about Gavin Menzies. The academic world had scorned him, and then some. Well-placed and respected historians and scholars had dismissed him with contempt. You can hardly welcome such attitudes, but, more certainly, you don't want to be on the receiving end of them. Menzies had been so ridiculed that I had to consider that no one but my family might ever believe me. Could I actually announce such a discovery without so much as a supporting visit or a contemporary photograph of the site?

I decided to stop this line of thought. I would do what I could do. The organization and writing easily fell into three categories: the European reports of ruins on Cape Dauphin, the Chinese ability and inclination to make such voyages, and the Mi'kmaq nation's cultural memory of foreign contact and settlement. As I wrote, the pieces slid logically into position. When the drug arrived in March, I started the new and even more complicated regime. I was used to medication's unpleasant effects. When I felt most sick, I thought of my Acadian ancestors who lived for hundreds of years with dire and painful experiences: families separated, homes torched, livelihoods destroyed.

But then something unexpected happened. By mid-April I was in the midst of an astonishing reversal. The regimen was working. New energy flooded me with a vitality I'd forgotten was possible. I started swimming again, as long-ebbed strength returned to my limbs. I walked everywhere, longer and longer distances.

By May I knew I could reach the summit of Cape Dauphin.

CHAPTER FIFTEEN

THE SUMMIT

I HAVE SELDOM done any serious hiking in the wilderness, and never alone. A solo climb to the summit of Cape Dauphin might be ill-advised, but I was reluctant to drag someone else along, especially if the whole thing proved pointless. It was also my habit to work on my own and discuss it later—a hard habit to break.

I knew the road I'd happened upon on my parents' anniversary offered a way up the mountain, and I knew how to read a map. I'd spent a long time studying the aerial photographs and topographic maps, and I felt I knew where I was going. Before

I'd fallen ill, I'd been a great lover of scuba diving and learned to handle a compass under water. Wayfaring on land had to be similar to finding north in a calm blue ocean. At this point I was driven by how much I had at stake, and I needed to prepare for the challenge: with months, years, of research behind me, I simply couldn't afford to fail. Now that I was feeling healthy again, I began to swim and walk to build my stamina for the climb, and, slowly, my body responded. My lungs wanted to breathe deeply again.

It was like coming alive once more. Having given such ideas up as lost, I now had a goal—a dream, perhaps—but with specifics attached and priorities defined. I had identified the areas of the site that were most interesting. I knew where I wanted to go and what I needed to see.

The timing would be crucial. In Cape Breton the snow in the highland forests is usually not fully gone until early May, when the first growth of spring is not yet thick enough to make hiking difficult. From the aerial photographs I could see smaller sites that could be reached only by bushwhacking through the forest as best I could. Much of the summit plateau was covered with dense spruce woods, rugged in part, and with boggy areas and streams I would have to cross. I decided I would go in late May 2004 in time for my forty-ninth birthday. I had not spent a birthday with my parents for years.

The flight from Toronto seemed longer than normal, and the last leg—from Halifax to Sydney aboard a crowded twin-propeller airplane—was less than smooth. Mom and Dad were waiting for me at the airport. They had recently moved to a smaller house, and this would be my first time sleeping in a strange bed in the new place. Over dinner we talked about the old place, the gardens, the good times. Mom said there can be good times anywhere or nowhere, depending on ourselves. I was preoccupied with thoughts of Cape Dauphin, and they found me more quiet than usual.

By the time I crawled between the covers, I was exhausted.

The alarm rang at six the next morning. The sun was already strong, and the breeze off the ocean was warm: a perfect day for hiking.

My mother had loaned me her car for the week, and I drove in the early morning traffic along the only road that goes north towards the highlands. At last the highway began climbing Kelly's Mountain, whose most seaward extension is Cape Dauphin. Here, as I remembered, was the dirt road that veered off sharply to the right, down towards the end of the cape. At this early hour it was deserted. I parked the car as close as I could remember to the spot where I had parked two years earlier and found the entrance into the forest.

I scrambled through the forest for half an hour, then stumbled on the remains of a path that led through a large, flat, open area of felled trees. Was this the logged area I remembered? I climbed higher and entertained the idea that *the* road—my road—might not be here at all, that I might have imagined it.

But, no, there it was. I paused to give it the briefest inspection, then started up it. That other summer I'd been grateful for the angle of its decline as I came down, but I'd forgotten how steep it was. Climbing was difficult.

The trees were thick and close enough to the edges of the road that the underbrush remained wet with dew long after the sun had risen. I climbed for over an hour, then struggled up a vast, rocky incline and out of the forest. I was wet with perspiration, and the wind was cold, but in some quite real part of me I felt entirely alive. I found a small but prominent rock outcropping facing the open water and sat down to rest.

This point was just below the summit of Cape Dauphin. The view was overwhelming. Ahead I could see the long, straight, dark blue horizon. To my right was the edge of the forest I had just climbed. To the left, the ocean was framed by an arm of land: this was the "coast that went north." The cape seemed to shrink to miniature proportions, dwarfed by the vastness of the ocean. I drank it in, almost shocked by what my eyes could see.

Immediately in front of my rock a rectangular stretch of cleared land sloped down gently to the Atlantic. I sat looking at it for some time as I caught my breath. Slowly it sank in that this terrain was the open site I had seen in the aerial photographs. From that evidence I'd thought that fires had perhaps burned the summit at various times — a not uncommon occurrence on the island. During certain seasons the site looked sparse, and I had been able to spot the outline of the large enclosing wall. In other photographs, thick vegetation all but

OPPOSITE, TOP: *The view of the site looking down, towards the Atlantic Ocean, with the highlands of Cape Breton in the distance.* BOTTOM: *Looking up the site towards the summit of Cape Dauphin, I could see the vestiges of terraces and the rubble of stone platforms.*

covered the area, and the wall could be glimpsed only through the dense groundcover. But all the photographs consistently showed one thing: a cleared space, roughly rectangular.

I still didn't move. In all the time I had spent looking at old ruins, exotic buildings and foreign settlements, and in the years I had spent teaching architectural history, I had never seen anything like this site. From my vantage point I could make out both the east and west edges of the cleared rectangle and the far north edge at the lower side. The edges were more jagged than I had expected from the photographs. Here and there a few spruce trees had forced their way into the strict geometry. But otherwise the site was clear—carpeted in low, thick, pale green moss with a light purple haze of wildflowers and a few low bushes, as if a meadow had been cut into the forest. In places the moss was so pale as to be almost white, and it seemed to cover every stone. The hard edges of some of these stones, highlighted by the morning light, marked what clearly had once been groups of buildings, which appeared to descend the hill in terraces. I knew it was an ancient settlement of some sort, but I did not recognize or understand the way it was laid out.

I had no training in archaeology, so surveying and dating this site was out of my hands. I had been hoping for a clear sign: "Made in China," "Made in France" or "Built by the English." And somewhere down in my Acadian soul I had been hoping the site would be French—perhaps that small Acadian chapel. Yet this was something strange. It looked like a ruined town, terraced into the side of a hill, with no obvious main street or roads of any kind, no clear remains

Images of the remains of the stone platforms built into the hillside.

of walls or chimney stacks, and no central open space or village green.

I got up and walked down the moss-covered site along the path of least resistance. I meandered back and forth, tripping over stones hidden by the mossy cover, following the terraces down the hill. If this was a town site, why could I see no remains of the walls of buildings or even the marks of their foundations and the outlines of fireplaces? Instead I was faced with stone outcroppings that resembled small stages scattered over the hillside. When I reached the bottom of the clearing and looked back up to where I had sat to rest, the terraces were even more distinct. This was certainly a constructed place.

I hiked around the site, following its forested edges along what appeared to have been its outer borders. Until I could describe the site to myself, I wouldn't be able to communicate it to anyone else.

To have repelled the advances of the surrounding forest so effectively, this rectangle must have been the scene of a great deal of activity at one time. But what kind of activity? I began to inspect the individual piles of stones. As I studied them, I gradually saw beneath the edges softened by thick moss their hard-edged geometry: there was no doubt that they had once been rectangular stone platforms built into the side of the hill. They were also connected by a path that criss-crossed down the terraces.

I bent to examine individual stones. They had finished edges, cut by masonry tools. These cut stones were scattered throughout the site and were mixed in with rough, uncut

Some of the many cut stones found littered over the site.

stones, simple boulders. It appeared that the platforms had been built of found stones of a fairly consistent size and that cut stonework had been used only where it had been needed. When I realized I was not looking at ruined walls and chimneys but, rather, rectangular platforms, the site began to make sense.

One of several groupings of rectangular stone platforms arranged around a central courtyard, with the author's drawing of this grouping from measurements taken on site.

In some places, small groupings of three stone platforms were built into the hillside at various heights surrounding an open, courtyard-like area, all oriented in the same direction. Some platforms were larger, particularly at the bottom of the hill, which made it more difficult to distinguish their exact edges.

What I had found was an array of stone platforms built into the side of a sloping hillside, far removed from the shoreline and any possible fishing base. It was a settlement near the summit of a hill in the wilderness, with no other obvious settlements nearby.

By this time, the sun was well into the west. I had to start down.

I was so tired when I got back to my parents' house that my father insisted on driving me to the one-hour photo shop to get my three rolls of film of the summit developed. I started to look at them in the car as he drove us back to the house. The day had been bright, the light perfect, and the site clear enough of undergrowth to reveal itself. By the time we were parked in the driveway, I had forgotten my fatigue. I sat down at the kitchen table and began to spread the pictures out while struggling to maintain some composure.

I'd asked the shop to make duplicates of everything, and there seemed to be stacks of photographs. At first glance, many appeared to show little more than stones on a mountainside.

"They do all look like ruins of something or other, Paul," my father said. I sensed he was trying to be reassuring.

Slowly, photograph by photograph, I showed my parents the rectangles, the ruined shapes that had once been stone platforms.

I gathered the photos in a stack and there, on the kitchen table, among the teacups, I spread out several books on Chinese architecture and construction. After a few minutes' study of the books' illustrations, my mother looked at one of the photographs, outlined the edges of a platform with her finger and pointed to where the stairs had been. It was not just I who was seeing them. It became clear why the ruins had been ignored for centuries. What can't be imagined can't be seen. Now the fog of confusion cleared. In that moment my parents realized that what I was seeing was real, and I realized that the key to anyone's understanding of Cape Dauphin was a simple explanation of Chinese architecture.

The Chinese traditionally built houses, temples and government buildings on raised stone platforms. Usually, but not always, the buildings constructed on top of the platforms would have been of wood. The platforms were essentially foundations, providing both a dry interior floor above the surrounding earth and a raised external walkway around the perimeter of the building. The builders of the main wooden structures of the Forbidden City in Peking had used this type of construction. I had brought from Toronto an entire suitcase full of books on Chinese architecture and Chinese construction techniques. I pulled out my copy of William Marsden's translation of Marco Polo and found the place where Polo writes about the house of Kublai Khan, which he claimed to have seen during his travels in China during the thirteenth century: "The paved foundation or platform on which it stands is raised ten spans above the level of the ground, and a wall of marble, two paces wide, is built on all sides. This wall serves as a terrace, where those who walk on it are visible from without."

The platforms were laid directly on the earth, with neither basements nor foundations as we know them in the West. For hundreds of years Chinese architecture has developed a subtle articulation of wooden ceiling beams and wall brackets, a structural system that sits atop stone bases. If that system had been used here, none of the wood was left. These ruins now looked like little more than rough stone outcroppings on the side of a hill. To Europeans—early French surveyors and map-makers—familiar only with their own buildings, these strange stone ruins would have been unimaginable as anything other than natural formations, unusual but not extraordinary. Once you recognize the Chinese connection, the layout of the site becomes understandable. The stones still lie for the most part in the rectangular geometric groupings in which they were laid. The town site conveys the sense of the small metropolis it once was, with both grand and simple structures arranged along footpaths that follow the contours of the hill.

Throughout the summer of 2004 I visited Cape Dauphin every month, from that first trip in May until August. On each visit I climbed to the site on three or four successive days, returning to my parents' house each evening. The drive to and from the site gave me time to think about what I was finding. I made the climbs in the early hours of each morning, then spent the day observing, photographing, measuring and simply visiting the various sites I had highlighted on my maps. It

TOP: *The largest set of ruins on the site, which has cut and laid stones still in place, with (bottom left and right) close-ups of those cut and laid stones in situ.*

was sometimes sunny, sometimes foggy and rainy, and sometimes all three in the same morning. I saw deer and moose and
wild grouse. I ran out of water and learned it was wise always
to carry more than I needed. Week by week I grew stronger.

On two occasions I failed to allow for the notoriously thick
and sudden Cape Breton fog. Just as the Labrador Current
and the Gulf Stream converge near Cape Breton, so the cold
air stream from the north meets the warm moist breezes that
accompany the southern current. The result is a fog that can
descend within minutes and shroud even the closest natural
markers without warning. Several years earlier I had been
scuba diving off the coast near Louisbourg on a bright and
sunny August morning, but when I came to the surface after
thirty minutes in the water I found myself in an opaque fog
that covered the shore, the dive boat and even the bobbing
heads of my companions. That had been sobering. But as I
was exploring the Cape Dauphin site, I stupidly became lost
more than once because of unpredictable weather.

As my work progressed, I ascertained that the stone platforms,
though they varied in size, had been laid into the side of the
hilly site with their outside edges facing the expanse of open
ocean. That arrangement alone points to Chinese origins. The
town is built into the side of a hill, not on its summit, as would
be expected of a European town, and it replicates similar settlements in China.

Close to the top of the site and along its eastern edge I found
a single structure that was unlike the others. Even in its
tumbledown state, it appeared to have been a free-standing

TOP: *An image of the stone quarry, with paving tiles (bottom)*
arranged in typical pattern.

building of more than one storey. Its ruins were taller and more substantial than the surrounding platforms, and its stone construction was more complex. It was the only structure on the site that seemed to have been built primarily of stone. Whatever doubts I may have entertained on the first day were put to rest as I examined this peculiar construction more closely.

I could have attributed the way in which the structure had fallen into disarray to centuries of wild storms blowing in off the Atlantic, but most of its large stones appeared to have been thrown about by force, while a few cut stones remained in place. It looked as though it had been deliberately destroyed.

I was descending the hillside road late one afternoon when the slanting sun lit the surface of a rocky cliff face I had hiked by many times. I was tired, but not too tired to notice shapes with clean straight lines. I stopped and climbed up. The stones in this face were cut into precise diamond shapes of the same size, but varying thickness. Some stones had been only partially cut, others had been cut but now had corners broken, and still others were near-perfect diamonds. I arranged several of them to see if they actually fit together, and they did, perfectly. They were paving stones. This cliff had been a quarry.

Given the scale of the overall site, I had been expecting some remains of paved walkways, but I found none. Now here were paving stones such as those used for walkways, but of a size and shape particular to China. I held them in my hands in the waning light. I thought: a Chinese settler in the New World was the last person to touch these stones.

CHAPTER SIXTEEN

THE WALL AND BEYOND

ON THE EVENING of my second day of exploring, I was in bed in my parents' new house with the aerial photographs spread around me. I picked up the most detailed of the series to stare at the wall. It was large enough to be seen clearly from the air. It enclosed the roughly rectangular area, about twice as long as it was wide, and bordered on the north side by a narrow stream. When I looked closely, I could see that the wall followed the river for about seven hundred metres, then climbed up both sides of the incline and followed a higher plateau just below the summit. It looked about three kilometres long.

But at the summit I had seen no wall. Indeed, my whole attention had been absorbed by the town site.

The next morning after breakfast I spread out my books on Chinese building techniques. Chinese wall-construction methods, it seemed, were also unlike those familiar to us. The Chinese built their walls of earth, using stone only as a base or sometimes as a facing material. They constructed the Great Wall in this way, laying a low stone base about the same width as the wall was high directly on the natural terrain. Then they compacted earth using rectangular wooden frames, similar to the smaller versions of the movable frames now used for pouring concrete. With the frame positioned on top of the stone base, they filled it with loose soil, then tamped it down using tools specially designed for the job. After the first layer of soil was compressed to the hardness of cement, they repositioned the frame and added another layer, then another, until the wall was as high as needed. In essence, Chinese walls were nothing more than the surrounding earth from which they were built.

Such walls at one time encompassed most traditional small towns in China. Needless to say, they required constant maintenance. When well maintained, they remained strong, but left unattended for more than a few years, they began to crumble. Even though the Great Wall's outer surface is covered with flat cut stones, it has required constant repair. Sections of it have simply dissolved.

Now I climbed back up Cape Dauphin, looking for the remnants of such a wall. The only pieces still here are wide sections of the low stone base, like a river of stones flowing up and

OPPOSITE: *Method of Chinese wall construction showing earth fill over a stone base. As with the Great Wall of China, the exposed faces of the wall pictured here are clad in stone.*

Chinese illustration showing method of wall construction where loose earth is collected between two wooden frames and tamped down before the frame is removed and repositioned.

down over the hills. Many of the stones have been swallowed by the forest, but where I could still see parts of the wall, it varied in width from five to six metres.

It was built to snake over steep slopes and to enclose much more territory than needed to mark the boundary of the town. It was far removed from any harbour and designed without apparent military intent. I had been looking for something taller and more pronounced, while hiking over the remains of something typically Chinese. The earthen upper part of the wall had dissolved long ago. Like visitors who may also have seen the ruins over the centuries, I hadn't been able to understand what I was seeing. When I was actually on the site, the wall was almost invisible. When I climbed that last steep hill on the first morning, I had walked over it. I had been standing on top of it without noticing.

The scale of the wall is remarkable, though at first glance — even to an architect — the remains of the stone base appear no more unusual than any collection of natural rough stones in a rocky terrain.

I sat in the sunlight on the stones of the southern wall, and the weight of the thing sank in on me. This site had once seen an immense undertaking, yet its builders had all but escaped history.

In China, so fundamental was the connection between a wall and the town it enclosed that the same written character

Section of ruined base of wall.

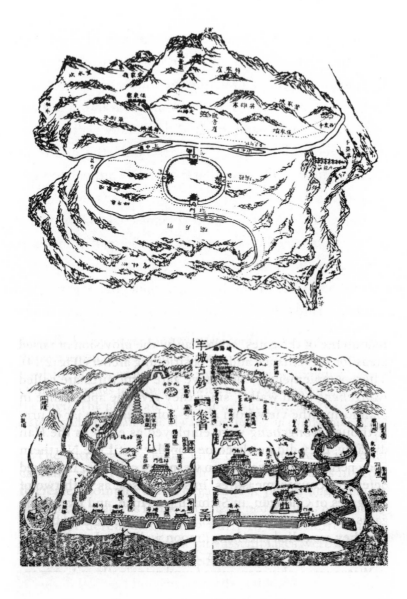

TOP: *A Chinese illustration of a walled city built on a mountainous site next to a river.*

ABOVE: *In this illustration, the city wall follows the topography of the site and includes an extension added to encompass more territory.*

is used for both. The Chinese city wall was a necessity but, unlike those of European towns, not a defensive necessity. The wall was intended to define the town's presence, marking not only its markets and government buildings but also its gardens and parks and the land deliberately left wild and uncultivated. Like a typical Chinese wall, the main wall here had gaps for entrances that traced the cardinal points of the compass.

I studied the earliest aerial photographs, taken soon after a fire had swept over the summit in the earlier part of the twentieth century. In these photos I could make out another wall just north of the centre of the larger rectangular clearing and enclosing an area about two-thirds as big. This wall was similar in width and form to the large wall, and ran along the same hilly terrain. Its appearance was slightly less distinct in the photos, and I suspected it to be an older construction.

I returned to Cape Breton in June. The forest had grown thicker and wild flowers—especially mayflowers, the official flower of Nova Scotia—were everywhere. Hiking was now more difficult, but I wanted to go beyond the wall to the west, following the road to its end. More recent colour aerial photographs showed the road more clearly than the black and white photographs I'd looked at first, but I had not paid much attention to the section of the road beyond the wall. From my photos, I could trace it as it wound through a portion of the surrounding plateau that spread over the top of the mountain.

On the morning of June 18 I set off along the west road. This stretch was more open in parts than the eastern section I had climbed and more consistent in width, with a harder, less-ruined surface. For about thirty minutes I walked along it easily as it curved through the forested plateau. Suddenly, I realized that the landscape around me was familiar. My God, I thought, these are fields and they've been farmed—recently. Then I considered where I was. Within the ruins of Louisbourg, open fields still lay barren two hundred years after the fortifications were destroyed. Cape Breton is rock, and I was standing on rock covered by a thin veneer of soil. Once cleared and left unattended, this place allowed only the roots of moss and wildflowers to take hold.

I followed the road as it forked, with branches sometimes leading in several different directions. Each intersection led to more of these small acreages cut into the forest. What had once been field was now meadow, and it was beautiful. Wildflowers I knew and many I didn't know were here in profusion, and they made me laugh as they rippled in the breeze. Different fields opened to different views. Some sat in slight valleys, and some covered the crest of gentle hills. Over the course of the remaining summer months, I was able to piece together the puzzle into a pattern that again appeared to point to Chinese origins.

I mulled over why every branch of the road came to a dead end in a rectangular open space. I counted six roads that dead-ended in this manner. To modern eyes, a flat, open, rectangular space at the end of a road looks like an old parking lot. I estimated that each of these clearings could have accommodated five or six mid-sized cars.

My father discovered that a series of higher-resolution and smaller-scale colour photographs was available from a local

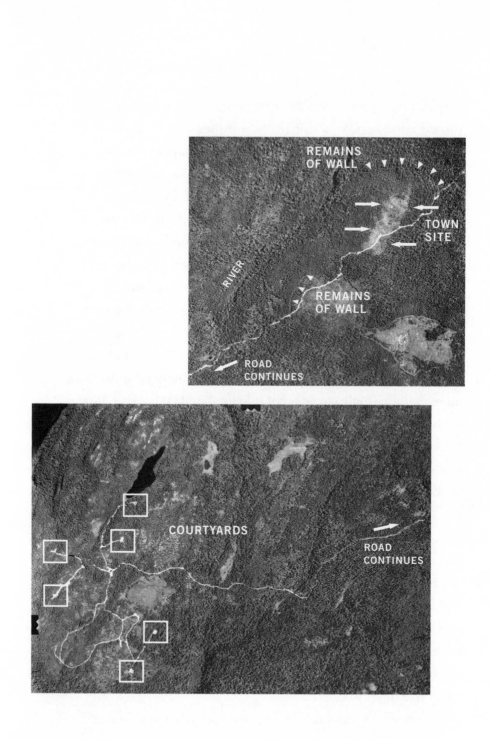

provincial government office. I purchased all the Cape Dauphin images and studied them closely. In colour, the dusty brown road contrasted sharply with the rich greens of the forest, and the plan of a Chinese village community jumped out at me from the photos, just as the wall had done the winter before.

For centuries, the Chinese have constructed small court-yards at the end of road branches, and around each courtyard they built village houses. These residences multiply around the courtyards as the villages grow over several generations. Beyond the houses lay the agricultural fields.

Nature's memory, in the type of moss and plants now growing in the areas once built upon, offers subtle clues as to what the six Cape Dauphin farming villages once looked like. The common Chinese village house had no base other than pounded earth. The builders laid the houses out on a rectangular grid pattern and compressed the ground under them with a tamping technique similar to that used in wall construction. They built wooden houses on top of these floors. In contrast to the simple rectangular structures of the town, the villages would have grown outwards more haphazardly, with new rooms and their adjacent open courtyards added as needed. In most of China, an organic grid of houses still encloses open areas of various sizes, all branching out from a main courtyard. And this pattern is what the aerial photographs of Cape Dauphin appear to show.

OPPOSITE: *Two large-scale aerial photographs of the site taken in the 1990s showing the road system on the plateau and the faint traces of the overgrown wall (see arrows). The town site is highlighted.*

In the main walled town, the remains of platforms mark the positions of vanished buildings, but the farming villages are outlined instead by vegetation patterns that seem to distinguish places where the earth had once been pounded into concrete-like hardness. When I digitally pushed the contrast of the aerial photos, plant growth in certain places appeared to outline the rectangles of past construction. The clues left behind consistently tell a Chinese story.

The Chinese frequently built new villages in outpost areas, and it was common practice to organize these new villages in groups of ten or more households. Families built basic units around a courtyard, adding rooms as they increased in size. Many generations of the same family lived within an extended complex of rooms built around various open courtyards. As children were born, older generations moved inwards from the more public outside rooms.

Such self-sufficient villages had a long history in China and received more support early in the Ming Dynasty, which enacted regulations for the building, organization and control of villages. Small groups of families, living in close proximity, were responsible for the conduct of their members. The village units were self-policing and depended on other villages for the food and labour they could not supply themselves. The local village was responsible for maintaining the public roads. Elders mediated internal disputes. A group of villages was governed by a civil service administration located in the nearest

OPPOSITE: *Author has adjusted the contrast and outlined the lighter areas to show the remains of platforms and courtyards.*

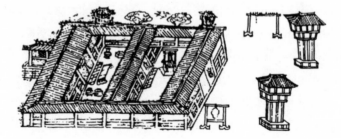

Illustration of a Chinese house showing the use of courtyards around which various-sized buildings are constructed.

town and headed by an appointed magistrate. A tax in the form of a percentage of the agricultural yield was paid to maintain the administration. Overall, the villages and the local town acted as an integrated, single community.

On Cape Dauphin I appeared to be looking at the physical remains of just such a political and social organization.

Along with the town and the villages, I found other areas dotted around the site that showed obvious signs of having been cleared in the distant past. In one case a clearing surrounded a small lake that I had seen in the aerial photographs and had often used to line up images taken at different scales. Its shape was consistent from season to season over decades. The very first time I noticed the lake, I thought its appearance was unusual, as though it were man-made.

One day in high summer I set out to look for it. It was some distance from one of the six courtyards, and I had to use all my compass skills to track around sections of forest that were too dense to hike through. In the aerial photographs it looked as though a path and other cleared sections had once led to this little body of water, but the land was now covered in low spruce. When I finally found the lake, I saw it was not much more than a pond. On the near shore was a row of almost perfectly round stones, placed in the manner of stepping stones. They seemed purposefully positioned, either as a foundation or as a walkway. The surrounding land appeared to have been cleared, much like the farmland I had seen, though on a smaller scale. Here was the human mind and hand at work.

One day I explored a short road along the edge of a meadow, a road that came from nowhere and went nowhere. Another time I found a stone platform that sat alone, outside the main wall, surrounded by forest. It was impossible for me to know exactly what this profusion of ruins had once been. The size and scale of the Cape Dauphin site was a challenge to my imagination.

Built into the hillside along a ridge just outside the north wall are large, nearly round, low piles of stone. Although now surrounded by thick forest, the area is one of the most beautiful and protected places on the site. The rough oval-shaped forms are several metres in diameter. They nestle into the slope overlooking a small valley, shielded from above and on both sides. The protected ridge offers a view much like the one from the summit, with the highlands and the Atlantic in the distance. In all aspects, these outcroppings resemble the round, stone gravesites found in China: built into the sides of mountains, protected by land on three sides, and with a view outward. For centuries such a site and such mounds have been the ideal form of Chinese tomb construction.

——

It was the road that led me to the top of Cape Dauphin. Roads are not unique to any civilization, but the quality of this road's construction, the low walls that still border it in places, and its consistent and specific width strongly suggest Chinese planning. Early in their history the Chinese brought organization and control to newly settled areas through the construction of government-sponsored highways, a system not unlike that of Rome. Unlike the Roman system, however, the Chinese system never went into decline, and civil engineering in China remained a science.

Chinese roads were built to consistent specifications. As early as two thousand years ago Chinese roads were based on a module called a "single width," derived from the size of a carriage or chariot axle. All public roads were multiples of that width. Small sideroads were one width, and grand, processional roads could be nine widths. The road on Cape Dauphin, almost nine kilometres in length, measures just under three metres wide in those sections that have suffered least over time. During the Ming Dynasty, the Chinese module for road widths was 1.435 metres, making a standard two-width Chinese road 2.9 metres wide: the width of the road on Cape Dauphin. Though Cape Dauphin would have been an outpost, it would likely have been built to Chinese government standards. The width of its roads met the specifications for regulations regarding the construction of public roads back in China.

As the summer wore on, I was puzzled by the varying quality of the road. The two main sections, the east road and the west road, were entirely different. In the space of nine kilometres the road went from being an obscured forest path to a byway that could be mistaken for a modern, heavily travelled road. The section leading up the steep side of the mountain from the shore to the town—the road I found during my first hike in the summer of 2002—is today, even in spring, mostly overgrown; in summer the forest encroaches enough in places to obscure it completely. But the upper section of the road, which links the town with the plateau beyond, has long sections that are wide and clear and still in excellent condition. The road at the top of the mountain is in far better condition than the road leading up the mountain.

A section of the road on the plateau of Cape Dauphin, showing typical width and condition.

Of course, no part of this road is modern. Even tractors could not climb the steep hill on the eastern slope of the mountain, and that is the only way up. The road switches back and forth as it climbs, often at angles far too steep to manoeuvre heavy equipment. It is not a logging road, and there is no evidence of recent work. But the road that runs along the plateau on the top of the mountain is long and wide and still looks well used. Unlike the road up the side, it clearly *was* well used at one time.

My guess is that, when the Chinese lived here, the road up the hill from the shoreline was a link to the water, but it saw little traffic. This settlement had to have been self-sufficient. The road up the hill perhaps supplied fish and coal, but may have been heavily travelled only when ships arrived. In contrast, so well trodden was the west road that its soil remains impoverished and compacted, and the trees still stop short of its borders. Its pristine length, perhaps more than any artifact on Cape Dauphin, contradicts the notion of a rough settlement and remains an enduring emblem of an advanced civilization.

CHAPTER SEVENTEEN

PARALLEL THREADS

THROUGHOUT THE SUMMER of 2004, week by week, my health improved. Each visit to the mountain—difficult and often tiring—brought me increased strength and a greater drive to continue. By the end of the summer I had begun to forget about my old battle with the HIV virus. I was alive and in the midst of a fascinating investigation.

I knew by now that the Chinese had a navy and a technology that would have allowed them to cross the Atlantic. But as my work progressed, it became ever clearer that these ruins had not been left by one or two shipwrecked vessels. This had been a major undertaking. The wall alone would have required thousands of man-hours to build. The road, the farms, the town, the tombs: this place was not a temporary station. It was organized, planned, big. At some point in Chinese history, as I was now convinced, this project had been taken on with considerable foresight, expense and government control. By mid-summer I realized how important a settlement Cape Dauphin had harboured.

During the fifteenth century the Chinese were the only nation on earth with the ability to make such a long ocean journey in large, expertly equipped ships—to sail out and return on a regular basis, maintaining contact with a settlement that numbered in the hundreds, if not thousands. Only China had the long history of technical accomplishments and the trained and disciplined individuals to allow her to build a successful colony on the wild coast of an island in the far North Atlantic, a colony cut off from most contact with the mother country.

As evidenced in the ruins, the people who landed on Cape Dauphin built a life for themselves, constructing a formidable walled town and an extensive road system. They developed farmlands that could have fed hundreds. The size of the project continued to surprise me as I discovered more and more of it. Every history of the East I read reminded me that Chinese civilization had claimed extraordinary achievements early in human history. During the period in which I suspected the Cape Dauphin settlement to have been built—up to the early fifteenth century—China was a nation unique in the world.

The Chinese themselves recognized this uniqueness. Over three thousand years ago, they developed an artistic language that was recognizable as a product of their particular culture. Artists perfected specialized techniques for lacquer decoration and for the weaving of cloth from the unwound cocoons of silk worms. China had invented a sophisticated technology in the casting of massive bronze vessels, some weighing over ninety kilograms. It was exploring and expressing itself as a unified culture when Europeans were barely out of neolithic caves.

Even then a crowded society, the Chinese evolved a highly articulated philosophy and a set of successful rules for acceptable behaviour to govern the individual, the family and the wider community—a philosophy that was to last until the twentieth century. At the scale of the nation-state, emperors organized and maintained their vast lands and, if necessary, could put massive armies into battle. An efficient road and canal system linked the far-flung regions of the empire. And in this same period of early growth, a strong intellectual base was established that was to last throughout Chinese history. Very early in that history, China had become a great nation—a greatness that would eventually lead to her naval explorations.

Well before the Roman Empire rose to glory, the separate kingdoms of ancient China had been brought under the control of a central authority, which extended the frontiers almost to their modern borders. During its formative period, China was for the most part cut off from other developing civilizations. The Chinese believed in no supernatural supreme being and saw themselves as responsible for their own history. The nation drew its strength from the power of organization and co-operation. China's ability to employ efficiently a large and well-organized workforce—on projects from the building of villages to the damming of powerful rivers—allowed it to undertake feats of civil engineering unattained and, indeed, unimagined elsewhere. The Great Wall is only one example.

The country's strong intellectual foundations and the presence of scholars at all levels of government meant that historical records were maintained. The written history of China is the oldest in the world. Even thousands of years ago, accounts, records, royal instructions and edicts were written on bamboo slats and bound together in collections. Politics and civil administration were not the only subjects: Chinese authors wrote on history, music, ritual, poetry and philosophy. Widespread exposure to the written word facilitated the development of the philosophical base that underpinned Chinese culture. When Socrates was teaching in the West, China was developing the world's most successful and influential system of personal and social ethics, much of it the work of Confucius, a penniless scholar who wrote on the attainment of a good, simple and productive life. Confucius is considered to be China's greatest teacher, and his thoughts were discussed, elaborated and refined by generations of Chinese philosophers. His views on ethical behaviour have been the basis of the Chinese educational system and a fundamental aspect of the Chinese understanding of self, family and nation for over 2,500 years.

Along with the works of Confucius, literate Chinese looked to two other books: *Mencius*, by the sage of the same name, a disciple of Confucius and a commentator on Confucian thought; and *Tao Te Chin*, a philosophical how-to book written in the form of poetry by the legendary monk Lao Tzu. Confucius, Mencius and Lao Tzu have influenced the governing of China for most of its history. All three were required reading for anyone working within the vast civil service. These men set the standards against which behaviour at every level of life was organized and judged. It's rare in human history for a few writers to have defined the individual and collective identity of a large nation for over two millennia.

For two thousand years, young men, often the most promising from every class of society, were recommended from the various districts for training in the classics, an education that would lead to an examination for a possible appointment to the civil service. Every level of government bureaucracy and every official post was staffed by a scholar who had been examined according to rigorous standards. The teachings of Confucius stressed self-respect and discipline, devotion to the principle of fairness, concern for others, the understanding of ritual within society and loyalty to superiors. The writings of Lao Tzu concentrated on the notion that great goodness is possible in the world and that each person is responsible for that goodness.

No other society developed such a scholar elite. These men, and they were all men, provided much of the cohesive stability of their society. The system gave opportunities for advancement to the high-born as well as those born in poverty or obscurity. By the early twelfth century, there were over 200,000 students in the Chinese national school system. Of those students, half were candidates for the official government exams, which awarded only five hundred passing degrees. Even those students who failed the exams were distinguished by their training and education and usually found positions as local leaders in their home districts. Part of China's strength lay in the civil service, which remained constant throughout the growth and decline of various dynasties. This historically tested wisdom became the foundation for even the most minor of Chinese policies and practices, from the grand scale of an emperor's edicts to simple village documents.

China developed over many centuries without having to reinvent itself in a renaissance such as Europe experienced at the end of the Middle Ages. The Chinese frequently improved on technical innovations made thousands of years earlier. Traditions were built, and success bred success.

The Chinese invented paper and printing: printed books were available by the middle of the ninth century, and movable type existed by 1030. Broad swatches of the population had access to the country's history, traditions, laws and philosophy. Paper and printing made Chinese philosophy, history, literature and poetry readily available, disseminated technical information, accelerated the learning of vocabulary and guided farmers to the most efficient methods for planting and harvesting.

China was the first country to understand agriculture in a scientific way and was able to produce high-quality food in large quantities well in advance of any other. Some basic agricultural techniques not used in Europe until the eighteenth century had already been in common practice among Chinese farmers for over a thousand years. *Master Lu's Spring and Autumn Annals,* a Chinese farming manual written about 2,500 years ago, recommended planting crops in rows, to allow adequate space for their growth and for proper wind circulation around the young plants. The Chinese invented iron ploughs centuries before anything comparable occurred elsewhere. Advanced iron-casting techniques and the development of a non-brittle cast iron highly suited to the design and construction of farm tools allowed the Chinese to become productive farmers in almost all types of soil. Efficient ploughs made it possible for a new settlement to begin the tilling of soil immediately. Chinese irrigation techniques were so far in advance of those in Europe and the Middle East that Chinese hydraulic engineers were called in to direct the irrigation of the Tigris and Euphrates basin after the Mongol siege of Baghdad in the thirteenth century.

China, primarily an agrarian nation, grasped the means to feed its people early in its history—and prospered.

For centuries, Chinese society remained malleable enough to accept foreign influence and, in turn, influenced the peoples the Chinese considered barbarians. Foreign invaders such as the Mongols from the north were quick to assimilate vital aspects of Chinese culture and cheerfully adopted Chinese organization, writing, rituals and social ethics. During the reign of the Mongols the Chinese political system and the civil service that made it run continued to play a crucial role in maintaining good government.

The Mongols came to power in China when Chinggis (Ghengis) Khan had taken control of most of Asia in a thirteenth-century military sweep—one of the most astonishing conquests in world history. When Chinggis died in 1227, the empire he had forged, which stretched from the East China Sea to the Caspian, was divided into four territories ruled by four of his descendants. His grandson Kublai Khan took the title of Emperor of China in 1271. The Mongols helped build great public works, including major sections of the Grand Canal system, and maintained the structure of Chinese society. They also maintained an ocean-going navy. The Chinese people, however, felt themselves to be overtaxed and poorly treated by these foreign leaders. The Mongols lacked sensitivity and wisdom, they claimed, and were viewed by them as aggressors and barbarians. Mongol rule collapsed in 1368 in the face of rebellions by Chinese peasant groups eager to return to true Chinese tradition.

The Mongols were replaced by the Ming Dynasty, which was to rule China from 1368 until 1644, during a time of enormous international upheaval. The Ming was established by a man who had once been a beggar and rose through a rebel group to become emperor. It was a minor renaissance of sorts: the foreigners were thrown out and China felt itself capable of anything. This flowering of thought, culture and technology was to mark one of the highest points in the history of Chinese civilization. Under newly invigorated Chinese leadership, the people of China, from the peasant class to the scholarly gentlemen of the bureaucracy, were anxious to reaffirm the greatness of their culture and its accomplishments. Being ruled by three successive Mongol tribes had been more humiliating than destructive.

The Ming Dynasty, in the early ambition of its reign, set out to see the world. In the fourteenth century Chinese voyages of exploration were launched to reaffirm China's sense of its power and influence. Like any confident and successful nation, China took an interest in the lands beyond her own borders. We need think only of those African giraffes in the Forbidden City. By 1400—and perhaps much earlier—China had the inclination and the ability to send the best, the brightest and the most energetic out into unknown seas.

These mariners would have had the knowledge necessary to establish and govern a new settlement in a foreign country. They had the ships and the sailors, training in government, efficient agricultural skills, maturity of purpose, and a belief in the righteousness of their nation and the goodness of its collected wisdom.

Over the summer of 2004 I came to accept that the Cape Dauphin ruins were those of a Chinese settlement. I understood much of the how and something of the why of this remarkable outpost. But what was it that had allowed the Chinese settlement to succeed—so long, at least, as they chose to pursue it—while the later Europeans stumbled over and over again in their efforts to survive on this challenging coast?

One simple but fundamental difference between this Chinese settlement on Cape Dauphin and the early European attempts at colonization is that the Chinese appear to have come in peace. The Mi'kmaq people who still inhabit this region seem to have had every reason to remember the Chinese well. And if the legendary figure of Kluscap—the wise teacher who came by sea from the south and who left the Mi'kmaq just as Europeans started to arrive — does indeed represent the Chinese (either a specific leader or the Chinese settlement in general), those earliest visitors still hold a place of honour in Mi'kmaq memory.

Neither the Mi'kmaq nor the Chinese were aggressive, although China, as the inventor of gunpowder, had the ability to wage war. But the Chinese were armed primarily with their technology, their social organization and their Confucian ideals. Even before its emissaries left its borders, Chinese society had proven that it possessed an attractive logic and wisdom. The Mongols had shown how readily a foreign nomadic people could assimilate Chinese culture. In the Mi'kmaq legends I found consistently respectful references to these earliest visitors, references that contrasted sharply with the anger, fear and hatred the native nations directed at the Europeans who were to arrive later.

The educated Confucian elite acted as the overseers of life in China. They researched, debated and managed any adventure that the Emperor undertook. China's ability to send elaborate diplomatic missions beyond its borders depended on these highly trained, loyal and disciplined decision-makers. When I contemplate the ruins on Cape Dauphin and consider how the Chinese could have built such an impressive settlement on the other side of the world, the maturity and strength of these individual leaders seem particularly important. Most early European attempts to colonize America met with disaster primarily because of untrained leadership and lack of preparation. Despair and fear would have been great adversaries at the end of such long, difficult and uncharted sea voyages. When faced with the possibility of beginning a new life outside the framework of the known world, a community could survive only under the guidance of the strongest and most confident of leaders. Only a sophisticated command of civil government could direct the successful construction of roads, stone walls and farming villages. The scholarly bureaucracy in China could provide such a class of leaders.

If my theory of Cape Dauphin's history is correct, the Chinese leaders who accompanied the overseas fleets would have had neither hellfire nor eternal damnation with which to threaten the Mi'kmaq. On the evidence of the Mi'kmaq legends, Chinese teaching of farming and fishing techniques, of map-making and astronomy, and of medicine and good government may have been offered in kindness. In the early fifteenth century the Mi'kmaq were living in the Stone Age. Suddenly a highly evolved and successful community from an advanced civilization may have dropped into their midst. If the Mi'kmaq legends can be believed, the colony of strangers, living under harsh circumstances far from home, seems to have followed the Confucian code that all Chinese memorized as children: "Dwell at home in humility. Conduct your business in reverence. And in your dealings with others, be faithful. Even if you go east or north to live among wild tribes, these are things you must never disregard."

On the lonely mountaintop of Cape Dauphin, the Chinese built roads and town walls, fed hundreds of people and maintained social order. Such activities were intrinsic to their culture. The Mi'kmaq had to have been impressed.

———

Across the centuries, scholars, researchers and writers have regarded the Mi'kmaq artistic tradition as remarkable among the early North American aboriginal peoples. Their starkly different aesthetic is unique among their neighbours. They were the people who produced the Cross-Bearers, and they had their own written language.

I had assembled a large file on clothing and pattern-making among the Mi'kmaq, but it really represented a series of questions. Now I opened the files I had closed many months ear-

A Mi'kmaq family, pre-1902.

lier in the rush to complete a record of my research and began
to organize and distill some of the intricate parallels between
Mi'kmaq dress and the patterns and clothing styles of China.

I had already noticed that the distinctive hats once worn
by Mi'kmaq women bore obvious similarities to styles worn by
various Chinese minority groups. There are even more striking similarities between the traditional clothing styles of the
Chinese and those of the Mi'kmaq. In black and white photographs of the nineteenth century and in earlier painted illustrations, Mi'kmaq women appear in short jackets with loose
sleeves, the edges of which are often bordered with a plain or
patterned design. The short jacket is layered over a dark dress
that reaches to the floor. The dresses are similarly bordered
along the bottom with coloured and embroidered banding.
The Mi'kmaq men wear knee-length jackets, sometimes
trimmed along the edges, either belted or tied at the waist and
worn over simple trousers. These early designs—the layering,
the patterns and the placement of ornamentation—all have
direct parallels in traditional clothing worn by the Chinese
before the twentieth century.

The similarities were compelling enough at first glance to
suggest an important relationship between the two cultures.
As I looked more closely at the patterns made by Mi'kmaq
artisans, and as I studied their history, I could see why they
had perplexed early scholars. The Mi'kmaq were noted
pattern-makers when the first Europeans arrived. They
became famous for their embroidery and their quillwork
designs using coloured porcupine quills. They used these patterns on the borders of their clothing and on small boxes they

TOP: *Mi'kmaq woman in traditional dress, 1913.*

ABOVE: *A Chinese woman and her servant, 1902, showing the traditional jacket, bordered along the edges, worn over a long skirt.*

TOP: A *Mi'kmaq man*, c. 1920–1930.

ABOVE: *One of many styles of traditional men's clothing in China.*

TOP ROW: *Images of Mi'kmaq women in traditional pointed hats.*
BOTTOM ROW: *Women from the Minority Peoples of China wearing typical hats.*

TOP ROW: *Line drawings of Mi'kmaq petroglyphs from Kejimkujik, showing women in ceremonial headdresses.*
BOTTOM ROW: *Left, a woman of the Minority Peoples of China in headdress. Right, a Chinese empress.*

TOP: *Two Mi'kmaq women's hats showing the typical double-curve pattern. The one on the left is from c. 1770–1790. The hat on the right is from 1909.*

MIDDLE: *Detail from a Mi'kmaq chief's coat, 1841, also showing the double curve.*

BOTTOM: *An example of the double curve from clothing worn by the Minority Peoples of China.*

fashioned of birchbark. I noticed both their simplicity and their remarkable sophistication. When historians wrote about these designs, they regarded them as specific to the northeast coast of Canada. The Government Printing Bureau in Ottawa published an article in 1915 on a shape the author Frank Speck called the double-curve pattern—two matched curved lines—found among the native people of the Northeast. Speck traced the design through the various aboriginal nations and concluded that it originated in the most eastern regions of North America. Its use then migrated westward, its form becoming less and less pure as it strayed from the source. This pattern is typical of what happens to style: as Roman architecture evolved from Greek architecture, the original simplicity was lost through elaboration over distance and time. A German High Baroque cathedral represents an elaboration of simpler—arguably more elegant—earlier forms. Even though neighbouring aboriginal nations used the double-curve pattern, Speck observed that the Mi'kmaq examples were the most symmetrical, as though the Mi'kmaq held the visual copyright and all future editions were knock-offs. Without actually stating that the double-curve could have had such a limited and specific point of distribution on the continent, Speck suggested as much in the way he analyzed and displayed his data.

Mi'kmaq sophistication has amazed everyone who has studied these people. Lescarbot, Le Clercq and Nicolas Denys described the patterns and colours used by the Mi'kmaq, sometimes in great detail. Denys, the rough-hewn businessman interested only in codfish, was especially fascinated by

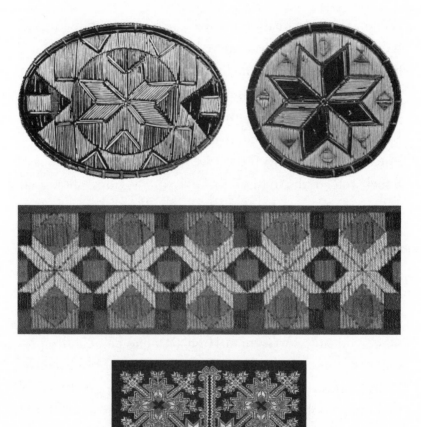

TOP: *Two examples of Mi'kmaq boxes decorated with porcupine quills in the eight-legged starfish pattern.*
MIDDLE AND ABOVE: *Examples of a similar embroidery pattern from the Minority Peoples of China.*

Mi'kmaq pattern-making: "In summer the men have robes of Moose skin, well dressed, while, ornamented with embroidery two fingers' breadth wide from top to bottom, both close and open work. Others have three rows at the bottom, some lengthwise, and others across, others in broken chevrons, or studded with figures of animals, according to the fancy of the workman."

Most French observers commented on the visual language of pattern and colour employed by the Mi'kmaq to decorate objects of everyday life. But reading between the lines, I felt that modern historians such as Speck struggled with the evidence. How were they to account for this remarkable—seemingly unique—artistic tradition among such an isolated people?

In an important work on the subject of Mi'kmaq quillwork published by the Nova Scotia Museum, Ruth Whitehead assigns the terms "flyfot" and "eight-legged starfish" to certain Mi'kmaq patterns. She says that the flyfot pattern is untraceable to other local sources and suggests it might have evolved from other forms or been adopted from European iconography. But the flyfot and the eight-legged starfish—distinctively Mi'kmaq—as well as the double curve are all common among the Chinese. With the ruins on Cape Dauphin as a starting point, I asked myself what could have been the origin of these patterns, these ways of dressing, this language, this technical knowledge, and all the remarkable differences between the Mi'kmaq and other aboriginal peoples observed for centuries?

Speck, writing about the double-curve pattern, offers this answer: "It may have originated in the northeast and drifted westward, or it may have been derived from an original old

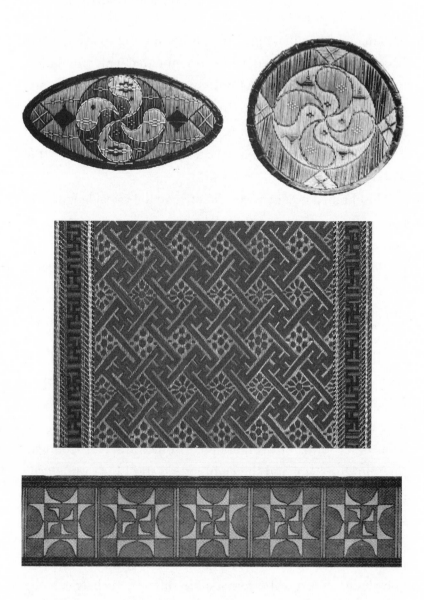

TOP: *Two samples of Mi'kmaq boxes decorated with porcupine quills in the flyfot pattern.*

MIDDLE AND BOTTOM: *Flyfot-like embroidery patterns from the Minority Peoples of China.*

American design element that became remodeled and specialized to its present form among some of these tribes and was subsequently adopted by their neighbors in general." He's saying that the pattern either originated where his research says it did or made its way up from the middle of the continent, skipped over the neighbours, settled among the Mi'kmaq to enjoy a flowering of classical brilliance, then found its way, battered and bruised, back towards the interior. Speck claims that "the latter supposition seems a little more plausible." On that single sentence hinges the attitude of the majority of contemporary researchers. No one studying Mi'kmaq culture has been able to plausibly explain how anything so marvellously sophisticated could have originated from a tiny piece of land in relative isolation on the edge of the continent.

CHAPTER EIGHTEEN

GAVIN AND GOLD

THROUGH THE AUTUMN and early winter of 2004 I sat in my Toronto apartment, my research arrayed around me, and wrote. At the end of the first week of December I was done. I carefully tapped into alignment three hundred pages of research and illustrations, as well edited and readable as I could make them. I set them in the middle of the desk.

I carefully wrapped the bundle and sent it with a cover letter to a well-respected Toronto agent. I called several days later to see if she had received my package, and she explained that she could not invest the time to read it because such a book would never sell. I wasn't crushed, because I wasn't trying to write a best-seller. She hadn't read the manuscript, so her rejection was not a reflection on it but rather was based on her assessment of public interest in archaeological stories.

I sent the manuscript to Tim Brook, a respected Vancouver historian and someone who knew both Chinese history and early Canadian history. He was kind enough to read it and to respond, but his answer demonstrated something I'd already realized: how much professional scholars disliked Gavin Menzies. Dr. Brook's response became a stage from which to criticize Menzies, though he courteously expressed the hope that I was right. I reread his letter several times. He offered no explanation for the ruins even though he knew the history of the area. Perhaps he entertained the possibility that they weren't there. I was either very wrong indeed or the ruins had eluded the realm of professional scholarship.

Together, the agent and the scholar made it clear I was going to have difficulty getting anyone to take me seriously. Through the lens of traditional history, my conclusion was simply untenable.

I decided to send a note to Gavin Menzies, who until now knew nothing of my research. I anticipated that this story, coming out of nowhere, would be a shock. I first sent an e-mail to his 1421 website, describing my background and how my Acadian ancestry and ties to Cape Breton had led to the research and the discovery. I attached a two-page description of the find and a summary of the history surrounding it. I also offered to send my manuscript to England if he wanted to read it.

Menzies was back to me within a day, excited and anxious to see the research. He immediately saw the logic behind a Chinese settlement on Cape Breton Island. As a mariner, he understood the profound determinant of ocean currents on Cape Breton's importance when control of the oceans meant control of the land. Perhaps my research into the Gulf Stream and the critical position it played in the island's history had given my reasoning substance in Menzies's eyes. Whatever the case, I was delighted: someone was interested. The next afternoon, just a couple of days before Christmas 2004, I sent him a copy of the manuscript.

Menzies and I corresponded over the Christmas holiday, and then he was off on another world trip. On his way back to England from China via Central America, he would stop in Toronto to see me.

I met with Menzies and his wife, Marcella, at the King Edward Hotel, one of the few lovely old hotels remaining in Toronto. Menzies looks much younger than his seventy years, his face full of youthful excitement. We talked through dinner; at times he seemed almost to vibrate with enthusiasm as we pulled different papers and files from the stacks of books we had arranged on the floor around us in several lopsided piles. I kept trying to apologize to his wife for monopolizing the dinner conversation with the subject of Cape Dauphin, but she listened with as much enthusiasm as Menzies. We'd been corresponding for only a few weeks, and I was surprised at the man's grasp of the material I'd put at his disposal. I was also surprised when he brought up the subject of gold while we were talking about Chinese motivations for coming this far.

"Don't forget that you may be looking at more than an agricultural economy," he said. "Gold was a great motivator, especially then. You may find evidence of smelting on Cape Dauphin."

"I've never heard anything about gold mining in the area."

"It would have been reason enough to found a colony. Or if not, the later discovery and production of a valuable metal—gold, perhaps—might have been enough to sustain a colony."

"I'll look into it."

"In fact, I should tell you that I came across an old Cape Breton tourist brochure in London. It mentions the remains of a long-dead gold mine down there."

"Really?"

"And don't forget that name Bras d'Or. That could be significant."

Then Menzies made an offer. In mid-May he was to take part in an international symposium at the Library of Congress in Washington sponsored by the library's Asian Division. It would be a one-day meeting with a long lineup of speakers who would address the early Chinese voyages. Officially, the topic was to be the voyages of Zheng He, to mark the six hundredth anniversary of his first voyage in 1405, but the papers to be presented had a much wider range than that. To the library's credit, they had included Menzies and other researchers who were working on early Chinese visits to the Americas and the subsequent mapping of the coasts of both North and South America. The symposium would constitute a review of current knowledge of these early maps and cover all the known Chinese and early European world maps.

Unofficially, the library was asking a question: Did enough evidence exist to suggest that China mapped the Americas first? Had Europeans of the late fifteenth and early sixteenth centuries then relied upon and copied Chinese maps for their own adventures? Menzies invited me to present my research in Washington.

As we talked about what that might mean, Marcella, half jokingly, told me that I should be careful—her husband had had his life threatened in Lisbon by someone who felt that the Portuguese role in the discovery of the Americas had been muddied by Menzies's stories of Zheng He's exploits.

I said goodbye to the Menzies that night and went home both excited and worried. Speak at an international symposium of academics? That seemed a far cry from my little apartment in Toronto or the almost childlike adventure of exploring the top of Cape Dauphin. I had to admit that my head was somewhat turned, though perhaps I had been indiscreet. Menzies was a bright—even brilliant—amateur with a genuine knack for promotion. Had I told him too much or needlessly exposed my remarkable site to public scorn or, worse, damage?

Over the next few weeks, the idea that the Chinese might have used the island for mining and producing metals plagued me. Certainly I was wary. To the delight of his detractors, Menzies has a tendency to hyperbolize. He often described his revelations as being the best, the biggest and the greatest even before they had been thoroughly studied and understood. He has something of a showman's instinct, and it has proved both advantageous and otherwise for his work. After our Toronto meeting, I was afraid he would unintentionally let slip to the press that gold might have lured the Chinese to the shores of Cape Breton. Images of gold have a way of clouding people's senses. I imagined planeloads of treasure seekers and vandals landing on this precious site. Yet the man had a point. Evidence of mining would suggest one more substantial reason for a Chinese settlement.

I knew that if gold had been found on Cape Breton, it would have been reported and recorded in official government publications.

Mid-nineteenth century reports quickly revealed that Nova Scotia and Cape Breton not only had gold mines but their very own gold rush. It was a far cry from the Californian or Yukon rushes, but there was gold here. Typical was a British government report entitled *The Gold Yield of Nova Scotia*, which covered the period from 1860 to 1872: "The proximity of Nova Scotia to the Mother-Country, its accessibility from all points by land or sea, its excellent harbours, innumerable rivers, immense forests, extensive deposits of coal, iron, and gold, and above all its wholesome climate and law-abiding population are claims worth considering by capitalists who invest in mining ventures." This and other government reports were clear: gold was among the wealth of minerals found in the area. Production in 1867 was 27,583 ounces, a total matched in 1868. But the local gold rush was short-lived, and I got the impression that only the easily accessible gold in Nova Scotia was mined. The remaining gold seams posed technical challenges that the mining entrepreneurs of the time were unable or unwilling to tackle. Investors lost interest.

But as I read through these reports, I was surprised to discover evidence that the area had long been associated with gold. In a report from 1868 titled *A Practical Guide to the Gold Fields of Nova Scotia*, the author writes: "The French names of Bras d'or, Cap d'or and Jeu d'or (now corrupted into Jeddore) strongly confirm the belief that the presence of gold, in those localities especially, was not unknown to the first Acadian settlers." Often British government reports made special note of Cape Breton and cited the possible importance of the name Bras d'Or—arm of gold—the island's inland lake system. The opening from the sea to Bras d'Or flows by Cape Dauphin. While these government reports were being written, mines were dug at both Ingonish and Chéticamp, though neither mine was particularly successful.

When loose gold is found in river bottoms, geologists term the material that carries the gold *auriferous*. And so, when these nineteenth-century British engineers reported that "the sands of some of the rivers of Cape Breton Island were auriferous," they were claiming, as the Seven Cities legend had four centuries earlier, that there was gold in the sand.

I returned to research on the Seven Cities legend that I had been compiling for publication. I had left out certain elements of the fifteenth-century stories because they seemed too far-fetched, too mythical. I had included the references to the Portuguese bishops because I felt they explained how Europeans might have made sense of the reports of settlements, but I had left out the section of the legend that mentioned "gold in the sands." It was not that I wished to omit evidence; it was just that I had never seen mention of it in any general history of the area. And then there was the possibility, however remote, that dreams of treasure might quickly turn a pristine site into a shambles of overturned rubble. At any rate, I had ignored the mention of gold in the legends, though I kept files and copies of the original documents pertaining to these and other miscellaneous subjects.

A Portuguese report from 1447 claimed that a ship had been blown off course, sailed into the Gulf Stream and landed on an island. A crew member returned to Portugal with sand from the shore that he sold "unto a goldsmith of Lisbon, out of which he had a good quantitie of gold." It was also reported that Portuguese sailors brought home sand they had collected on the shore to repack their firebox, only to discover it was flecked with tiny pieces of gold. The Zeno brothers had reported that the island had "all kinds of metals, but especially . . . gold." The Corte-Real brothers had returned with a gilded sword. The interior of the island is still called the Arm of Gold. And now the geological reports concurred: centuries ago there had been gold in the sands of Cape Breton Island.

CHAPTER NINETEEN

WASHINGTON

I was grateful for Menzies's invitation to present my findings, but the four-month deadline seemed too short. I was just finishing the research, the Nova Scotian government had not been notified of the discovery and the site was not protected in any way. If I was right, a few careless visitors could spoil what might be one of the most significant new archaeological sites in the world. A public presentation would leave it open to vandals. I asked Menzies for time to think.

Speaking at the Library of Congress might prove disastrous for the site; not speaking might mean it would never be recognized.

I decided to inform the Nova Scotia government and, specifically, the Nova Scotia Museum. I sent the manuscript to the curator of archaeology, where I was reasonably confident the research would be taken seriously and the significance of the find carefully considered. I received a reply: there were hundreds of sites in Nova Scotia, and many such claims were received each year. Sincerely, etc.

I was stunned. Respect from the local authorities was crucial if the project was to have any future. If they did not believe in it, the site would not officially exist.

On reflection, I couldn't blame them. There *are* many archaeological sites in Nova Scotia. This area has some of the earliest New World settlements; European interest was concentrated on this region for a long period. A recent book had been published, and a documentary was planned on ruins that are reported to have been left by early Scottish settlers in the region who had some sort of connection to the Holy Grail legend.

In late January I followed every official channel to persuade those in authority to make some acknowledgement of the ruins. When nothing was forthcoming, I contacted Menzies and agreed to make the discovery public at the one-day symposium in Washington—under specific restrictions. I would show maps and diagrams of the site and disclose its location, but only in general terms. I would identify the coastline, but not the specific cape. I would keep the position vague enough to discourage casual visits but specific enough to explain why Cape Dauphin was such an important point on the island. Still, I was concerned that this sort of circumlocution would lead serious scholars to suspect a hoax, and the public to discount the whole thing. If I would not say where it was, what was I hiding? But a public announcement of the exact location seemed more dangerous in the long term, and certainly foolish at this early stage.

Menzies and I agreed that I would speak openly and freely about what I had found, with the stipulation that I would not reveal the exact location of the site. If I could make the presentation clear enough, those in the audience would appreciate the reason for my reticence.

The symposium was a little over three months away. I was accustomed to speaking to large groups of students and using pictures to show them a way of seeing. But students are generally not skeptics. Now I faced the prospect of speaking to a room full of skeptics—intelligent skeptics. Yet that was everything I could hope for. It was a challenge, and I had grown ready for the challenge. I would have fifteen minutes to present, and fifteen minutes it would be—surely enough time to give world history a little shake.

I needed to eliminate everything that was non-essential to the discovery—much of the supporting history—but I did need to show the ruins, explain why I thought they were Chinese and how they contrasted with European ruins. I had to make clear why the Chinese would have built where they did, deal somehow with the important connections between the Mi'kmaq and the Chinese, and include the significance of my extensive collection of European reports and maps. Finally, I would have to explain my Cape Breton and Acadian connections and why I, unknown to the archaeological community, had found the ruins. In fifteen minutes. My friends saw little of me for these months; my family even less.

Since first testing positive for HIV, I've learned to fear stress. It can sicken even the healthiest body, and I have seen what it can do to a weakened immune system. I avoid stress by organizing and preparing with a thoroughness often remarked on by students. I brought the same approach to the symposium talk and, by the first week of May, I had my presentation down to fourteen minutes, had memorized the opening and spaced the written text like lines of poetry. My inspiration at this point came from knowing that the ruins were real, I had exhausted my intellect to prove they couldn't possibly be Chinese and then had been forced to admit that they were. They were not going away. When I was ready, I had to face the disconcerting prospect that what people now chose to believe was beyond me.

When I lived in Washington during the early 1990s, I fell in love with the city and its architecture. It seemed always in bloom, and its museums are some of the best in the world. In May 2005 it was still beautiful, and the museums still had my favourite paintings on display, but Washington is a city more southern than northern, and I found the heat stifling. The increased security over the past few years had taken its toll, and fences and barriers marred buildings where I remembered walking freely. Beautiful old tree-lined streets were closed even to foot traffic.

I arrived a couple of days before the symposium so I could visit the monuments and the paintings I liked most. Of all the public buildings on Capitol Hill, the Jefferson Building, the oldest section of the Library of Congress, is one of the most striking, with its imposing dome based on the design of the Paris Opera. Above the dome, a statue of the ancient goddess of Wisdom holds the torch of learning high above the library. To have spoken here, in some hallowed hall under the dome of the original neo-classical building, would have delighted me, but I was denied this architect's romantic fantasy. The symposium was held in the Mumford Room of the much newer Madison Building across the street. I was presenting a new idea to an institution that was built on ideas. The architecture of the lecture hall aside, I was thrilled.

By chance I ran into Menzies on Sunday, the day before the symposium. We spent an hour in conversation and I realized for the first time how important my talk was to him, to the other speakers, and to many who were planning to attend. The prospect that a large archaeological site might prove what Menzies and others had been saying, often in direct opposition to the most influential and respected scholars, gave my fifteen minutes considerable weight. Menzies was to some degree trusting me with his reputation. If my research was poorly received or could not hold up under public scrutiny, I would look bad, Menzies would look bad and the plausibility of early Chinese voyages would be damaged.

The day of the symposium was hot, bright and humid. In the hall, before the morning session, Dr. John R. Hébert, the moderator for my part of the day and the head of the Geography and Map Division of the library, introduced himself as a fellow

Acadian—a Cajun from Louisiana. We figured we were probably cousins.

Meanwhile my brother Gregory, who was trying to get here from Halifax, found that his flight was delayed and quickly booked a roundabout by way of New York. He arrived late in the morning with a grin, looking as though he had run all the way from Canada. We had a quick lunch together at the library restaurant, but I was too nervous to sit for long. We walked over to the Capitol building together to look out over the mall and the Lincoln Memorial in the distance.

"Wonder what all this would have looked like if they'd stayed on?" he asked.

"Who?"

"The Chinese."

I laughed.

"Don't ask that at the symposium," I said.

As it happened, the speakers who preceded me all, in their own way, helped set the stage. Their insights into the maps, the types of settlements the Chinese constructed, and advanced Chinese navigational methods made Chinese ruins at Cape Dauphin a real possibility. Early in the day we became aware that a small group of people had attended only to hector any notion of Chinese voyages. Their questions were unfortunately petty and ill-phrased, but their anger towards Menzies was real. Some of these individuals had spread a rumour on the Internet that they would stage demonstrations, and the Library of Congress had assigned extra security. In the end, the few in the audience who still considered Menzies either a charlatan or a heretic were silenced by the wealth of fact contained in the presentations. Even for them, these early Chinese voyages became a remote possibility.

By mid-afternoon I stood to face an audience that was willing to accept Chinese mastery of the oceans before the fifteenth century as a likely, if not a proven, fact. I explained exactly what I had found. I described how the stone wall, the platforms and the road, taken together, pointed specifically and uniquely to China. I concentrated on what I had seen and researched and only on what I knew. I tried to let the information speak for itself. Near the end of my fifteen minutes I used the Columbus Map, which showed the Island of Seven Cities, to link that legend to Cape Breton, and I used the Mi'kmaq writing to introduce the wide-ranging influence that the Chinese might have had. I could have spoken for hours, but instead I tried to allow the power and clarity of the visual images to carry the message: the ruins were Chinese in origin, Europe knew about this strange island as early as the mid-fifteenth century, and there was reason to believe that aspects of traditional Chinese life had been absorbed into native culture. Less had to be more.

When I was done and the floor was opened to questions directed at all the speakers from the afternoon session, I could see Gregory at the back, watching and listening.

"Where is it?" people wanted to know.

"Are there graves?"

"Have you dug yet?"

"What about the Nova Scotia government?"

So many questions were directed at me that I was swallowing up time that should have belonged to other speakers.

Then it was over, and I was startled by a burst of applause. Gavin Menzies actually bounded up the aisle.

"Brilliant!" was all he said.

Then Gregory slipped through the crowd. "You blew them away, Paul," he whispered as he wrung my hand.

Others crowded around, and it was only then I realized how excited people were. A line formed of those waiting to shake my hand, many of them Chinese. I fielded very specific questions about the architecture and the gravesites. A couple of people from Yale introduced themselves, along with an engineering professor from the Catholic University of America who was familiar with my work there some years before. Gregory disappeared. I found out later he had slipped out of the library to phone my parents, who were waiting anxiously at home.

Dr. Hébert asked me if I had considered — with L'Anse aux Meadows to the north — if Cape Dauphin could be a Viking settlement. I said that I had addressed this idea in my research but had no time during the presentation to explain the difference between a typical Viking settlement, even an extremely large one, and the ruins on Cape Dauphin. Dr. Hébert smiled. "Laisser les bonnes temps rouler," he said in Cajun French.

It seemed that I had plausible answers to everything I was asked, which told me — and Menzies — that I had missed no obvious elements. During the ebbing of that long day, I was convinced that Cape Dauphin was truly the discovery I believed it to be. I had put the research to a public forum, and it stood firm on its foundations. It had not been condemned as some modern heresy, and no one had offered a persuasive counter-explanation or proclaimed my findings a hoax.

In the days that followed I received many notes, though few I appreciated more than the one from archaeologist Betty Meggers of the Smithsonian, who had attended the symposium. My careful work, she wrote, was "a model for others to follow."

CHAPTER TWENTY

THE FIRST VISITORS

CAPE BRETON WAS STILL COLD in late May. After the unseasonable heat of Washington, the travelling was beginning to take its toll on me. But I had promised to get together in Sydney on Wednesday evening with Menzies and his friend Cedric Bell, and I had promised Menzies I would take him to see the site.

I owed it to him, but it was still a hurdle to be overcome. The summit of the cape had been mine, visited only rarely by hikers and hunters walking into the wilderness. Even they might pass through only in the late summer or fall, when the secret of the

ruins was closely guarded by the dense green cover that flour-
ished in the warm sunlight and light rains of the area. Now I
was giving it away. It was a transition, a change, an ending and
a beginning—and beginnings and endings are difficult for me.

At a less subtle level, I knew Menzies to be a writer and a
public man. I was giving him the inside track on a project that
had not been published and might turn the head of the history
world. If so, it would certainly be an important victory for
Menzies and his team. I didn't own the site and had presented
it but once in public. I debated with myself whether this
guided tour was wise. Bell, an amateur archaeologist, had
researched the remains of a Chinese junk found in New
Zealand and, through Menzies, he too had access to all my
maps and charts and knew exactly where the site was.

In the end, I had to trust both of them to respect my claim.

I flew from Toronto on Wednesday afternoon. As the plane
taxied along the runway to the Sydney terminal, I could see
that Cape Breton had donned her finest in frigid greys. It had
snowed that morning. My parents had gone away on a short
holiday, so I had to take a taxi in from the airport. The keys to
my mother's car were on the kitchen table, with a short note
telling me to be careful because of the snow. I had just enough
time to unpack, turn around, and drive out to meet Menzies,
Bell, and Bell's wife for dinner. They had rented a rustic log
cabin for themselves near the town of Baddeck on the Bras
d'Or Lakes, not far from Cape Dauphin. Menzies had arrived
the day before from Washington.

The cabin was well off the main highway, down a winding,
hilly and mostly dirt road through the forest. I arrived around

four in the afternoon. Menzies made the introductions all around.

Bell was a marine engineer from northern England, a tall and jolly fellow in his mid-seventies with a mop of white hair and the air of a slightly mad professor. He wore the rumpled clothes of a hiker and had the glowing complexion of a man who happily spends his days out of doors. He had been retired for years, and he and his wife, Patricia, whom he called Paddy, now spent many of their days searching for Roman ruins along the back roads of Cumbria. I warmed to him. He was my father's age, and he treated me a bit like a young apprentice. He eagerly demonstrated a curious divining-rod contraption he had learned to use during his days as an engineer. Once he'd used it to find burned pipes, when he'd worked for a large oil company. Now he put it to the service of uncovering Roman ruins.

Paddy cooked a fine dinner for all of us, but the talk centred around the Cape Dauphin site and the following day's hike. The Bells had been on the island for several days already and, before the brief snowstorm, had been able to make a couple of hikes around the summit of Cape Dauphin.

"Paul, you've definitely found a Chinese town." Bell leaned close to me. "I *also* think there was a smelting operation here. There's lots of iron ore around the site, and we found smelters."

"Smelters?"

"Yes, indeed. Stone smelters. But you have to know what to look for. They might look like a couple of hills and a few bumps to someone unfamiliar with this sort of thing. But

when properly understood—even ruined and grown over—
there they are. You have smelters on your site. *And* standard
36 by 4 metre Chinese barrack blocks. And a system of canals."

I looked at him with a mixture of wonder and skepticism.

"Let me say something more about the smelters," he continued. "In the middle of an otherwise flat area you'll find a
raised rectangle, about the size of this cottage and ramped on
all sides. When you look carefully in the immediate vicinity,
you'll see the remains of a system of aqueducts used to drive
the water wheel that operated a bellows forcing combustion
air into the smelter bowls. The Chinese used the same layout
and same sizes as the Romans used. Ramp, aqueducts, smelter
bowls—the ruins are all there."

He sat back, his face aglow.

"But"—I was a little alarmed at this precipitous rate of
discovery—"I don't think the Chinese came all the way here
for iron ore."

"No!" Bell nodded in vigorous agreement. "I suspect there
was also gold. The site was very secure. Too secure for the simple mining of iron ore."

"What do you mean?"

"On the road up, we found evidence of over twenty gate-
ways, and that is just leading to the main walled town. There is
another and smaller secure section located along the road
which was controlled by a separate gatehouse and appears to
have been surrounded by a double-walled enclosure. It had its
own separate barracks block and its own smelter. There was
something going on there that needed to be kept secure."

"Good Lord," I said.

"*And* Gavin says he found mention of there having been gold in Nova Scotia."

"And what about the name of this lake?" Paddy called from the kitchen. "The Bras d'Or—the Arm of Gold? That name must come from somewhere."

I felt I owed such enthusiasm a larger share of my findings, or at least my opinion.

"Okay"—I drew a breath—"In fact, this may have been a much larger and more important settlement than I first thought."

Menzies adjusted the flame on the lamp that hung over the table. Everyone looked at me intently.

"I haven't said much to you about this up to now. Our whole emphasis has been on the Cape Dauphin site and the Chinese link. But you do know that I spent more than a year searching out primary documents that might explain the ruins. And you'll remember my saying in Washington that the Island of Seven Cities as it appears on the Columbus Map closely resembles Cape Breton."

"A remarkable observation," Menzies said.

"I don't know if I was the first to notice this resemblance. But the Seven Cities truly was a fabled island and it was all the talk in the fifteenth century. Sailors claimed to have seen it and returned. There were reports of sand samples brought back to Europe—sand that was full of gold. Columbus drew the place on his maps, and Cabot claimed to have found it."

"Did he?" Bell exclaimed.

"Yes, he did. And he gave its precise latitude—that is, Cape Breton's latitude."

"Really?"

"So it looked like game, set and match for Cape Breton. But then something surprising happens. The discovered Island of Seven Cities doesn't fulfill its promise, and its whereabouts shifts from place to place on the maps of later years. Finally it disappears."

"You mean no one spoke of it."

"Exactly. The island itself didn't go anywhere. It stayed right there. Meanwhile, some maps of this period—the Lopo Homem Map of 1554 is the best example—show Cape Breton Island, including seven distinct place names, six of them in Mi'kmaq and the seventh shown as 'C dos bretois'—the Cape of the English."

"How many names?"

"Seven. The number varies on later maps, but the first time they appear, on this 1554 map, it appears to be seven. And these Mi'kmaq names are said by Ganong, the granddaddy of the early cartography of the North Atlantic coast, to constitute the most ancient native Indian place names recorded in New France and most likely in all of the Americas."

I saw Menzies glance at the Bells, wild surmise in his eye.

"You know," I said, "at first, this all looked like a red herring to me. I barely noted it. Apparently Cape Breton was the only place in North America to have native place names recorded, located and mapped this early in European discovery. Interesting. A coincidence. I didn't even twig when I began to study Nicolas Denys's writings on Cape Breton from the mid-1600s. By then those Mi'kmaq names were mostly forgotten, but Denys also lists the seven names given by European visitors to the Cape Breton ports with good harbours. They were all well known to Europeans by the seventeenth century. Of course, I couldn't know if the Mi'kmaq locations and the European ports were the same places, but, frankly, the coastal geography of the island suggested they were."

"Wait a minute," Bell interrupted. "What *are* those ports?"

"There was Campseaux, which is present-day Canso. There was Fort St. Pierre, now St. Peters. There was Le Chadye, which became Chéticamp—that's where my ancestors settled. There was St. Anne—that's now Cape Dauphin. There was Niganiche, where the Portuguese had their fishing camps—it's now Ingonish."

"St. Peters?" Bell interjected.

"Yes, in fact we have authoritative histories that report Mi'kmaq traditions claiming that earth mounds at St. Peters were built by white men before the arrival of the French. And there are earthworks at Ingonish that many people believe to be older than the French era. Of course, everyone assumed they were Portuguese. As I began to see the Chinese connection, I started to ask myself if there might be ruins at other places on the island. What would be the logic of building only one tiny city on an island on the far side of the world? But I was still reluctant to make the leap to seven cities.

"Then I looked at St. Peters in particular. There were several historic documents and maps of the area that mentioned ruins. And I remembered that Nicolas Denys claimed to have eighty arpents of land under cultivation at St. Peters. I'd initially skimmed over that report, but then I read a commentary written in the English translation of Denys's book. It called Denys's claim of eighty arpents 'a gross exaggeration.' That caught my eye. The extent of land Denys claimed to have under cultivation was so vast that scholars dismissed it. But I had become a bit wary of scholarly dismissal by then. What if Denys was telling the truth? The area he reported as cleared was on the top of a steep hill, the same area where the old maps and reports located pre-European ruins. A light went on. Even before European settlement, this was an island with seven distinctly named places, at least two of which had ruins that were thought to be pre-European. Suddenly I was faced with the possibility that there had been seven cities on the island—that this was in fact the Island of Seven Cities, just as Columbus and Cabot had claimed."

There was a silence. I thought I'd better stop. My mouth was dry, and I took a long drink of water. I'd probably persuaded these people that I was a madman who had just accidently stumbled on a previously undiscovered archaeological site.

Finally Bell spoke or, rather, cackled.

"I *told* you!" He shot a triumphant look at Menzies.

Now *I* was puzzled.

"Told him what?" I asked.

"Told him! Paddy and I have *been* to both Louisbourg *and* St. Peters."

"Really? When?"

"Just the other day. We don't have time to fool around. And you know what we saw at Louisbourg? We were astonished, believe me. Along the edge of a boggy shore was the outline of what looked to me like two Chinese finger docks. They're the long thin docks that jut out like fingers and are custom-made for the ships they're supposed to serve. Yes, the ones at

Louisbourg are all covered now in tall grass and thick bushes, but under all that bog their outline is obvious. And then we went to St. Peters and there, along the shore, we saw what looked to us like stonework—far older and more massive than they could explain with their local history."

Menzies smiled. "The whole drive down from Halifax," he said, "Cedric was trying to convince me that this was a much bigger discovery than you had suggested."

"Gavin," I said. "I owe *you* a bit of an apology on this gold business. I was reluctant even to investigate it, but it turns out there was not one mine but two gold mines on Cape Breton Island during the nineteenth century: one at Ingonish and one at Chéticamp, where my father was born. I have government reports from the nineteenth century that describe the gold as present in Cape Breton sands. It's hard for me not to think about the story of a sailor who took a bag of Seven Cities sand to a fifteenth-century Lisbon jeweller. The sand was full of gold."

"Well, well," said Menzies.

"Well, well, well," said Bell and his wife.

It was getting late, and I wanted to get home to Sydney. The next day would be a long one, and we needed our sleep. Bell walked me to the car.

"Do you think Gavin will have trouble on the climb tomorrow?" I asked.

Menzies was five years younger than Bell, but Bell and his wife were accustomed to hiking through the hills of Cumbria. Menzies was more accustomed to the inside of his office or the seat of an airplane.

"He had some heart problems a while back. Paddy and I have talked about it. We'll go slowly tomorrow."

The next day was cold and wet. As I pulled up to my regular parking spot at the base of Cape Dauphin, I saw Menzies and the Bells decked out like professional hikers in full rain gear.

I discovered that the road up, even in a cold rain, was much easier in the company of others. The Bells and I were relatively sure-footed, even though the snow and rain had made the rocky sections of the hike slippery and dangerous in parts. We watched out for Menzies, but he too made the hike without complaint. As we reached the summit, even though the air was dense with fog, he was visibly excited.

"Remarkable," he exclaimed. He looked down the long slope of the site. "Truly remarkable. So much bigger than I imagined."

As the four of us started to climb down the terraces, we walked around one of the platforms, finding the corners, mentally making note of the beginnings and endings. We talked a great deal about the construction of the town wall. Menzies asked about a theory I had described to him in January, of the older wall that appeared in the earliest aerial pictures of the summit. I believed the area it enclosed had been expanded during a second major period of construction.

He nodded.

"The first construction could have been during the voyages of Kublai Khan's fleets," he said. "And the second at the time of Zheng He." Such assertions were part of Menzies's style. He could certainly be entirely wrong, but it was just this sort of bold leap that had allowed him to open minds to new possibilities.

They wanted to see the graves. I had not spoken about the mounds at the Library of Congress, but I had told Menzies about them during our first meeting in Toronto. A Cape Breton fog was coming in, and I sensed he was a bit uncomfortable. I asked if he was all right.

"I'm a bit disoriented, that's all. Fog is the mariner's nightmare," he said.

I went on ahead by myself, down the ridge beyond the wall and into the woods, looking for the graves. The fog was thick now, and I could not risk any of us becoming lost in this forest. I wanted to find a path we could backtrack out on easily. I jumped over the stones and plunged into the woods. This was a place I knew, even in the fog.

I led them to the low, carefully arranged, oval-shaped mounds built into the side of the slight ridge. That they might be Chinese tombs came as no surprise to the Bells, whose search for things Roman often disclosed the remains of other things not so ancient, including graves. As an amateur archaeologist, Bell had surveyed many such mounds.

"Never touched one, though," he confided. "I leave that to others." In silence, we circled one specimen.

I explained how the Chinese built their tombs: round and of stone, located outside the town wall and usually on the side of a hill.

Menzies was quiet and, in spite of his rain gear, he was wet. He had taken off his gloves and his hands looked raw and cold. He shook his head in wonder.

"Ming Dynasty graves," he said softly. "I believe I have just seen Ming Dynasty graves, untouched, forgotten. Amazing."

I felt these mariners had much to teach me about seeing ruins, but it was already mid-afternoon. We had not rested since we began—and the rain had not let up. It was time to head back down to some place warm.

We trudged down the mountainside in the rain, more thoroughly soaked with every step. We spoke only once or twice, but I was happy. I had been right to bring them. Now I was one of a group, and each of us was witness to the evidence of a history that had long lain hidden.

CHAPTER TWENTY-ONE

FAMILY REUNIONS

IN JULY 2005 I joined my family on Prince Edward Island for our annual holiday. Everyone wanted me to re-enact the Washington presentation; all they'd heard so far was Gregory's biased reporting of the event. I had planned a working week-end and had loaded dozens of new images into my series of presentation slides: the Mi'kmaq patterns and clothing, more information on the Seven Cities legend, copies of the Portuguese royal decrees sending ships out to look for the island, and a rather complicated explanation of how John Cabot determined latitude and his reference to the Bordeaux

River. I would spend the weekend on the beach putting my notes in order, then try out the new speech to my family on Sunday evening. For the first time my parents had not been able to make the trip because my mother had had a minor operation on her knee.

Everyone else except me was staying—as we usually did— at Cavendish on the northern shore. Like most of the island, Cavendish has miles of sandy beach made a pale shade of earthy red by the local soil. My family likes Cavendish because of its golf course, and every year they rent cottages and spend early mornings on the links. I somehow failed to inherit the golf gene. This year I was just as happy to stay farther down the shore, away from golf clubs and birdies and eagles.

The grand old Dalvay-by-the-Sea Hotel, famous as one of the stately inns of Canada, is on a spectacular site thirty min-utes' drive along the northern shore from Cavendish. The wooden, three-storey, multi-gabled lodge was built during the late nineteenth century and perches on a low hill surrounded by manicured lawns. The foundations are of local fieldstone, round boulders the colour of the island's soil. The main sec-tion of the hotel is inlaid with a painted timber framework attached to the exterior wall—a finely drawn grid that gives the massive gables the smaller scale of a country house. The dozens of windows are outlined in the same crisp white frames, and the peak of each gable is painted a dark forest green. The overall effect is one of comfort and solidity. The hotel is an often-used location for the television adaptation of *Anne of Green Gables,* and Japanese tourists on *Gables* pil-grimages snap photographs around the grounds. Just to the north over the dunes are a wide and seemingly endless sandy beach and the long, straight, uninterrupted horizon of the Gulf of St. Lawrence. It was here that Jean Alfonce gave his directions to Tartary in the mid-sixteenth century.

I decided to squeeze in some exploring, not for Tartary but along this shore, which interested me more than the grand hotel itself. Across from the entrance, over the two-lane road that follows the northern shore, is one of the island's several public beaches. Yet even in the height of summer there are seldom more than a dozen families here, their blankets and picnic baskets spread on the sand. As children, we'd climbed these grassy dunes during our summer vacations. A wooden boardwalk from the road to the beach protects them now. Just a fifteen-minute walk to the east of the entrance to the board-walk is the area once known as L'Étang des Berges, the home-stead of Jacques Chiasson during the 1750s. I had been aware of the place for years, searched for it on old maps, and, every time I visited PEI, spent a bit of time snooping around.

A narrow stream flows through the dunes to a tiny lake just south of the seashore. It is easy to miss. You can splash through it almost without noticing: at its deepest point the water is not much higher than your ankles.

On Saturday, after breakfast on the deck of the Dalvay, I set out along the shoreline and up the course of the stream. I waded up the middle, following the brackish flow until it began to widen into the lake and became too deep for me to go farther. The lake is surrounded by low spruce forest, tall beach grasses and sand dunes. This was L'Étang des Berges — the Pond of Shores. Somewhere at the edge of this miniature lake my ancestors lived for almost a generation. Remnants of their farmhouse may lie hidden here. The stream was like a small, loose thread, visible to the world. If I tugged on it, perhaps it might unravel a story not only of Acadians and the British but also of my own family.

I spent most of the next morning on the veranda of my hotel, looking out over the flawlessly still lake as a couple squabbled and struggled with a canoe, which they finally capsized near the shore. The howls and accusations echoed against the backdrop of a perfect blue sky and the softly golden sand dunes. It was all too interesting and, before I knew it, the afternoon was half gone and I still hadn't prepared my presentation. Maybe the family would forget about it.

I drove to the cottages my family rent. At various points the road skirts sand dunes, the ocean and the few small harbours that still support a fishing industry. Then I turned inland through the low hilly farmland that is the backbone of the Prince Edward Island economy: gentle rolling fields divided into crisp rectangles, with neat edges of green and gold pastures receding into the distance. Just as I settled peacefully into this pastoral dream, the coastline appeared again, and the road wound along the bays, inlets, cliffs and beaches of the north shore.

The three family cottages are in a single line, and the doors are always open, with children and adults tripping from one to the next. We like to cook, and dinner is generally prepared in all three cottages as a team effort. Bernie's wife, Debbie, had made a huge platter of grilled shrimp, and my brothers opened bottles of wine. Gregory had managed to set up a computer and a projector against the wall of his and Joann's cottage. The adults had showered and changed, but the kids were still in their swimsuits. There was a poignancy in not seeing my parents in their usual places.

My presentation was clear in some parts and, frankly, confusing in others. I saw the parts that were easy to understand, the boring parts, and the glazed looks when I started explaining John Cabot's use of latitude.

When I was done, my young nephew Conor suddenly spoke up. "How do you know the Chinese were there? Can you prove it?"

Everyone looked to see how I would respond to something so guileless and direct.

"That's *the* question, Conor," I said. "It's about evidence. The evidence isn't just one or two things, but many things that point in the same direction. There are so many pieces of the story, like the pieces of a huge jigsaw puzzle. They all fit together *once* you see that it is a Chinese puzzle."

He looked at me, a little blankly.

"Imagine," I said. "Imagine you were trying to put a jigsaw puzzle together but you didn't know what it would look like when you were done. It would be just about impossible to identify the little pieces or to figure out how each one of them fits into the whole picture. Maybe you'd study each piece over and over, but no matter how carefully you'd examine it, it wouldn't make sense. Maybe you'd try to fit it into another piece, but it wouldn't quite fit."

"Pretty impossible," Conor said.

"Exactly. But then one day you find the top of the puzzle box under the sofa. Suddenly you see what the puzzle should actually look like. That's what happened to me. It was like seeing for the first time what the picture should look like. Then all the pieces—all those pieces that never really fit well—clicked into place like a puzzle should. That's what the ruins are. They're like the puzzle box that was lost under the sofa. They showed the real picture for the first time. The facts, the puzzle pieces, did the rest."

Conor was smiling.

That's when Gregory brought out the T-shirts. He had had them custom-made with COLUMBUS printed in big block letters, then boldly crossed out. Underneath, in Chinese-like lettering, were the words *Zheng Who*.

Gregory was straight-faced. "There are still some people who don't know who this Zheng He is."

We all pulled the shirts on over our clothes and, for the rest of that night, we looked like the team we are.

CHAPTER TWENTY-TWO

BEFORE THE SNOW

THE LAST EDGES of an October storm had blown in overnight, and I woke up at first light to what local weather broadcasters regularly call "cold drizzle and intermittent fog." It was not the day I had hoped for, but I had come equipped this time with my own outfit of new rain gear.

I had been writing and organizing data most of the summer, and now I wanted to see the ruins again before winter set in and the mountain was blanketed in white. I had hoped to take my parents up this time, but, with the weather as it was, it was out of the question until at least the following spring. My mother's knee had healed somewhat, but she still needed a cane to walk any great distance. My father had recently had a hip replaced, and the other hip was in poor shape.

Mom was up when I came into the kitchen, filling a thermos with hot milky tea.

"All I need is water, really," I protested.

"No, that's not all you'll need. It's October. You're to take this, too."

"What's that?"

"A bag of trail mix."

"Oh, all right."

"And be careful."

"I'm always careful."

As I drove out from Sydney, the birch and maple trees in the low areas near the rivers and lakes had not only changed colour but had already begun to lose their leaves. I anticipated that the early frost would have killed much of the summer's growth on Cape Dauphin, but I hadn't been to the site this late in the season and didn't really know what to expect. Certainly this cold rain and fog would make the climb miserable. I hoped that the storm would blow over during the morning and that I might have some sunshine in the late afternoon.

I parked my mother's car on the side of the road, as I had so many times over the past couple of years. In a way, the site was more home to me now than anywhere else. At this point on the dirt road, the trees at the entrance to the forest had always seemed to me a gateway to a private world. I had come to the end of the beginning of this project, and the autumn forest made tangible that sense of a turning point.

The steep rocky sections of the climb had been difficult for me at the best of times. This day, I found them gruelling. Fallen leaves covered some of the rockiest sections, and I was unsure of every step.

The rain showed no sign of stopping, but as I climbed higher the fog began to lift. The yellow leaves and stark white bark of the birch trees gave way to the sombre green of the spruce forest. Where the fog still hung among the branches, the woods looked almost black. The road smelled of nature—not the spring smell of young green but the musty smell of a forest dying once again in advance of the winter snows.

I stopped in my tracks, something I seldom did on this climb. The only sound was the dripping of water through the branches: harsh and cold, gentle and reassuring at the same time. When this track had been a road travelled by the Chinese, how many men had stood here for a minute, alone in the cold rain? I had a palpable sense of these people, not very different from me, alone perhaps but going about their business six centuries ago. The whole idea was suddenly perfectly normal and real.

The last leg of the climb had always been my favourite part, where the road is wider and more obvious. I always looked forward to this section, not only because it signalled the last push on the hike up but because, over the top of this last incline, the remains of the settlement would open up to me as it spread down the north side of the mountain.

This time, though, it was something of a struggle. The rain had all but stopped, but the rocks were slippery and I fell twice, scratching my hands each time. My rain gear kept me dry, but my face was dripping and my hands were cold and impressively bloody. Then I came over the top edge, and the ragged sense of cold loneliness imparted by the weather and the dark forest dissolved like the fog. Here was the site, my site, and I felt home again.

I blessed my mother as I gulped the hot milky tea and dug into the bag of trail mix. The single stone outcropping near the top of the site, where I'd rested the first time and many times since, now seemed far less wet and cold than it probably was. The walk had taken much longer than usual: it was already noon.

The rain stopped. I could see the ocean and the faint outline of the highlands in the distance. I suspended searching and just looked. The ocean partly covered in fog, the rain deciding whether to stay or move out to sea, the simple starkness of the woods, almost black against the white sky: this had been the setting for the lives of generations of Chinese men and women. I was certain of it.

I finished the thermos of tea, wrapped my handkerchief around the scrape on my left hand, and started to walk around the platforms. Since my Library of Congress presentation, anyone with the willingness to put the various newspaper articles and interviews together, and with a rudimentary knowledge of currents and cartography, could have found the site without too much difficultly. I knew I no longer had any real control over it. I walked among my ruins, wondering whether they had been touched.

I had forgotten how thickly the mosses grew, or perhaps I had expected them to have died back as winter approached. Certainly they had lost much of their colour—the various pale shades of green were bleached to a muted grey—but they were still thick. I knew the site well, and I was comfortable hiking quickly over the uneven surface. But the tiny roots that held the various mosses to the sides of rocks, now soft and full of moisture, fell away easily under a misplaced boot, and several times I leapt from stone to stone to avoid falling. I knew I couldn't stay long. Twilight approaches quickly in mid-October, and I couldn't imagine heading down the hill in the dark.

It was hard to leave. My architect's heart and mind finds something satisfying about being in the presence of ruins, perhaps less from a sense of nature humbling our follies than a marvelling at our ability to create structures with enough care and consideration that they leave their story behind when we are gone. But I didn't look back as I left the summit. The sun had started to sink quickly now, and I was cold. The ruins on Cape Dauphin had waited for centuries, and they'd wait a little longer for the others who were sure to follow me.

CHAPTER ONE

7   *named it Acadia, after the mythical Arcady*

        Samuel Eliot Morison, *The European Discovery of America: The Northern Voyages, A.D. 500–1600* (New York: Oxford University Press, 1971), 195.

        John Mack Faragher, *A Great and Noble Scheme: The Tragic Story of the Expulsion of the French Acadians from Their American Homeland* (New York: Norton and Company, 2005), 6.

    the young French explorer Samuel de Champlain

        Samuel de Champlain, *The Works of Samuel de Champlain*, 6 vols. (Toronto: Champlain Society, 1922–36).

8   *L'Acadie became known as a place that might offer settlers a better life*

        There are many books published on Acadian history. The most complete and readable account is Faragher, *A Great and Noble Scheme*.

12   *and came back with a little clothbound book written in* 1975

        The first printing of Lamb's book may be difficult to find, but the more recent edition is widely available.

        James B. Lamb, *Hidden Heritage: Buried Romance at St. Ann's, Cape Breton Island* (Wreck Cove, Cape Breton Island: Breton Books, 2000).

    Yet far and away the most intriguing and puzzling

        Lamb, *Hidden Heritage*, 33–35.

16   *I came across a nineteenth-century history entitled*

        F.G. Speck, "Beothuk and Micmac." *Indian Notes and Monographs* no. 22 (New York: Museum of the American Indian, Heye Foundation, 1922).

Speck's article includes a map entitled "Hunting Territories of the Micmac Indians of Nova Scotia," which locates Kluscap's travels.

17   *Louisbourg, after all, was just an hour's drive down the coast*
       The classic history of the French occupation of Louisbourg is J.S. McLennan's *Louisbourg from Its Foundation to Its Fall, 1713–1758* (Sydney, N.S.: Fortress Press, 1969).

CHAPTER TWO

27   *map-makers began to draw maps that represented the observations of sailors*
       John Wilford's book is an easily available general introduction to the history of Western cartography and is useful as a concise reference.
       John Noble Wilford, *The Mapmakers* (New York: Vintage Books, 2001).

29   *The cartographer Martin Behaim*
       Ibid., 70.

30   *The notion that there were islands off the European coast*
       The following offer a general review of these legendary islands, where they were, and what became of them: William H. Babcock, *Legendary Islands of the Atlantic: A Study in Medieval Geography* (New York: American Geographical Society, 1922). J. de Courcy Ireland and D.C. Sheehy, "Atlantic Islands." *European Approaches to North America, 1450–1640.* Ed. David Quinn (Aldershot, U.K.; Brookfield, Vt.: Ashgate/Variorum, 1998), 1–17. Donald S. Johnson, *Phantom Islands of the Atlantic* (Fredericton: Goose Lane, 1994).

31   *the Benincasa Map of 1482 gave these bays place names*
       Babcock, *Legendary Islands of the Atlantic*, 70.
    Below the drawing of the island, Behaim wrote
       De Courcy Ireland and Sheehy, "Atlantic Islands," 10.

33   *Las Casas reported that*
       The Las Casas report, "Fifteenth-century indications of unknown lands in the Atlantic," first printed in *Historia de las Indias*, 1552, is found in James A. Williamson, *The Cabot Voyages and Bristol Discovery under Henry VII* (Cambridge: Hakluyt Society at the University Press, 1962), 175.

34   *Ferdinand Columbus claimed that his father*
       Fernando Colon, *The Life of the Admiral Christopher Columbus by His*

Son Ferdinand. Trans. Benjamin Keen (New Brunswick, N.J.: Rutgers
University Press, 1959), 27.

from the writings of a fifteenth-century historian named Galvano
Babcock, *Legendary Islands of the Atlantic*, 72.

The royal charter read in part
Williamson, *The Cabot Voyages*, 184.

35   *In 1486 another grant was awarded to Fernão Dulmo*
Ibid., 186.

shipping documents from the harbour at Bristol
Ibid., 188.

36   *Toscanelli sent him back a copy of a letter*
Colon, *The Life of the Admiral Christopher Columbus*, 21.

Here is the island of the Seven Cities
G.R. Crone, "The Mythical Islands of the Atlantic Ocean: Suggestion as
to Their Origin." *Comptes Rendus du Congrès International de
Geographie Amsterdam 1938* (Leiden: E.J. Brill, 1938), 170.

37   *a thin, illustrated book, the* Atlas of Columbus and the Great Discoveries
Kenneth Nebenzahl, *Atlas of Columbus and the Great Discoveries*
(Chicago: Rand McNally, 1990). Further information on the Columbus
Map can be found in Michel Mollat du Jourdin et al., *Sea Charts of the
Early Explorers, 13th to 17th Century.* Trans. L. le R. Dethan (London:
Thames and Hudson, 1984).

40   *gathered from letters written over several generations by the Zeno family*
Babcock, *Legendary Islands of the Atlantic*, 72.
Richard H. Major, trans. and ed., *The Voyages of the Venetian Brothers
Nicolo and Antonio Zeno to the Northern Seas in the XIVth Century.
Comprising the Latest Known Accounts of the Lost Colony of Greenland
and of the Northmen in America before Columbus* (London: Hakluyt
Society, 1873).

41   *A reference to Zeno's book I found in an eighteenth-century history*
John Pinkerton, *The History of Scotland from the Accession of the House of
Stuart to That of Mary* (London: C. Dilly, 1797), 261.

a fair and populous city, where the king of the place
Babcock, *Legendary Islands of the Atlantic*, 128.

CHAPTER THREE

43   *In 1497 King Henry VII of England sent Cabot*
The following offer accounts of both John and Sebastian Cabot:
H.P. Biggar, *The Voyages of the Cabots and of the Corte-Reals to North America and Greenland, 1497–1503* (Paris: [s.n.] 1903). (Short title:) *Voyage of the Cabots.*
Peter E. Pope, *The Many Landfalls of John Cabot* (Toronto: University of Toronto Press, 1997).
Williamson, *The Cabot Voyages.*
George Parker Winship, *Cabot Bibliography, with an Introductory Essay on the Careers of the Cabots Based upon an Independent Examination of the Sources of Information* (New York: Burt Franklin, 1900).

45   *foreign ambassadors sent out letters to their European courts*
These letters are found in translation in the following: H.P. Biggar, *The Precursors of Jacques Cartier, 1497–1534: A Collection of Documents Relating to the Early History of the Dominion of Canada* (Ottawa: Government Printing Bureau, 1911).
Williamson, *The Cabot Voyages.*
a single English letter in the Spanish archives
Ibid., 211.

54   *which was awarded to Cabot by the English King and dated February 3, 1498*
Biggar, *The Precursors of Jacques Cartier*, 22.

55   *"The 27 being Monday*
Pope, *The Many Landfalls of John Cabot*, 55.

56   *"repeatedly and deliberately misrepresented his role*
Ibid., 58.

57   *the so-called Paris map of 1544*
Ibid., 58.

59   *A map, believed to have been drawn in 1508*
Babcock, *Legendary Islands of the Atlantic*, 74.
a region simply called the Seven Cities was thought by the Spanish
The following review the Seven Cities and Cibola legend as it reappeared in the northwestern United States in the mid-sixteenth century: A.F. Bandelier, *The Gilded Man (El Dorado) and Other Pictures of the Spanish Occupancy of America* (New York: D. Appleton, 1893). C. Gregory Crampton, *The Zunis*

of Cibola (Salt Lake City: University of Utah Press, 1977). Charles Wilson Hackett, ed., *Historical Documents Relating to New Mexico, Nueva Vizcaya, and Approaches Thereto, to 1773*, vol. 1 (Washington: Carnegie Institution of Washington, 1923). George Parker Winship, "Why Coronado Went to New Mexico." *Annual Report of the American Historical Association for the Year 1894* (Washington: Government Printing Office, 1895).

60   *"all the pulpits of the order resounded with the stories*
           Ibid., 88.

CHAPTER FOUR

63   *had divided any newly found overseas lands into two zones*
           George Patterson, "The Portuguese on the North-East Coast of America and the First European Attempt at Colonization There. A Lost Chapter in American History." *Proceedings and Transactions of the Royal Society of Canada for the Year 1890* 8 (1891): 142.
        the King of Portugal issued a Letters Patent
           Biggar, *The Precursors of Jacques Cartier*, 65.

64   *[They are] very wild and barbarous*
           Samuel Eliot Morison, *Portuguese Voyages to America in the Fifteenth Century* (New York: Octagon Books, 1965), 70.

65   *The Venetian ambassador to Portugal, Pietro Pasqualigo*
           Biggar, *The Precursors of Jacques Cartier*, 65.

68   *the Portuguese government levied a royal tax of ten percent*
           Morison, *Portuguese Voyages to America in the Fifteenth Century*, 225.
        he was given a Letters Patent granting him ownership of the lands
           Biggar, *The Precursors of Jacques Cartier*, 127.

69   *A Portuguese report written fifty year later*
           Ibid., 195.

CHAPTER FIVE

74   *In the letter that Raimondo de Soncino sent to the Milanese Duke*
           Ibid., 17.

75   *La Cosa labelled as* Cauo Descubierto
           W.F Ganong, *Crucial Maps in the Early Cartography and Place-*

Nomenclature of the Atlantic Coast of Canada (Toronto: University of Toronto Press with the Royal Society of Canada, 1964), 150.
I wondered if La Cosa's use of the term descubierto *might not be significant* Morison, *Portuguese Voyages*, 3–10.

77   *"the leading historians of Portugal and Brazil assert it*
      Ibid., 3.

78   *began to refer to the island as Cape Breton*
      Ganong, *Crucial Maps*, 168.

80   *Verrazano, when sailing past Cape Breton on his return trip to France*
      Ibid., 189.

82   *It was during this second voyage in 1535*
      H.P. Biggar, *The Voyages of Jacques Cartier* (Ottawa: Printed by F.A. Acland, 1924), 237.

83   *John Cabot's observations had proven true*
      "Second Dispatch of Raimondo di Soncino to the Duke of Milan, 18 December 1497." H.P. Biggar, *The Precursors of Jacques Cartier*, 17.
      Until the fifteenth century, the European cod industry had relied
      A concise history of the early cod industry is found in H.P. Biggar, *The Early Trading Companies of New France: A Contribution to the History of Commerce and Discovery in North America* (Clifton, N.J.: Augustus M. Kelley, 1972), 18–37.

85   *These are believed to be the first native names mapped*
      Ganong, *Crucial Maps*, 165.

86   *"Terra de Muyta Gemte"*
      Ibid., 146.
      "a townie of fourscore houses"
      Richard Hakluyt, *A Discourse on Western Planting Written in the Year 1584*. Ed. Charles Deane (Cambridge: Maine Historical Society, 1877), 122.

87   *Hakluyt cautioned his government in 1584*
      Ibid., 102.

88   *Alfonce suggested that there may have been a Portuguese settlement*
      Ganong, *Crucial Maps*, 365.

CHAPTER SIX

93 *In 1603, the French King, Henry IV, appointed Pierre du Gua de Monts*
W.J. Eccles, *France in America* (Markham, Ont.: Fitzhenry and Whiteside, 1972), 14.

94 *Samuel de Champlain and Marc Lescarbot*
Champlain, *The Works of Samuel de Champlain.*
Marc Lescarbot, *The History of New France.* Trans. W.L. Grant (Toronto: Champlain Society, 1907).

95 *"l'isle du cap Breton qui est par la hauteur de*
Champlain, *The Works of Samuel de Champlain*, vol. 1, 466.
Champlain believed that it had been Portuguese
Ibid., 468.

97 *Lescarbot mentioned ruins on the island*
Lescarbot, *The History of New France*, 187.

99 *In 1621 King James I of England granted Sir William Alexander*
These early settlement projects are described in George Pratt Insh, *Scottish Colonial Schemes, 1620–1686* (Glasgow: MacLehose, Jackson and Company, 1922).
Lord Ochiltree, was given royal authorization
David Laing, *Royal Letters, Charters, and Tracts Relating to the Colonization of New Scotland, and the Institution of the Order Knight Baronets of Nova Scotia, 1621–1638* (Edinburgh: Bannatyne Club, 1867), 54.

100 *"to bring assistance and provisions to the Sieur de Champlain*
Champlain's letter, "The Narrative of the Voyage Made by Captain Daniel of Dieppe," is included in Champlain, *The Works of Samuel de Champlain*, vol. 6, 153.

101 *In 1635 Father Perrault, a visiting missionary*
The letter from Father Julien Perrault, "Relation of Certain Details regarding the Island of Cape Breton and Its Inhabitants," is included in Rueben Gold Thwaites, ed., *The Jesuit Relations and Allied Documents: Travels and Explorations of the Jesuit Missionaries in New France, 1610–1791. The Original French, Latin, and Italian Texts with English Translations and Notes*, 74 vols., vol. 8 (Cleveland: Burrows Brothers Company, 1898), 157.

102 *A report filed in Paris by Champlain*
Champlain, "The Narrative of the Voyage Made by Captain Daniel of Dieppe," 159.

103 *Vieuxpoint had been rescued by a Basque fishing vessel*
"Letter from the Reverend Father l'Allemand to the Reverend Father Superior, at Paris," November 22, 1629. Thwaites, ed., *The Jesuit Relations*, vol. 4, 235.

105 *The name Cibo appears to have been in long use*
Nicolas Denys, *The Description and Natural History of the Coasts of North America (Acadia)*. Trans. and ed. William F. Ganong (Toronto: Champlain Society, 1908), 182n.3.
"the river called by the Indians the Grand Cibou"
Champlain, "The Narrative of the Voyage Made by Captain Daniel of Dieppe," 156.

106 *"thirty days' journey to the north"*
George P. Hammond and Agapito Rey, *Narratives of the Coronado Expedition, 1540–1542* (Albuquerque: University of New Mexico Press, 1940), 140.

CHAPTER SEVEN
108 *"laden and provided with everything that was necessary*
Champlain, "The Narrative of the Voyage Made by Captain Daniel of Dieppe," 200.
They made regular reports to France, and these Jesuit Relations
Thwaites, ed., *The Jesuit Relations*.

110 *In the spring of 1634 Father Julien Perrault*
Ibid., vol. 8, 157.

112 *Denys, a businessman, had been in Acadia since 1632*
Ganong's translation of Denys's *Description and Natural History* reviews his Acadian career.

114 *In an 1885 article entitled "Lost Colonies of Northmen and Portuguese"*
R.G. Haliburton, "A Search in British North America for Lost Colonies of Northmen and Portuguese." *Proceedings of the Royal Geographical Society and Monthly Record of Geography* 7 (1) (1885): 25–38.

115   The chapter summary reads: "The Island of Cap Breton
        Denys, *The Description and Natural History*, 175.

118   In 1677 he obtained an ordinance from the intendant at Quebec
        "Ordinance of M. du Chesneau, Intendant in Canada in the Interest of
        Sieur Denis," August 21, 1677. Ibid., 57.

120   A government accountant named Gargas
        William Inglis Morse, ed., *Acadiensia Nova (1598–1779): New and
        Unpublished Documents and Other Data Relating to Acadia* (London:
        Bernard Quaritch, 1935).

CHAPTER EIGHT
129   settlers from Newfoundland–116 men, 10 women and 23 children
        McLennan, *Louisbourg*, 12.

130   "There is not in all the island land suitable
        Faragher, *A Great and Noble Scheme*, 139.

132   the French produced over five hundred surveys
        John Fortier, "The Fortress of Louisbourg and Its Cartographic Evidence."
        Association for Preservation Technology Bulletin 4 (1–2) (1972): 2–173.
        "Beyond the Bastions: French Mapping of Cape Breton
        Joan Dawson, "Beyond the Bastions: French Mapping of Cape Breton
        Island, 1713–1758." *Nova Scotia Historical Review* 10 (2) 1990: 6–29.

135   "is one of the finest harbours to be seen for wood and land
        George Geddie Patterson, *Patterson's History of Victoria County, Cape
        Breton, Nova Scotia* (Sydney: College of Cape Breton Press, 1978), 30.
        "the bay of Ste. Anne's was the locality
        Ibid., 30.

137   "the finest harbour in the world"
        Ibid., 30.

140   the population of slaves in the French Caribbean islands
        Eccles, *France in America*, 168.

141   a crucial centre for trade in the North Atlantic
        John Robert McNeill, *Atlantic Empires of France and Spain: Louisbourg and
        Havana, 1700–1763* (Chapel Hill: University of North Carolina Press, 1985).

142   *Two weeks later, a detachment of English soldiers*
         Patterson, *Patterson's History*, 37.
         A census in 1752 listed fewer than twenty people
         Sieur de La Roque, *The 1752 Census of Isle Royale (Known as Cape*
         Breton Island) as a Result of the Inspection Made by Sieur De La Roque
         (Pawtucket, R.I.: Quinton Publications, 1997), 42.

143   *"the said Fortress, together with all the works*
         McLennan, *Louisbourg*, 290.
         A census of Nova Scotia taken in 1766
         Samuel Holland, *Holland's Description of Cape Breton Island and*
         Other Documents (Halifax: Public Archives of Nova Scotia, 1935), 10.
         in 1774, an Englishman named Samuel Holland
         Ibid., 63.

CHAPTER NINE

146   *The name Chéticamp may derive from an earlier Mi'kmaq name*
         Denys, *The Description and Natural History*, 185n.2.

147   *Three of the first families were Chiassons*
         Sally Ross and Alphonse Deveau, *The Acadians of Nova Scotia: Past and*
         Present (Halifax: Nimbus Publishing, 1992), 106.

148   *"as thickly planted there as the hairs upon his head"*
         Thwaites, ed., *The Jesuit Relations*, vol. 1, 177.

149   *claim that the unlimited introduction of alcohol by European fishermen*
         Denys, *The Description and Natural History*, 445.
         Antoine Simon Maillard, *An Account of the Customs and Manners of the*
         Micmakis and Maricheets Savage Nations (London: Hooper and Morley,
         1758), 49.
         It was "a town of about 50 hovels"
         Philip A. Buckner and John G. Reid, eds., *The Atlantic Region to*
         Confederation (Toronto: University of Toronto Press, 1998), 190.

150   *under the leadership of the Reverend Norman McLeod*
         In *Hidden Heritage*, chapter 3, James B. Lamb profiles the Reverend
         McLeod.

152   *The first had been the French map from 1733*
         Dawson, "Beyond the Bastions," 12.

CHAPTER TEN
158   *Father Chrestien Le Clercq*
       Chrestien Le Clercq, *New Relation of Gaspesia with the Customs and
       Religion of the Gaspesian Indians.* Trans. and ed. William F. Ganong
       (Toronto: Champlain Society, 1910).

160   *"This new world has been peopled by certain individuals*
       Ibid., 85.

164   *I found a 1997 copy of the* Mi'kmaq Concordat with the Vatican
       James Youngblood Henderson, *The Mikmaw Concordat* (Halifax:
       Fernwood Publishing, 1997).

165   *The legend of the Great Kluscap*
       The following cover the Mi'kmaq legends in detail:
       Silas Tertius Rand, *Legends of the Micmacs* (New York: Longmans,
       Green, 1894).
       F.G. Speck, "Beothuk and Micmac."
       ——— "Some Micmac Tales from Cape Breton Island." *Journal of American
       Folklore* 27 (107) (1915): 59–69.
       Wilson D. Wallis and Ruth Sawtell Wallis, *The Micmac Indians
       of Eastern Canada* (Minneapolis: University of Minnesota Press, 1955).

167   *a telling description of the Mi'kmaq*
       Thwaites, ed., *The Jesuit Relations*, vol. 3, 75.

168   *"knowledge of letters"*
       Le Clercq, *New Relation of Gaspesia*, 86.
       "making marks with charcoal upon birch-bark"
       Ibid., 131.

172   *According to a later writer, Silas Rand*
       Silas Tertius Rand, *A Short Account of the Lord's Work among the Micmac
       Indians* (Halifax: William MacNab, 1873), 5.

174   *"the darkness, superstition and bigotry of Romanism"*
       Ibid., 34.
       I learned from Olive Dickason
       Olive Patricia Dickason, *The Myth of the Savage and the Beginnings of
       French Colonialism in the Americas* (Edmonton: University of Alberta
       Press, 1984), 104.

175   *"nothing enchants those people more than a style of metaphors*
       Maillard, *An Account of the Customs and Manners of the Micmakis and*
       Maricheets Savage Nations, 3.

176   *They knew the North Star as a stationary point*
       Rand, *Legends of the Micmacs*, xli.
       "much ingenuity in drawing upon bark a kind of map
       Le Clercq, *New Relation of Gaspesia*, 137.

177   *the Mi'kmaq reached Newfoundland before Europeans*
       Alan D. McMillan, *Native Peoples and Cultures of Canada* (Vancouver:
       Douglas and McIntyre, 1995), 56.
       an account written in 1593 by Richard Strong
       Ruth Holmes Whitehead, *Nova Scotia, the Protohistoric Period, 1500– 1620:*
       Four Micmac Sites (Halifax: Nova Scotia Musuem, 1993), 19.

178   *"infallible remedy" for epilepsy*
       Sieur de Dièreville, *Relation of the Voyage to Port Royal in Acadia or*
       New France. Trans. Alice Webster (Toronto: Champlain Society, 1933),
       181.

179   *they could cure themselves of death itself*
       Ibid., 180.

CHAPTER ELEVEN

182   *"the traces of wide and well-built roadways*
       Lamb, *Hidden Heritage*, 34.
       I set up a sort of on-screen air-intelligence lab
       All aerial photographs were ordered from the National Air Photo Library
       in Ottawa. The Cape Dauphin area has a history of forest fires, and testing
       on the site indicates a major fire in the early part of the twentieth century
       that left the site bare. The earliest air photo is from August 1929.
       Subsequent aerial photographs have shown the wall and town site with
       progressively more ground cover.

188   *"after the manner of the Chinese"*
       Rand, *A Short Account of the Lord's Work among the Micmac Indians*, 5.

189   *"possibly some light might be got into it*
       Maillard, *An Account of the Customs and Manners of the Micmakis and*
       Maricheets Savage Nations, 33.

191   *From Menzies and other writers and historians*
       Gavin Menzies, *1421: The Year China Discovered the World* (London:
       Bantam Press, 2002).
       The early naval strength of China is also covered in the following:
       Louise Levathes, *When China Ruled the Seas: The Treasure Fleet of the
       Dragon Throne, 1405–1433* (New York: Simon and Schuster, 1994).
       Joseph Needham, *Science and Civilisation in China*, vol. 4, pt. 3
       (Cambridge: Cambridge University Press, 1954).

CHAPTER TWELVE

195   *I began to read Chinese history of the period.*
       The following is the list of general histories consulted for this book:
       Patricia Buckley Ebrey, *The Cambridge Illustrated History of China*
       (Cambridge: Cambridge University Press, 2003).
       John King Fairbank and Merle Goldman, *China: A New History*
       (Cambridge, Mass.: Belknap Press of Harvard University Press, 2001).
       Jacques Gernet, *A History of Chinese Civilization*. Trans. J.R. Foster
       and Charles Hartman (Cambridge: Cambridge University Press,
       1999).
       W. Scott Morton, *China: Its History and Culture* (New York: McGraw-
       Hill, 1995).
       Frederick W. Mote and Denis Twitchet, eds., *The Cambridge History of
       China*, vol. 7: *The Ming Dynasty, 1368–1644* (Cambridge: Cambridge
       University Press, 1988).

196   *Chinese ships had sailed the full extent of the Indian Ocean*
       Needham, *Science and Civilisation in China*, vol. 4, pt. 3, 486.

199   *By the late thirteenth century, Marco Polo reported*
       A.C. Moule and Paul Pelliot, trans., Marco Polo, *The Description of the
       World* (London: Routledge, 1938), 320.

200   *The Mongols, for instance, using experienced Chinese sailors*
       Fairbank and Goldman, *China: A New History*, 123.

201   *of ships from the tenth and eleventh centuries with six masts*
       Morton, *China: Its History and Culture*, 104.
       A description written in 1178 reported
       Needham, *Science and Civilisation*, vol. 4, pt. 3, 464.
       the significant community of Nestorian Christians living in China
       J.P. Wiest et al., "Christianity in China." *The New Catholic Encyclopedia*

(Detroit and Washington, D.C.: Thomson/Gale; Catholic University of America, 2003).

Chinese sailors and a small Christian community
Needham, *Science and Civilisation, vol. 4, pt.* 3, 508.

203   *a number used by scholars of Chinese naval technology*
Ibid., 480.

205   *"they also add certain other wholly ridiculous circumstances*
Le Clercq, *New Relation of Gaspesia*, 85.
The island settlement described by Zeno did not exist
Babcock, *Legendary Islands of the Atlantic*, 131.

206   *"the particulars of this affair seem to have been carefully concealed*
Faragher, *A Great and Noble Scheme*, 463.

208   *A 1432 memorial to the fleet's commander, Zheng He*
Needham, *Science and Civilisation*, vol. 3, 557.

210   *"anticommercialism and xenophobia won out*
Fairbank and Goldman, *China: A New History*, 139.

CHAPTER THIRTEEN

215   *the Mi'kmaq took every opportunity to recite their ancestry*
The following are the earliest descriptions and observations of life among the Mi'kmaq:
Pierre Baird (1567–1622)
Reuben Gold Thwaites, ed. *The Jesuit Relations*, vols. 1, 2, 3.
Nicolas Denys (1598–1688)
Denys, *The Description and Natural History.*
Sieur de Dièreville (?–c. 1711)
Sieur de Dièreville, *Relation of the Voyage to Port Royal in Acadia.*
Chrestien Le Clercq (c. 1641–1695)
Le Clercq, *New Relation of Gaspesia.*
Marc Lescarbot (c. 1570–1642)
Marc Lescarbot, *Nova Francia: A Description of Acadia*, 1606. Trans. P. Erondelle (London: George Routledge and Sons, 1928).
Pierre Maillard (c. 1710–1762)
Maillard, *An Account of the Customs and Manners of the Micmakis and Maricheets Savage Nations.*

216   *Throughout history, Chinese tombs have been the depository of stores*
        The following were my primary sources for information on Chinese rituals
        surrounding death:
        Justus Doolittle, *Social Life of the Chinese: Daily Life in China* (London:
        Kegan Paul, 2002).
        John Henry Gray, *China: A History of the Laws, Manners and Customs of
        the People.* Ed. William Gow Gregor (London: Macmillan, 1878).
        Edwin D. Harvey, *The Mind of China* (Westport, Conn.: Hyperion Press,
        1973).
        Michael Loewe, *Chinese Ideas of Life and Death: Faith, Myth and
        Reason in the Han Period (202 BC–AD 220)* (London: George Allen and
        Unwin, 1982).
        "Some do cover him with many skins of beavers
        Denys, *The Description and Natural History*, 439.
        "when these relatives die they wear mourning for a full year
        Antione Silvy, *Letters from North America.* Trans. Ivy Alice Dickson
        (Belleville, Ont.: Mika Publishing, 1980), 212.

217   *"quite round, of the form of a well, and four to five feet deep*
        Le Clercq, *New Relation of Gaspesia*, 300.
        "On account of the depth of the grave
        Thwaites, ed., *The Jesuit Relations*, vol. 3, 129.

CHAPTER FOURTEEN

229   *"there is found a sort of black stone*
        Marco Polo, *The Travels of Marco Polo, the Venetian.* Trans. William
        Marsden, ed. Manuel Komroff (New York: Liveright Publishing, 2003),
        170.

CHAPTER FIFTEEN

244   *The Chinese traditionally built houses*
        The following were my primary sources for information on Chinese
        architecture and planning:
        Chao-Kang Chang and Werner Blaser, *China: Tao in Architecture* (Basel:
        Birkhauser Verlag, 1987).
        Ronald G. Knapp, *China's Traditional Rural Architecture: A Cultural
        Geography of the Common House* (Honolulu: University of Hawaii Press,
        1986).
        ——*China's Vernacular Architecture: House Form and Culture*
        (Honolulu: University of Hawaii Press, 1989).
        ——*China's Walled Cities* (Hong Kong: Oxford University Press, 2000).

Ssu-ch'eng Liang, *A Pictorial History of Chinese Architecture: A Study of the Development of Its Structural System and the Evolution of Its Types*. Ed. Wilma Fairbank (Cambridge, Mass.: MIT Press, 1984).

Laurence G. Liu, *Chinese Architecture* (New York: Rizzoli, 1989).

Ann Paludan, *The Ming Tombs* (Hong Kong: Oxford University Press, 1991).

Laurence Sickman and Alexander Soper, *The Art and Architecture of China* (Baltimore: Penguin Books, 1956).

Osvald Siren, *The Imperial Palaces of Peking* (Paris: G. van Oest, 1926).

"The paved foundation or platform on which it stands
Marco Polo, *The Travels of Marco Polo*, 130.

247   *it replicates similar settlements throughout China*
Although the style and scale of construction are different, much of the site plan of the Putuoshongcheng Temple Complex at Chengde is similar to the site plan at Cape Dauphin.
Liu, *Chinese Architecture*, 126.

CHAPTER SIXTEEN

251   *Chinese wall-construction methods*
Needham, *Science and Civilisation in China*, vol. 4, pt. 3, 45.

254   *the same written character is used for both*
Knapp, *China's Walled Cities*, 1.

261   *The Chinese frequently built new villages*
Fairbank and Goldman, *China: A New History*, 129.
Gernet, *A History of Chinese Civilization*, 393.

264   *For centuries such a site and such mounds*
Paludan, *The Ming Tombs*.
Chinese roads were built to consistent specifications
Needham, *Science and Civilisation in China* vol. 4, pt. 3, 5, note d.

CHAPTER SEVENTEEN

270   *Along with the works of Confucius*
Confucius, *The Analects*. Trans. David Hinton (Washington: Counterpoint, 1998).
Lao Tzu, *Tao Te Ching*. Trans. David Hinton (Washington: Counterpoint, 2000).
Mencius, *Mencius*. Trans. David Hinton (Washington: Counterpoint, 1999).

272 *China was the first country to understand agriculture*
Robert Temple, *The Genius of China: 3,000 Years of Science, Discovery, and Invention* (New York: Simon and Schuster, 1986), 15.

278 *Across the centuries, scholars, researchers*
"They astonished the first Europeans with the sophistication of their birch-bark canoes, their snowshoes, and other technological products so suited to their sometimes harsh environment. More than this, they amazed the first whites with the complexity of their arts: some of their weaving and dyeing, for example, was considered superior to any found in France."
"'I Fashion Things': The Micmacs' Surprising Legacy," *Canadian Heritage*, April 1980, 25.

285 The Government Printing Bureau in Ottawa *published an article in 1915*
Frank G. Speck, *The Double-Curve Motif in Northeastern Algonkian Art*, Geological Survey of Canada, Memoir 42 (Ottawa: Government Printing Bureau, 1914), 1–17.
the Mi'kmaq examples were the most symmetrical
Ibid., 5.

287 *"In summer the men have robes of Moose skin*
Denys, *The Description and Natural History*, 411.
Ruth Whitehead assigned the terms
Ruth Holmes Whitehead, *Micmac Quilllwork: Micmac Indian Techniques of Porcupine Quill Decoration, 1600–1950* (Halifax: Nova Scotia Museum, 1982).
the flyfot pattern is untraceable to other local sources
Ibid., 193.
"It may have originated in the northeast
Speck, *Double-Curve Motif*, 3.

CHAPTER EIGHTEEN

295 *Typical was a British government report entitled*
A. Heatherington, *The Gold Yield of Nova Scotia, 1860–1872* (London: Mining Journal Office, 1873), 4.
Production in 1867 was 27,583
Wyatt Malcolm, *Gold Fields of Nova Scotia*, Geological Survey of Canada, Memoir 156 (Ottawa: Printed by F.A. Acland, 1929), 4.

296 *The French names of Bras d'or, Cap d'or and Jeu d'or*
A. Heatherington, *A Practical Guide for Tourists, Miners and Investors, and All Persons Interested in the Development of the Gold Fields of*

Nova Scotia (Montreal: Printed by John Lovell, 1868), 20.

"the sands of some of the rivers of Cape Breton Island were auriferous
Gillian Rosemary Evans, "Early Gold Mining in Nova Scotia." *Collections of the Nova Scotia Historical Society* 25 (1942): 21.

297   *"unto a goldsmith of Lisbon*
Babcock, *Legendary Islands of the Atlantic*, 72.
"all kinds of metal, but . . . especially gold
Ibid., 128.

CHAPTER TWENTY

312   *including seven distinct place names, six of them in Mi'kmaq*
Ganong, *Crucial Maps*, 165.

313   *claiming that earth mounds at St. Peters were built by white men*
R.G. Haliburton, "Lost Colonies of Northmen and Portuguese." *Popular Science Monthly*, May 1885, 48.
Patterson, 169.
"earthworks at Ingonish that many people believe to be older than the French era
Patterson, *History of Victoria County*, 168.

LIST OF ILLUSTRATIONS

The author would like to acknowledge the kind permission of the following rights holders to reprint from their material. Every effort has been made to contact copyright holders; in the event of an inadvertent omission or error, please notify the publisher.

348

Clarence Webster Canadiana Collection, 1939, W3975. Bottom left, image from *Costumes of the Minority Peoples of China* (Kyoto: Binobi, 1982), 240. Bottom right, image from Margaret Campbell, *From the Hands of the Hills* (Hong Kong: Media Transasia, 1978), 76.

Page 283. Top row, tracings of the Mi'kmaq petroglyphs at Kejimkujik Lake by George Creed, from Marian Robertson, *Rock Drawings of the Micmac Indians* (Halifax: The Nova Scotia Museum, 1973), figs 184, 183, 182. Bottom row, Minority Peoples headdress from *Ethnic Costumes and Clothing Decorations from China* (Hai Feng Publishing Company), 39. Image of Chinese empress from Zhou Xun and Gao Chunming, 151.

Page 284. Women's hats with double curve, courtesy the Nova Scotia Museum, NSM 13.6/09.8, and reproduced in Ruth Whitehead, *Elitekey: Micmac Material Culture from 1600 A.D. to the Present* (Halifax: The Nova Scotia Museum, 1980), 23. Detail of embroidered chief's coat courtesy of Canadian Museum of Civilization, artifact III-F-306, photograph by Harry Foster, image S77-1842. Chinese example of the double-curve, bottom, from *Embroidery Designs of the Miao People of China Collected by the National Minority Literary and Art Team of the Central Institute for Nationalities and the Research Group of the Art Department of the Cultural Bureau, Kweichow Province* (People's Fine Arts Publishing House, 1956), 28.

Page 286. Example of Mi'kmaq eight-legged starfish pattern at top left, courtesy of Nova Scotia Museum, NSM 69.184.1. Reproduced in Ruth Whitehead, *Micmac Quillwork: Micmac Indian Techniques of Porcupine Quill Decoration, 1600–1950* (Halifax: The Nova Scotia Museum, 1982), 177. Example at top right, courtesy of Nova Scotia Museum, NSM 76.70.11. Also reproduced in Whitehead, 177. Examples of similar Chinese embroidery pattern, middle, courtesy of *Ethnic Costumes and Clothing Decorations from China* (Hai Feng Publishing Company), 266, and at bottom, courtesy of Textile Museum of Canada, T92.0288b.

Page 288. Flyfot-decorated box, top left, courtesy Nova Scotia Museum, NSM 76.70.18, reproduced in Whitehead, *Micmac Quillwork*, 194. Top left, courtesy Nova Scotia Museum, NSM 76.70.3, reproduced in Whitehead, 194. Flyflot-like Chinese embroidery patterns, middle, from *Ethnic Costumes and Clothing Decorations from China*, 155. Sample at bottom from *Embroidery Designs of the Miao People of China*, 38.

BIBLIOGRAPHY

CAPE BRETON HISTORY, GEOLOGY, AND GEOGRAPHY

Bourinot, J.G. "Cape Breton and Its Memorials of the French Regime." *Proceedings and Transactions of the Royal Society of Canada for the Year 1890* 8 (1891): 173–339.

Brown, Richard. *The Coal Fields and Coal Trade off the Island of Cape Breton.* London: Sampson Low, Marston, Low, & Searle, 1871.

Calder, John H., et al. *One of the Greatest Treasures: The Geology and History of Coal in Nova Scotia.* Halifax: Nova Scotia Department of Natural Resources, 1993.

Dawson, Joan. "Beyond the Bastions: French Mapping of Cape Breton Island, 1713–1758." *Nova Scotia Historical Review* 10 (2) 1990: 6–29.

Denys, Nicolas. *The Description and Natural History of the Coasts of North America (Acadia).* Trans. and ed. William F. Ganong. Toronto: Champlain Society, 1908.

——*Description Géographique et Historique des Costes de 1'Amérique Septentrionale avec l'Histoire Naturelle du Païs.* Paris: Claude Barbin, 1672.

Donovan, Kenneth, ed. *The Island: New Perspectives on Cape Breton History, 1713–1990.* Fredericton: Acadiensis Press, 1990.

Evans, Gillian Rosemary. "Early Gold Mining in Nova Scotia." *Collections of the Nova Scotia Historical Society* 25 (1942): 17–47.

Fletcher, Hugh. *Descriptive Note on the Sydney Coal Field, Cape Breton, Nova Scotia.* Ottawa: S.E. Dawson, 1900.

Gordon of Lochinvar, Sir John. *Encouragements, for Such as Shall Have Intention to Bee Under-takers in the New Plantation of Cape Breton, Now New Galloway in America.* Edinburgh: John Wreittoun, 1625.

Guillet, G.R., and Wendy Martin. *The Geology of Industrial Minerals in Canada.* Montreal: The Canadian Institute of Mining and Metallurgy, 1984.

Haliburton, Thomas C. *History of Nova Scotia*. Belleville, Ont.: Mika Publishing, 1973.

Heatherington, A. *A Practical Guide for Tourists, Miners and Investors, and All Persons Interested in the Development of the Gold Fields of Nova Scotia*. Montreal: Printed by John Lovell, 1868.

——*The Gold Yield of Nova Scotia, 1860–1872*. London: Mining Journal Office, 1873.

Holland, Samuel. *Holland's Description of Cape Breton Island and Other Documents*. Halifax: Public Archives of Nova Scotia, 1935.

Lamb, James B. *Hidden Heritage: Buried Romance at St. Ann's, Cape Breton Island*. Wreck Cove, Cape Breton Island: Breton Books, 2000.

Lavery, Mary, and George Lavery. *Tides and Times: Life on the Cape Breton Coast at Gabarus and Vicinity*. Scarborough, Ont.: M. and G. Lavery, 1991.

Malcolm, Wyatt. *Gold Fields of Nova Scotia*. Geological Survey of Canada. Memoir 156. Ottawa: Printed by F.A. Acland, 1929.

McNeill, John Robert. *Atlantic Empires of France and Spain: Louisbourg and Havana, 1700–1763*. Chapel Hill: University of North Carolina Press, 1985.

Moore, Christopher. "The Maritime Economy of Isle Royal." *Canada: An Historical Magazine* 1 (4) (June 1974): 33–46.

Morrison, Murdoch D. "The Migration of Scotch Settlers from St. Ann's, Nova Scotia, to New Zealand, 1851–1860." *Collections of the Nova Scotia Historical Society* 10 (1933): 73–95.

Patterson, George Geddie. *Patterson's History of Victoria County, Cape Breton, Nova Scotia*. Sydney: College of Cape Breton Press, 1978.

Pichon, Thomas. *Genuine Letters and Memoirs relating to the Natural, Civil, and Commercial History of the Island of Cape Breton and Saint John from the First Settlement there to the Taking of Louisbourg by the English in 1758*. London: J. Nourse, 1760.

Roque, Sieur de La. *The 1752 Census of Isle Royale (Known as Cape Breton Island) as a Result of the Inspection Made by Sieur de La Roque*. Pawtucket, Rhode Island: Quinton Publications, 1997.

CHINESE HISTORY, PHILOSOPHY, AND SOCIETY

Anderson, Mary M. *Hidden Power: The Palace Eunuchs of Imperial China*. Buffalo: Prometheus Books, 1990.

Barker, R. "The Size of the 'Treasure Ships' and Other Chinese Vessels." *Mariner's Mirror* 75 (1989): 273–75.

Chang, Chao-Kang, and Werner Blaser. *China: Tao in Architecture*. Basel: Birkhauser Verlag, 1987.

Chang, K.C., ed. *Food in Chinese Culture: Anthropological and Historical Perspectives*. New Haven: Yale University Press, 1977.

China House Gallery. *Richly Woven Traditions, Costumes of the Miao of Southwest China and Beyond.* New York City: China Institute in America, 1987.

Confucius. *The Analects.* Trans. David Hinton. Washington, D.C.: Counterpoint, 1998.

Costumes of the Minority Peoples of China. Kyoto: Binobi, 1982.

Dillon, Michael, ed. *China: A Historical and Cultural Dictionary.* Richmond, Surrey: Curzon, 1998.

Doolittle, Justus. *Social Life of the Chinese: Daily Life in China.* London: Kegan Paul, 2002.

Ebrey, Patricia Buckley. *The Cambridge Illustrated History of China.* Cambridge: Cambridge University Press, 2003.

Fairbank, John King, and Merle Goldman. *China: A New History.* Cambridge, Mass.: The Belknap Press of Harvard University Press, 2001.

Filesi, Teobaldo. *China and Africa in the Middle Ages.* Trans. David L Morison. London: Frank Cass with the Central Asian Research Centre, 1972.

Gernet, Jacques. *A History of Chinese Civilization.* Trans. J.R. Foster and Charles Hartman. Cambridge: Cambridge University Press, 1999.

Goodrich, L. Carrington. *Dictionary of Ming Biography, 1368–1644.* New York: Columbia University Press, 1976.

Graham, David Crockett. *Folk Religion in Southwest China.* Washington, D.C.: Smithsonian Institution, 1961.

Gray, John Henry. *China: A History of the Laws, Manners and Customs of the People.* Ed. William Gow Gregor. London: Macmillan, 1878.

Hansen, Henny Harald. *Mongol Costumes.* Ed. Ida Nicolaisen. London; Copenhagen, New York: Thames and Hudson, Rhodos International Science and Art Publishers, 1993.

Harvey, Edwin, D. *The Mind of China.* Westport, Conn.: Hyperion Press, 1973.

Hommel, Rudolf. *China at Work: An Illustrated Record of the Primitive Industries of China's Masses, Whose Life Is Toil, and Thus an Account of Chinese Civilization.* New York: John Day, 1937.

Keith, Donald H., and Christian J. Buys. "New Light on Medieval Chinese Seagoing Ship Construction." *International Journal of Nautical Archaeology and Underwater Exploration* 10 (1) (1981): 119–32.

Knapp, Ronald G. *China's Traditional Rural Architecture: A Cultural Geography of the Common House.* Honolulu: University of Hawaii Press, 1986.

——*China's Vernacular Architecture: House Form and Culture.* Honolulu: University of Hawaii Press, 1989.

——*China's Walled Cities.* Hong Kong: Oxford University Press, 2000.

Lai, T.C. *To the Yellow Springs: The Chinese View of Death.* Hong Kong: Joing Publishing Company with Kelly and Walsh, 1983.

Lao Tzu. *Tao Te Ching.* Trans. David Hinton. Washington, D.C.: Counterpoint, 2000.

Lee, Sherman E. *Chinese Landscape Painting*. Cleveland: Cleveland Museum of Art, 1962.

Levathes, Louise. *When China Ruled the Seas: The Treasure Fleet of the Dragon Throne, 1405–1433*. New York: Simon and Schuster, 1994.

Liang, Ssu-ch'eng. *A Pictorial History of Chinese Architecture: A Study of the Development of Its Structural System and the Evolution of Its Types*. Ed. Wilma Fairbank. Cambridge, Mass.: MIT Press, 1984.

Liu, Laurence G. *Chinese Architecture*. New York: Rizzoli, 1989.

Loewe, Michael. *Chinese Ideas of Life and Death: Faith, Myth and Reason in the Han Period (202 BC–AD 220)*. London: George Allen and Unwin, 1982.

Mencius. *Mencius*. Trans. David Hinton. Washington, D.C.: Counterpoint, 1999.

Menzies, Gavin. *1421: The Year China Discovered the World*. London: Bantam Press, 2002.

Mitamura, Taisuke. *Chinese Eunuchs: The Structure of Intimate Politics*. Trans. Charles A. Pomeroy. Rutland, Vt.: Charles E. Tuttle Company, 1970.

Morton, W. Scott. *China: Its History and Culture*. New York: McGraw-Hill, 1995.

Mote, F.W. *Imperial China, 900–1800*. Cambridge, Mass.: Harvard University Press, 1999.

Mote, Frederick W., and Denis Twitchet, eds. *The Cambridge History of China*, vol. 7: *The Ming Dynasty, 1368–1644*. Cambridge: Cambridge University Press, 1988.

National Minority Literary and Art Team of the Central Institute for Nationalities and the Research Group of the Art Department of the Cultural Bureau, Kweichow Province. *Embrodiery Designs of the Miao People of China*. Peking: People's Fine Arts Publishing House, 1956.

Needham, Joseph. *Science and Civilisation in China*. 6 vols. Cambridge: Cambridge University Press, 1954.

Paludan, Ann. *The Ming Tombs*. Hong Kong: Oxford University Press, 1991.

Polo, Marco. *The Travels of Marco Polo, the Venetian*. Trans. William Marsden. Ed. Manuel Komroff. New York: Liveright Publishing, 2003.

——*The Description of the World*. Trans. A.C. Moule and Paul Pelliot. London: Routledge, 1938.

Serruys, Henry. *The Mongols and Ming China: Customs and History*. Ed. Francoise Aubin. London: Variorum Reprints, 1987.

Sickman, Laurence, and Alexander Soper. *The Art and Architecture of China*. Baltimore: Penguin Books, 1956.

Siren, Osvald. *The Imperial Palaces of Peking*. Paris: G. van Oest, 1926.

Sleeswyka, André. "The Liao and the Displacement of Ships in the Ming Navy." *Mariner's Mirror* 82 (1) (1996): 3–13.

Sullivan, Michael. *Symbols of Eternity: The Art of Landscape Painting in China*. Oxford: Clarendon Press, 1979.

Temple, Robert. *The Genius of China: 3,000 Years of Science, Discovery, and Invention.* New York: Simon and Schuster, 1986.

Wiest, J.P., et al. "Christianity in China." *New Catholic Encyclopedia.* Detroit: Washington, DC: Thomson/Gale; Catholic University of America, 2003.

Worchester, G.R.G. *The Junks and Sampans of the Yangtze.* Annapolis, Md.: Naval Institute Press, 1971.

Zhou, Xun, and Chunming, Gao. *5000 Years of Chinese Costumes.* San Francisco: China Books and Periodicals.

——*Le Costume Chinois.* Fribourg: Office du Livre, 1985.

EUROPEAN EXPLORATION, DISCOVERY, AND SETTLEMENT

Alfonce, Jean. *Les Voyages Avantureux du Capitaine Ian Alfonce, Sainctongeois.* Poitiers: Pelican par Ian de Marnef, 1559.

Andrews, K.R., N.P. Canny, and P.E.H. Hair, eds. *The Westward Enterprise: English Activities in Ireland, the Atlantic, and America, 1480–1650.* Liverpool: Liverpool University Press, 1978.

Biggar, H.P. *A Collection of Documents Relating to Jacques Cartier and the Sieur de Roberval.* Ottawa: Public Archives of Canada, 1930.

——*The Early Trading Companies of New France: A Contribution to the History of Commerce and Discovery in North America.* Clifton, N.J.: Augustus M. Kelley, 1972.

——*The Voyages of the Cabots and of the Corte-Reals to North America and Greenland, 1497–1503.* Paris: [s.n.] 1903.

——*The Voyages of Jacques Cartier.* Ottawa: F.A. Acland, 1924.

——, ed. *The Precursors of Jacques Cartier, 1497–1534: A Collection of Documents relating to the Early History of the Dominion of Canada.* Ottawa: Government Printing Bureau, 1911.

Buckner, Philip A., and John G. Reid, eds. *The Atlantic Region to Confederation.* Toronto: University of Toronto Press, 1998.

Champlain, Samuel de. *The Works of Samuel de Champlain.* 6 vols. Toronto: Champlain Society, 1922–36.

Charlevoix, P.-F.-X. *History and General Description of New France.* Trans. John Gilmary Shea. 6 vols. Chicago: Loyola University Press, 1962.

Clark, Andrew Hill. *Acadia: The Geography of Early Nova Scotia to 1760.* Madison: University of Wisconsin Press, 1968.

Collège Sainte-Marie. *Liste des Missionnaires-Jesuites: Nouvelle-France et Louisiane, 1611–1800.* Montreal: Collège Sainte-Marie, 1929.

Colon, Fernando. *The Life of the Admiral Christopher Columbus by His Son Ferdinand.* Trans. Benjamin Keen. New Brunswick, N.J.: Rutgers University Press, 1959.

Cook, Ramsey, ed. *The Voyages of Jacques Cartier.* Toronto: University of Toronto Press, 1993.

Cortesao, Armando. *History of Portuguese Cartography.* 2 vols. Coimbra: Junta de Investigacoes do Ultramar, 1969.

Cuthbertson, Brian. *John Cabot and the Voyage of the Matthew.* Halifax: Formac Publishing, 1997.

Daigle, Jean, ed. *The Acadians of the Maritimes: Thematic Studies.* Moncton: Centre d'etudes acadiennes, 1982.

Dawson, Joan. *The Mapmakers Eye: Nova Scotia through Early Maps.* Halifax: Nimbus Publishing with the Nova Scotia Museum, 1988.

Dawson, Samuel Edward. *The Saint Lawrence, Its Basin and Border-Lands: The Story of Their Discovery, Exploration and Occupation.* Toronto: Copp, Clark, 1905.

Diereville, Sieur de. *Relation of the Voyage to Port Royal in Acadia or New France.* Trans. Alice Webster. Toronto: Champlain Society, 1933.

Eccles, W.J. *France in America.* Markham, Ont.: Fitzhenry and Whiteside, 1972.

——*The French in North America, 1500–1783.* Markham, Ont.: Fitzhenry and Whiteside, 1998.

Entremont, Clarence-Joseph de. *Nicolas Denys: Sa Vie et Son Oeuvre.* Yarmouth, N.S.: L'impremerie Lescarbot, 1982.

Faragher, John Mack. *A Great and Noble Scheme: The Tragic Story of the Explusion of the French Acadians from their American Homeland.* New York: Norton and Company, 2005.

Fortier, John. "The Fortress of Louisbourg and Its Cartographic Evidence." *Association for Preservation Technology Bulletin* 4 (1–2) (1972): 2–173.

Ganong, W.F. *Crucial Maps in the Early Cartography and Place-Nomenclature of the Atlantic Coast of Canada.* Toronto: University of Toronto Press with the Royal Society of Canada, 1964.

Griffiths, Naomi E.S. *The Contexts of Acadian History, 1686–1784.* Montreal and Kingston: McGill-Queen's University Press, 1992.

Hakluyt, Richard. *A Discourse on Western Planting Written in the Year 1584.* Ed. Charles Deane. Cambridge: Maine Historical Society, 1877.

——*Hakluyt's Voyages: The Principal Navigation Voyages Traffiques and Discoveries of the English Nation Made by Sea or Over-land to the Remote and Farthest Distant Quarters of the Earth at Any Time within the Compasse of These 1600 Yeeres.* Ed. Irwin R. Blacker. New York: Viking Press, 1965.

Haliburton, R.G. "Lost Colonies of Northmen and Portuguese." *The Popular Science Monthly* 27 (May-October 1885): 40–51

Harley, J.B., and David Woodward, eds. *The History of Cartography.* Vol. 1. Chicago: University of Chicago Press, 1987.

Harrisse, Henry. *The Discovery of North America: A Critical, Documentary and Historic Investigation.* London: Henry Stevens and Son, 1892.

Hoffman, Bernard G. *Cabot to Cartier: Sources for a Historical Ethnography of Northeastern North America, 1497–1550.* Toronto: University of Toronto Press, 1961.

Insh, George Pratt. *Scottish Colonial Schemes, 1620–1686.* Glasgow: MacLehose, Jackson and Company, 1922.

Jacobson, Timothy. *Discovering America: Journeys in Search of the New World.* Toronto: Key Porter, 1991.

Jones, Elizabeth. *Gentlemen and Jesuits: Quests for Glory and Adventure in the Early Days of New France.* Toronto: University of Toronto Press, 1991.

Kershaw, Kenneth A. *Early Printed Maps of Canada, 1540–1703.* Ancaster, Ont.: Kershaw Publishing, 1993.

Krause, Eric R. "Private Buildings in Louisbourg, 1713–1758." *Canada: An Historical Magazine* 1 (4) (1974): 47–59.

Laing, David. *Royal Letters, Charters, and Tracts relating to the Colonization of New Scotland, and the Institution of the Order Knight Baronets of Nova Soctia, 1621–1638.* Edinburgh: The Bannatyne Club, 1867.

Le Clercq, Chrestin. *New Relation of Gaspesia with the Customs and Religion of the Gaspesian Indians.* Trans. and ed. William F. Ganong. Toronto: Champlain Society, 1910.

Lescarbot, Marc. *The History of New France.* Trans. W.L. Grant. Toronto: Champlain Society, 1907.

——*Nova Francia: A Description of Acadia, 1606.* Trans. P. Erondelle. London: George Routledge and Sons, 1928.

Major, Richard H., trans. and ed. *Select Letters of Christopher Columbus, with Other Original Documents relating to His Four Voyages to the New World.* London: Hakluyt Society, 1857.

McGhee, Robert. *Canada Rediscovered.* Ottawa: Canadian Museum of Civilization, 1991.

McLennan, J.S. *Louisbourg from Its Foundation to Its Fall, 1713–1758.* Sydney, N.S.: Fortress Press, 1969.

Meinig, D.W. *The Shaping of America: A Geographical Perspective on 500 Years of History.* New Haven: Yale University Press, 1986.

Mollat du Jourdin, Michel, et al. *Sea Charts of the Early Explorers, 13th to 17th Century.* Trans. L. le R. Dethan. London: Thames and Hudson, 1984.

Moogk, Peter. *Building a House in New France: An Account of the Perplexities of Client and Craftsmen in Early Canada.* Markham, Ont.: Fitzhenry and Whiteside, 2002.

Morison, Samuel Eliot. *The European Discovery of America: The Northern Voyages, A.D. 500–1600.* New York: Oxford University Press, 1971.

——*Portuguese Voyages to America in the Fifteenth Century.* New York: Octagon Books, 1965.

Morse, William Inglis, ed. *Acadiensia Nova (1598–1779): New and Unpublished Documents and Other Data relating to Acadia.* London: Bernard Quaritch, 1935.

Paine, Lincoln. *Ships of Discovery and Exploration.* New York: Houghton Mifflin, 2000.

Patterson, George. "The Portuguese on the North-East Coast of America and the First European Attempt at Colonization There. A Lost Chapter in American History." *Proceedings and Transactions of the Royal Society of Canada for the Year 1890* 8 (1891) 127–73.

Pinkerton, John. *The History of Scotland from the Accession of the House of Stuart to That of Mary.* London: C. Dilly, 1797.

Pope, Peter E. *The Many Landfalls of John Cabot.* Toronto: University of Toronto Press, 1997.

Portinaro, Pierluigi, and Franco Knirsch. *The Cartography of North America, 1500–1800.* New York: Charwell Books, 1987.

Pothier, Bernard. "Acadian Emigration to Ile Royale after the Conquest of Acadia." *Histoire Sociale/Social History* 6 (November 1970): 116–31.

Rochemonteix, Camille de. *Relation par Lettres de l'Amerique Septentrionalle (1709–1710).* Paris: Letouzey, 1904.

Ross, Sally, and Alphonse Deveau. *The Acadians of Nova Scotia: Past and Present.* Halifax: Nimbus Publishing, 1992.

Skelton, R.A. *Explorers' Maps: Chapters in the Cartographic Record of Geographic Discovery.* New York: Frederick A. Praeger, 1958.

Thwaites, Reuben Gold, ed. *The Jesuit Relations and Allied Documents: Travels and Explorations of the Jesuit Missionaries in New France, 1610–1791. The Original French, Latin, and Italian Texts with English Translations and Notes.* 74 vols. Cleveland: Burrows Brothers, 1898.

Wilcox, R. Turner. *The Mode in Furs: The History of Furred Costume of the World from the Earliest Times to the Present.* New York: Charles Scribner's Sons, 1951.

Wilford, John Noble. *The Mapmakers.* New York: Vintage Books, 2001.

Williamson, James A. *The Cabot Voyages and Bristol Discovery under Henry VII.* Cambridge: Hakluyt Society at the University Press, 1962.

—— *The Voyages of John and Sebastian Cabot.* London: G. Bell and Sons, 1937.

Winship, George Parker. *Cabot Bibliography, with an Introductory Essay on the Careers of the Cabots Based upon an Independent Examination of the Sources of Information.* New York: Burt Franklin, 1900.

Wright, Jonathan. *God's Soldiers: Adventure, Politics, Intrigue, and Power—A History of the Jesuits.* New York: Doubleday, 2004.

MI'KMAQ HISTORY, LANGUAGE, AND LEGENDS

Battiste, Marie, and James Youngblood Henderson. *Protecting Indigenous Knowledge and Heritage: A Global Challenge.* Saskatoon: Purich Publishing, 2000.

Cummins, Bryan D. *First Nations, First Dogs: Canadian Aboriginal Ethnocynology.* Calgary: Detselig Enterprises, 2002.

Dickason, Olive Patricia. *The Myth of the Savage and the Beginnings of French Colonialism in the Americas.* Edmonton: University of Alberta Press, 1984.

Hager, S. "Micmac Customs and Traditions." *American Anthropologist* 8 (1895): 31–42.

Harper, J. Russell. "Two Seventeenth-Century Micmac Copper Kettle Burials." *Anthropologica,* no. 4. Ottawa: The Research Centre for Amerindian Anthropology, 1957.

Henderson, James Youngblood. *The Mikmaw Concordat.* Halifax: Fernwood Publishing, 1997.

Kauder, Christian. *Buch das Gut: Enthaltend den Katechismus.* Vienna: Die Kaiserliche wie auch Kongliche Buchdrucherei hat es gedruckt, 1866.

Maillard, Antoine Simon. *An Account of the Customs and Manners of the Micmakis and Maricheets Savage Nations now Dependent on the Government of Cape Breton, from an Original French Manuscript-Letter, Never Published, Written by a French Abbot, Who Resided Many Years, in Quality of Missionary, amongst Them to Which Are Annexed Several Pieces relative to the Savages of Nova Scotia and to North America in General.* London: Hooper and Morley, 1758.

Mallery, Garrick. "Picture Writing of the American Indians." *Tenth Annual Report of the Bureau of Ethnology to the Secretary of the Smithsonian Institution, 1888–1889.* Washington, D.C.: Smithsonian Institution, 1893.

McDonald. Shayne. "Newfoundland and Labrador before the Arrival of Cabot: The Newfoundland Mi'kmaq Perspective." In Iona Bulgin, ed., *Cabot and His World Symposium: Papers and Presentations.* St. John's: Newfoundland Historical Society, 1997.

McMillan, Alan D. *Native Peoples and Cultures of Canada.* Vancouver: Douglas and McIntyre, 1995.

Rand, Silas Tertius. *Dictionary of the Language of the Micmac Indians Who Reside in Nova Scotia, Prince Edward Island, Cape Breton and Newfoundland.* Halifax: Nova Scotia Printing Company, 1888.

——*A First Reading Book in the Micmac Language: Comprising the Micmac Numerals, and the Names of the Different Kinds of Beasts, Birds, Fishes, Trees etc. of the Maritime Provinces of Canada.* Halifax: Nova Scotia Printing Company, 1875.

——*Legends of the Micmacs.* New York: Longmans, Green: 1894.

——*A Short Account of the Lord's Work among the Micmac Indians.* Halifax: William MacNab, 1873.

——*A Short Statement of Facts relating to the History, Manners, Customs, Language and Literature of the Micmac Tribe of Indians in Nova Scotia and P.E. Island.* Halifax: James Bowes and Son, 1850.

Ray, Arthur J. *I Have Lived Here since the World Began: An Illustrated History of Canada's Native People.* Toronto: Lester Books, 1996.

Robertson, Marion. *Rock Drawings of the Micmac Indians.* Halifax: The Nova Scotia Museum, 1973.

Schmidt, David L., and Murdena Marshall, eds. and trans. *Mi'kmaq Hieroglyphic Prayers: Readings in North America's First Indigenous Script.* Halifax: Nimbus Publishers, 1995.

Schwartz, Marion. *A History of Dogs in the Early Americas.* New Haven, Conn.: Yale University Press, 1997.

Silvy, Antione. *Letters from North America.* Trans. Ivy Alice Dickson. Belleville, Ont.: Mika Publishing, 1980.

Speck, F.G. "Beothuk, and Micmac." *Indian Notes and Monographs* no. 22. New York: Museum of the American Indian, Heye Foundation, 1922.

——*The Double-Curve Motif in Northeastern Algonkian Art.* Geological Survey of Canada, Memoir 42. Ottawa: Government Printing Bureau, 1914.

——"Some Micmac Tales from Cape Breton Island." *Journal of American Folklore* 27 (107) (1915): 59–69.

Unbylined article. "'I Fashion Things': The Micmacs' Surprising Legacy." *Canadian Heritage,* April 1980: 25.

Wallis, Wilson D., and Ruth Sawtell Wallis. *The Micmac Indians of Eastern Canada.* Minneapolis: University of Minnesota Press, 1955.

Whitehead, Ruth Holmes. *Micmac Quilllwork: Micmac Indian Techniques of Porcupine Quill Decoration, 1600–1950.* Halifax: Novas Scotia Museum, 1982.

——*Nova Scotia, the Protohistoric Period, 1500–1620: Four Micmac Sites.* Halifax: Nova Scotia Musuem, 1993.

——*The Old Man Told Us: Excerpts from Micmac History, 1500–1950.* Halifax: Nimbus Publishing, 1991.

Wicken, William C. *Mi'kmaq Treaties on Trial: History, Land and Donald Marshall Junior.* Toronto: University of Toronto Press, 2002.

OCEAN CURRENTS

Charton, Barbara. *The Facts on File: Dictionary of Marine Science.* New York: Facts on File Publications, 1988.

Department of Fisheries and Oceans. *Sailing Directions: Nova Scotia (Atlantic Coast) and Bay of Fundy.* Ottawa: Department of Fisheries and Oceans, 1990.

Ellis, Richard. *Encyclopedia of the Sea.* New York: Alfred A. Knopf, 2000.

Groves, Donald G., and Lee M. Hunt. *Ocean World Encyclopedia.* New York: McGraw-Hill, 1980.

Parker, Sybil P. *McGraw-Hill Encyclopedia of Ocean and Atmospheric Sciences.* New York: McGraw-Hill, 1980.

Stommel, Henry. *The Gulf Stream: A Physical and Dynamical Description.* Berkeley: University of California Press, 1965.

THE SEVEN CITIES LEGEND

Babcock, William H. *Legendary Islands of the Atlantic: A Study in Medieval Geography.* New York: American Geographical Society, 1922.

Bandelier, A.F. *The Gilded Man (El Dorado) and Other Pictures of the Spanish Occupancy of America.* New York: D. Appleton, 1893.

Courcy Ireland, J. de, and D.C. Sheehy. "Atlantic Islands." *European Approaches to North America, 1450–1640.* Ed. David Quinn. Aldershot, U.K.,; Brookfield, Vt.: Ashgate/Variorum, 1998: 1–17

Crampton, C. Gregory. *The Zunis of Cibola.* Salt Lake City: University of Utah Press, 1977.

Crone, G.R. "The Mythical Islands of the Atlantic Ocean: Suggestion as to Their Origin." *Comptes Rendus du Congres International de Geographie Amsterdam 1938.* Leiden: E.J. Brill, 1938.

Davis, W.W.H. "The Spaniard in New Mexico." *Papers of the American Historical Association* 3 (1) (1888): 164–176.

Hackett, Charles Wilson, ed. *Historical Documents relating to New Mexico, Nueva Vizcaya, and Approaches Thereto, to 1773.* Vol. 1. Washington D.C.: Carnegie Institution of Washington, 1923.

Hammond, George P., and Agapito Rey. *Narratives of the Coronado Expedition, 1540–1542.* Albuquerque: University of New Mexico Press, 1940.

Johnson, Donald S. *Phantom Islands of the Atlantic.* Fredericton: Goose Lane, 1994.

Major, Richard H., trans. and ed. *The Voyages of the Venetian Brothers Nicolo and Antonio Zeno to the Northern Seas in the XIVth Century Comprising the Latest Known Accounts of the Lost Colony of Greenland and of the Northmen in America before Columbus.* London: Hakluyt Society, 1873.

Nebenzahl, Kenneth. *Atlas of Columbus and the Great Discoveries.* Chicago: Rand McNally, 1990.

Winship, George Parker. "Why Coronado Went to New Mexico." *Annual Report of the American Historical Association for the Year 1894.* Washington D.C.: Government Printing Office, 1895.

ACKNOWLEDGEMENTS

This project started with a visit home and, fittingly, I am most grateful to my family for their support. Along with two close friends, Beth and Rob, they were the first to listen.

The research could not have been done without the patience and insight of the gentle, diligent staff of the Toronto Reference Library. For the help they provided on almost every aspect of this project, I owe them a heartfelt thanks.

My good counsel Marian Hebb was another one who listened, as did Anne Collins, my editor and publisher at Random House Canada. To both I am indebted.

Robert Buckland helped me find the words and the shape of the story. The following people read the manuscript and offered useful suggestions and criticisms: Gavin Menzies, Betty Meggers and George Gibson. By their individual and shared wisdom I am humbled. Thank you.

I'd like to thank Ron Eckel, Scott Richardson, Beate Schwirtlich, Jennifer Shepherd, Scott Sellers, Pamela Murray and Kylie Barker at Random House Canada, and freelance editors Rosemary Shipton and Curtis Fahey, for helping to make this book a reality. In the United States, I'd like to thank Michael Flamini and George Witte of St. Martin's Press.

INDEX

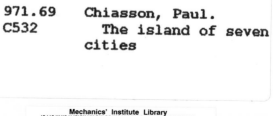